REMOTE**CONTROL**
New Media, New Ethics

From reality TV's fascination with the ordinary to the extraordinary world of pornography online, new media technologies and genres are confronting us with fresh ethical challenges that blur the boundaries between the producer and the consumer, the amateur and the professional, the private and the public.

Cash for Comment, Murdoch versus the Rabbitohs, payola in the food media and the high cost of a free lunch, the Wild West world of web journalism, advertising as entertainment – tackling these issues requires new ways of understanding media ethics.

Using accessible case studies and provocative interviews with some of Australia's foremost media practitioners – including Margo Kingston's reflections on online media, John Safran on media pranksterism, Mike Carlton on the ongoing issue of 'Cash for Comment' and Maxine McKew on the future of journalism – *Remote Control* is essential reading for anyone interested in the state of debate about media ethics in Australia.

As academics who write regularly in the mainstream media, the editors, Catharine Lumby and Elspeth Probyn, demonstrate that an intelligent and engaged discussion of these issues is vital to navigating the ethical dilemmas of our new mediascape.

Catharine Lumby is Associate Professor of Media Studies and Director of the Media and Communications Program, University of Sydney.

Elspeth Probyn is Professor of Gender Studies, University of Sydney.

REMOTE**CONTROL**
New Media, New Ethics

Edited by

CATHARINE LUMBY

ELSPETH PROBYN

CAMBRIDGE
UNIVERSITY PRESS

PUBLISHED BY THE PRESS SYNDICATE OF THE UNIVERSITY OF CAMBRIDGE
The Pitt Building, Trumpington Street, Cambridge, United Kingdom

CAMBRIDGE UNIVERSITY PRESS
The Edinburgh Building, Cambridge CB2 2RU, UK
40 West 20th Street, New York, NY 10011–4211, USA
477 Williamstown Road, Port Melbourne, VIC 3207, Australia
Ruiz de Alarcón 13, 28014 Madrid, Spain
Dock House, The Waterfront, Cape Town 8001, South Africa

http://www.cambridge.org

First published 2003

Printed in Australia by BPA Print Group

Typeface Cheltenham Light (*Adobe*) 10/14 pt. *System* QuarkXPress® [PC]

A catalogue record for this book is available from the British Library

National Library of Australia Cataloguing in Publication data

Remote control: new media, new ethics.

Includes index.
ISBN 0 521 53427 5

1. Mass media – Moral and ethical aspects. 2. Mass media –
Moral and ethical aspects – Australia. I. Probyn, Elspeth,
1958–. II. Lumby, Catharine.

175

ISBN 0 521 53427 5 paperback

Contents

Contributors

Kath Albury

Kath Albury is a writer, researcher and broadcaster, specialising in sexuality and popular culture. Kath is an Honorary Research Associate in the Media and Communications Program, University of Sydney, and a PhD candidate in the School of Media and Communications, at the University of New South Wales. She has been researching pornography since 1996, and is a chief investigator on the Understanding Pornography in Australia project. Her book *Yes Means Yes: Getting explicit about heterosex* was published by Allen & Unwin in 2002.

Mike Carlton

Mike Carlton is one of Australia's best known broadcasters and newspaper columnists. In a journalistic career spanning more than forty years, he has been a news reporter and editor, foreign correspondent, TV current affairs reporter and anchor, radio current affairs anchor, humorist and satirist. His foreign experience ranges from duty as a war correspondent in Vietnam in the 1960s and 1970s, through assignments in Asia, Africa and the United States. In the early 1990s he hosted a breakfast show on London radio which won major awards in the United Kingdom and at the New York Radio Festival. Mike is a regular columnist for the *Sydney Morning Herald*, and his 1997 novel *Off the Air*, published by Pan Macmillan, was an Australian bestseller. Mike is currently a radio broadcaster for Radio 2UE.

Kate Crawford

Kate Crawford is a lecturer in the Media and Communications Program at the University of Sydney, where she designed the first course on the theory and practice of online media. She has worked as a journalist for the *Sydney Morning Herald* and was the editor of *Internet.au* magazine. She is currently completing a PhD about the interplay of control and creativity on the Internet.

Milissa Deitz

Milissa Deitz is a Sydney journalist currently completing a PhD in the Media and Communications Program at the University of Sydney. She has taught media studies and journalism at the University of Newcastle, and Macquarie University. Her novel, *Bloodlust*, was published by Random House in 1999 and a non-fiction book about depression, *My Life as a Side Effect*, will be published by Random House in 2003.

Anne Dunn

Anne Dunn is a lecturer in the Media and Communications Program at the University of Sydney. Prior to this appointment Anne taught journalism at the University of Western Sydney and media production and online media at Charles Sturt University, Bathurst. Anne has spent more than twenty years working as a presenter, media researcher, journalist, producer and director, initially freelance, for commercial television, for SBS and for the ABC. Her work includes award-winning television and film documentaries. Anne is completing a PhD on policy and audiences in ABC Radio News. Her recent work includes 'What have you done for us lately? Public service broadcasting and its audiences' in Michael Bromley's *No News is Bad News* (Longman, 2001).

Ghassan Hage

Ghassan Hage is Associate Professor of Anthropology at the University of Sydney. He teaches and researches in the areas of migration, nationalism and racism. His works include *White Nation* (Pluto Press, 1998), *Arab-Australians: Citizenship and Belonging* (Melbourne University Press, 2001) and *Against Paranoid Nationalism* (Merlin Press, 2003).

John Hartley

John Hartley is Professor and Dean of Creative Industries, Queensland University of Technology. He is author, with Alan McKee, of *The Indigenous Public Sphere: The Reporting and Reception of Aboriginal Issues in the Australian Media* (Oxford University Press, 2000), and editor, with Alan McKee, of *Telling Both Stories: Indigenous Australians and the Media* (ECU/Arts Enterprise, 1996).

Duncan Ivison

Duncan Ivison teaches in the Department of Philosophy at the University of Sydney. He is the author of *The Self at Liberty* (Cornell University Press, 1997), *Postcolonial Liberalism* (Cambridge University Press, 2002) and co-editor of *Political Theory and the Rights of Indigenous Peoples* (Cambridge University

Press, 2000). In 2002–03 he was Laurance S. Rockefeller Visiting Fellow at the Center for Human Values, Princeton University.

Linda Jaivin

Linda Jaivin is a best-selling Australian author who has published four novels including *Eat Me* (Text Publishing, 1995), *Rock 'n Roll Babes From Outer Space* (Text Publishing, 1996), and *Miles Walker, You're Dead* (Text Publishing, 1999). She is also a specialist writer on contemporary Chinese culture. In 2001, she wrote a biography of Chinese songwriter and dissident Hou Deijan, called *The Monkey and The Dragon: A True Story About Friendship, Music, Politics and Life on the Edge* (Text Publishing, 2001). In the last two years she has become an outspoken advocate for refugees held in detention in Australia. She has written two plays, *Seeking Djira* and *Halal el Mashakel*, and is currently working on an opera about asylum seekers with musician Ed Kuepper to be performed in 2004. Her books have been translated into ten languages.

Margo Kingston

Margo Kingston is the political editor of the *Sydney Morning Herald* online, and runs *Webdiary*, a forum for reader opinion. She was a political journalist in Canberra for more than a decade, and is the author of *Off the Rails: The Pauline Hanson Trip* (Allen & Unwin, 1999) on Pauline Hanson's 1998 federal election campaign.

Catharine Lumby

Associate Professor Catharine Lumby is the Director of the Media and Communications Program at the University of Sydney. A widely published print journalist, Catharine has worked as a news reporter, feature writer and columnist for the *Sydney Morning Herald* and the *Age* newspapers. She has also worked as a news reporter for ABC television and currently writes a fortnightly column for the *Bulletin* magazine. Catharine is the author of two books, *Bad Girls: The Media, Sex and Feminism in the '90s* (Allen & Unwin, 1997) and *Gotcha: Life in a Tabloid World* (Allen & Unwin, 1999).

Maxine McKew

Maxine McKew, a Walkley Award-winning journalist, is one of Australia's most experienced and authoritative interviewers. A journalist who has anchored

ABC-TV's prestigious *Lateline* and *7.30 Report* programs, Maxine is a senior writer with the *Bulletin* magazine.

Michael Moller

Michael Moller recently completed a PhD in the Department of Gender Studies at the University of Sydney. His thesis, 'Reclaiming the Game: Rugby League, Globalisation and Masculinity', explores the social, economic and ethical aspects of rugby league. He has published another article about South Sydney's fans in *New Talents 21C*, a volume of the *Journal of Australian Studies* devoted to work by recent graduates. His research interests include masculinity in popular culture and the expression of ethics and community through consumption.

Jim Moser

Jim began his appointment as Managing Director of Clemenger BBDO Sydney in October 1999. Prior to his arrival in Australia he spent seven years with BBDO Europe, most recently as CEO of BBDO Milan. Jim was instrumental in merging the agency with local hot shop D'Adda Lorenzini Vigorelli – now known as DLV BBDO. Before Italy, Jim was CEO of BBDO Warsaw Group in Poland. An MBA graduate of the JL Kellogg Graduate School of Management at Northwestern University, Jim has also worked in New York and Chicago for DMB&B. He has experience on major global brands in Europe, North America and Asia.

Fiona Patten

Fiona Patten is a political lobbyist, consultant and spokesperson for the adult entertainment industry. In 1992 she established the EROS Foundation, Australia's foremost adult goods and services industry group, and served as its president from 1993 to 2000. As well as working as a health educator for sex workers, Fiona established the Scarlet Alliance, a national organisation for sex workers. A regular writer for the *EROS Journal*, Fiona has also contributed to *Pornography 101: Eroticism, Pornography, and the First Amendment* (Prometheus Books, 1997) and Jill Matthews' *Sex In Public: Australian Sexual Cultures* (Allen & Unwin, 1997).

Elspeth Probyn

Elspeth Probyn is Professor of Gender Studies at the University of Sydney. Her recent books include *Blush: Essays in Shame* (University of Minnesota Press, forthcoming) and *Carnal Appetites: FoodSexIdentity* (Routledge, 2000). She has published widely on different aspects of popular culture and media, and is co-chief investigator with Catharine Lumby of Girlcultures, a project focused on girls' use of the media. She writes a fortnightly column in the *Australian*'s Higher Education section.

Cherry Ripe

Cherry Ripe is Australia's most awarded food writer. She is a journalist, broadcaster and author of five books including *Goodbye Culinary Cringe* (Allen & Unwin, 1993), *Australia: The Beautiful Cookbook* (Weldon Owen, 1995), and *Ripe Enough?* (Allen & Unwin, 1999). She is now in her thirteenth year as food writer and occasional wine writer for the *Australian* and has contributed to many other publications including the *Observer* in the United Kingdom and the *Wall Street Journal*.

John Safran

John came to public attention in 1997 through the ABC travel show *Race Around the World*. He has provided content for numerous television stations and production companies, including Channel Seven, Channel Four in Britain and Viacom in the United States. He recently presented, co-wrote and co-produced the ten-part series *John Safran's Music Jamboree* for SBS television. He is currently working on a new religion-themed series for SBS.

Graeme Turner

Graeme Turner is Professor of Cultural Studies and Director of the Centre for Critical and Cultural Studies at the University of Queensland. He has published widely on media and cultural studies topics in Australia and internationally. Recent publications include *The Film Cultures Reader* (Routledge, 2002) (with Stuart Cunningham), *The Media and Communications in Australia* (Allen & Unwin, 2002), and the third, revised edition of *British Cultural Studies: An Introduction* (Routledge, 2002).

Acknowledgements

The editors would like to thank those who have worked on this project, including, of course, the contributors. We have been extremely fortunate to have the assistance of Adam Eldridge and Fiona Giles. The project started with funding from the University of Sydney and the research cluster on Popular Media and Ethics. The original members of that group were Joanne Finkelstein, Melissa Hardie, Duncan Ivison, Isabel Karpin, Catharine Lumby, Elspeth Probyn, and Stephen Garton. The editors have also benefited from funding from an ARC Large Grant on girls' use of the media.

1 Introduction: An Ethics of Engagement
ELSPETH PROBYN & CATHARINE LUMBY

A PRINCESS DRIVEN TO HER DEATH BY MANIACAL PAPARAZZI; REALITY shows where contestants cry, vomit and have sex on screen; radio hosts showered with vats of cash for editorial comment; an online world teeming with pornographers and Nazis; media moguls putting the boot into rugby league fans – in the past decade, media ethics have rarely been out of the media.

In their diversity and difference, the concerns raised by popular new media genres challenge the conventional framing of media ethics. Certainly the intensity, reach and variety of media formats today are unprecedented. From global news channels clogged with talking heads dissecting instantaneous satellite feeds to online web sites featuring people who live their entire life in front of a camera, our screens, magazines and airwaves are filled with images of what living is like. Driven by technological advances, increased competition, and the globalisation of capital and information flows, our contemporary mass media present the viewer, the reader and the Internet user at home with a host of ethical challenges.

Meanwhile, public debate brims with popular and scholarly commentators announcing the decline, degradation and even extinction of media ethics. In conventional terms, the story of the media is one of moral and professional decline, a tale of the steady erosion of codes and ideals which once guided mainstream journalistic practice and media production. And yet, as anyone who's worked in the media can attest, codes of ethics and journalistic ideals have always had a tenuous relationship with the messy realities of professional practice. The public might have been outraged by intrusions into Diana's privacy, but editors know photos of topless celebrities

#1

still sell magazines. And while current affairs shows have been savaged for unethical practices in the past decade, the mantra of TV journalism is still: get the story and get it first.

Faced with the realities of deadlines, frenzied competition for jobs, and continuous pressure from above to keep the ratings up and the costs down, it's no wonder that few media producers spend their time worrying about abstract ethical codes or ideals. Across the Western world, scholarly and popular debates about media ethics remain dominated by a belief in the efficacy of abstract, regulatory codes that attempt to define ethical behaviour in advance of practical dilemmas. Yet the very reason such codes are often derided or ignored by journalists is that they fail to take account of the realities and complexities of popular media practice. What's more, such codes are only held to apply to hard news and current affairs journalism, while increasingly many of the ethical dilemmas thrown up by the contemporary media relate to entertainment-oriented formats.

Remote Control offers a broader, more engaged and, we hope, more engaging framework for thinking about the ethical dilemmas thrown up by the contemporary media. Our contributors address the following questions: What are the limitations of current debates about ethics and the popular media? Do media consumers have the same kinds of ethical concerns as academic and media commentators who speak on their behalf? Should we have different ethical standards for information and entertainment media? Should we censor online media more or, conversely, less stringently than conventional formats? How much agency should we attribute to viewers and readers? When is it relevant to bring race or religion or gender into debates about crime and terrorism?

Conventional studies of media ethics tend to proceed on the basis that there are universally desirable political and social goals and ideals, and that a code of media ethics can be arrived at by measuring the extent to which a media practice supports such goals and ideals. These goals and ideals include the right to privacy; the importance of rationality, and the clear delineation of fact and opinion in public debate; the disclosure of all vested interests; and the separation of matters of public interest from matters which merely interest the public.

In contrast, we argue that any inquiry into the ethics of the contemporary popular media needs to begin by considering how emerging genres and technologies are re-shaping our public sphere, and how this might in turn cause us to rethink the assumptions grounding our ethical norms. The relationship between the media and ethics has to be understood as dynamic, not fixed. Similarly, the relationship between audiences and media products and technologies has to be seen as interactive. And as *Remote Control* demonstrates, there is ample evidence of experimentation on both sides of the screen and the page.

As Duncan Ivison writes in his chapter on the philosophical roots of debates about ethics and the public sphere:

> *Our philosophical orientation should be less towards consensus and more towards how we can live with the disagreements we have with each other. Since there is no standpoint outside of the conversations and arguments of the actual interlocutors that is rationally or morally authoritative on its own, we have to begin with the premises and beliefs that are brought to these arguments and work from there.*

In other words, not only is it OK to have heated debates about what counts as our values and ethics – it's essential.

In the course of her essay on the growth of the advertorial or infomercial, Anne Dunn makes a related point when she argues that: 'codes alone will never provide answers to the hard questions because ethical thinking and behaviour do not reside in codes. There is more to being ethical than following rules.' Ethics, Dunn suggests, have to be understood de facto, not de jure. Any organisation or profession can draw up a code of practice, but ethics inevitably come down to decisions made by individuals who have to balance self-interest and other pragmatic considerations with wider ideals.

ENGAGING WITH MEDIA

Any discussion of media ethics has to proceed from a detailed examination of how a given media text is organised, produced and consumed. We believe it's meaningless, not to mention pompous, to talk about media products and audiences in the abstract.

There is a long tradition within critical media studies of what Stuart Hall has called 'the encoding and decoding' processes. His framework directed attention to the different spheres that organise the production and the encoding of the media.[1] These have a direct impact on how different media are understood, engaged with, or decoded. The point of his model was to clarify the different types of restraints that affect the production of different media messages – from the infrastructure of each medium (e.g. commercial or state-funded), the choice of different genres and the public climate in which they are broadcast, to the position of consumers in terms of factors like social class. Hall argued that media reception always involves more than just the transmission of information. We extend this model while implicitly following its dictates. For instance, our interest in the new types of blurred genres on television (reality show meets game show) reveals that the types of issues presented by different media genres will be understood in particular ways by viewers.

None of us comes to the media as a blank slate. We all have histories and tastes, predilections and pet peeves. We bring expert knowledge, interests and preconceptions to what we read or watch or listen to. As Ghassan Hage points out in his essay, the ways in which we relate – or fail to relate – to others is also deeply ingrained. For Hage, at one level the ethics of journalism is simple: if you are *talking about* rather than *talking to* people, you are acting unethically. Hage uses the infamous example of the 'Muslim Lebanese rapes' as a prime instance of where the media *en masse* talked about 'the Lebanese problem', but rarely bothered to talk to Lebanese Australians. As he puts it, the question is not about whether to be nice – it's about recognising the other as fully human.

It is undeniable that media practitioners are fully a part of the society they report on. But they also have histories, and a knowledge of the history of the medium in which they work. One of the compelling aspects of *Remote Control* is the number of insights that practitioners offer in their interviews. They are up-front about the challenges they face in their professional lives. And while they are reflective, and sensitive to ethical dilemmas, they are also honest about the problems they face in living up to the codes of ethics that regulate their practice.

Contributors to this book all examine key ethical issues through a careful study of cases which have been the focus of both public and scholarly debate about media ethics in Australia over the past decade. We are less concerned with questions about what different media genres ought to do, and more with how they are actually organised, what practitioners endeavour to do in practice within the scope of their formats, and how viewers and readers navigate this new mediascape.

One of the guiding thoughts behind this book is that ethics emerge from encounters between the media text, the practitioner, the producer and the consumer. We propose that the focus on universal standards – which so often characterises discussions of ethics in general, and media ethics in particular – can cause a blindness to specifics. Too often, pronouncements are made about the ethics of a particular media product or event without any consideration of how a genre is organised, who consumes it and in what context. For instance, it makes absolutely no sense to take an ethical framework developed in the world of news journalism and apply it directly to the world of *Big Brother.*

Indeed, as Duncan Ivison argues in his overview of how ethics is understood within philosophical traditions, ethics must be understood as both situated and, of necessity, universalising. He draws our attention to why concepts like the public sphere and the right to engage in it are central to our democracies. Equally, the dizzying changes in the mediasphere, and the concomitant globalising and speeding up of information flows, bring new urgency and new inflections to old thoughts. How do we best ensure that the public sphere is a place where citizens can exchange and sometimes change their opinions and values? Ivison's down-to-earth discussion of values is a check to those who would decry any acknowledgement of *different* values as relativism or pluralism gone wrong. He also demonstrates how 'a vibrant, diverse, inclusive and critically engaged public' is the very cornerstone of our society. Intense discussions about values, about diversity and tolerance are, in other words, signs of life, not something to be deplored.

In simple terms, a renewed debate about ethics means taking new media genres and formats seriously. And to this end, the essays in *Remote Control* detail new media genres and practices. Kath Albury looks closely at the way ordinary people are participating in making and distributing porn on the Internet. What, she asks, happens to conventional ethical frameworks which denounce pornography for commercialising sex and exploiting female workers, when average people begin making porn for pleasure rather than profit? How applicable is the claim that porn commodifies bodies when many of the 'amateurs' represented have bodies which are too ordinary or tastes which are too kinky to be featured in mainstream pornography? As Albury states, while some may still argue that this kind of porn is immoral, it doesn't follow that the amateur community lives in an ethical vacuum. Indeed, participants in these online communities often operate with explicit codes of practice, internal value systems and ideas about best practice.

In another essay, Kate Crawford examines what constitutes acceptable speech on the Internet and how censorship is being practised. She locates two systems of control or censorship: one which operates in a targeted manner, such as defamation law, and one which is based in general moral principles, such as the anti-Internet porn legislation that has been introduced in Australia. Through a detailed examination of US and Australian case law and legislation, Crawford argues persuasively that these generalised principles are proving ineffective in censoring a medium as diverse and participatory as the Internet.

In her account of publishing an online webdiary, Margo Kingston also argues that the Internet poses specific ethical challenges and opportunities. Kingston writes as a print journalist who moves online and finds herself in a uniquely interactive world. Kingston's Webdiary has been an experiment for her, for Fairfax, and for her webdiarists. Online, her 'readers' become *contributors* – collaborators in the process of journalism, with some key resultant shifts in how Kingston understands her role and her ethical duties as a journalist. Her experience in the online media world leads Kingston to critique the conventional insistence on objectivity in journalism. She argues instead that objectivity is a ruse that 'hides the truth' and sets up the journalist as an 'observer/judge'. Fittingly, some of the most astute observations about media ethics are those she solicited from her contributors/readers. As one puts it, 'Knowing how to use power responsibly is the essence of ethics'.

From Kingston's comments it is evident that some genres facilitate and even demand a closeness between journalist and reader. This is at the heart of one of the basic principles of ethics that guide this book – the importance of honesty and accountability to an audience. In Elspeth Probyn's chapter, the world of food journalism and media is explored in terms of closeness and proximity. In one regard food journalism is one of the last bastions where certain unacceptable forms of subjective closeness are still practised. These include the ubiquity of freebies and complimentaries (known as comps), as well as, in certain cases, free meals for restaurant reviewers. These practices clearly contravene general ethical codes for journalism, as well as specific ones for food writers. But there are other forms of closeness which may provide inspiration for a wider ethics of engagement in terms of popular media and life-style genres. As John Newton, an established freelance food writer, comments, food journalism is a subjective, intimate and convivial form of journalism. Food journalists write about issues that are central to our lives, families, homes and health. Interviews with prominent food journalists provide a picture of their frustration at being dismissed as life-style writers, or worse – as gossip columnists. At the same time, they also speak to the incongruity of applying the subjective/objective distinction of conventional media ethics to popular, convivial and life-style journalism.

In John Hartley's chapter, another challenge is issued to the ethical norms of professional distance, detachment and objectivity. Hartley begins by asking what ethical journalism would look like from an Indigenous perspective. His interviews with several experienced Indigenous media practitioners uncover a set of very different ethical considerations. One of the key problems he and his interviewees identify is that Indigenous people have come to be identified with such a specific place in the mediasphere, that journalistic focus – positive or negative – inevitably frames them in narrow terms. Where, his chapter asks, are the business stories or the reports about Indigenous government issues? Where are the stories that portray Aboriginal life as anything other than one big problem – and implicitly or explicitly as a problem for whites? From the media practitioners he interviews, some clear-cut guiding principles emerge: the necessity for respect and of following protocols, and another sense of time other than that of the journalist. The stories also raise the need to identify a wider spectrum of leaders and spokespeople – like mainstream non-Indigenous Australia, Aboriginal Australia has many voices and differing points of view.

In Michael Moller's essay, the question of respect for difference is considered from another point of view – that of the grassroots fans who overturned a media mogul's decision to shut out a beloved local rugby league team. Moller follows the ways in which the supporters of the Rabbitohs (also known as Souths) used the media in their campaign to revoke the expulsion of South Sydney League Club from the National Rugby League – a decision made purely in terms of the interests of the commercial media. Moller's analysis does not come out against the broadcasting of rugby league games. On the contrary, he shows us the diversity of community that is fostered by sports media. It's a David and Goliath story of the battle by the fans, and their use of the Internet and traditional media to gain support for their cause.

In her account of the rise of media pranksterism in Australia, Milissa Deitz shows us how the media's heels are being nipped by the knowledgeable and audacious media practitioners of the future. Using handicams and web sites, young media consumers are increasingly turning the cameras on the received ideas and complacent media practices of mainstream journalism. Through her history of alternative media stunts, Deitz suggests that it's precisely the young people – normally portrayed as being in need of protection and correction by the popular media – who are familiar with its vocabulary, technology and formulas, and she shows how they use this knowledge to both develop and deploy an ethical critique of the industry.

In a quite different corner of the media, Graeme Turner takes us through some of the intricacies and the implications of the notorious Cash for Comment affair. Is John Laws an entertainer? Is Alan Jones a journalist? In examining the debate about where to draw the line between entertainment and information, radio host and commercial voice for hire, Turner raises crucial questions about the state of the media in general, and the case of talkback radio in particular. Turner argues that the fallout from the Cash for Comment episode provided a moment when there was active engagement by a number of parties – media practitioners, the Australian Broadcasting Authority, academics, and a plethora of voices talking back in the radio, in television, and in print. Though some ethics took a battering, the ensuing outcry and public inquiry provided a sense of what a working media ethics should do: provoke comment and reflection from all sides of the Australian public.

In Catharine Lumby's account of the appeal of reality TV we again hear from voices rarely heard in debates about media ethics. Drawing on research she conducted jointly with Elspeth Probyn, Lumby uses evidence from extensive interviews with teenage girls to show that fans of reality television are not the ethically vacuous dupes that some commentators have suggested. Rather, teenage girls use the scenarios in shows like *Big Brother* as a way of reflecting on the ethical dilemmas they face in their own lives. Teenagers today, she argues, are under constant surveillance and they are well aware of this, which may in part be why they understand and appreciate the ironies and the lessons of reality TV. In Lumby's description, a major part of the appeal of reality TV is that it 'presents us with individuals caught up in the process of negotiating the messy ethics of ordinary existence'. The lessons have to do with relationships, hopes and aspirations, as well as fears. In its showcasing of ordinary people, reality TV continually conveys the ordinariness of these questions.

As Anne Dunn concludes from her study of advertising techniques, 'ethics in advertising, as in any aspect of our lives, is about the quality of human relationships, the way we treat each other'. In a different articulation of the anxiety about the difference between the real and the manufactured, Dunn argues convincingly that some of the tricks of the ad trade may yet go awry. If the trend of camouflaging ads as content continues, she suggests, the advertising industry may be hoist with its own petard if the public becomes overly cynical. Indeed, she argues, it's a cynicism the advertising industry may already be detecting, resulting in a move away from the most devious forms of product placement. As people vote with their feet or with their credit cards, she says, the industry is being forced to engage with its public – to participate in a form of ethics in action.

The issues raised by an ethics in action are voiced in different ways in our interviews with some of the most prominent media practitioners in Australia. Their experience and candour are invaluable in providing insight and raising questions about the practice of ethics in this country. From their different points of view, Maxine McKew, Mike Carlton, John Safran, and Cherry Ripe speak honestly and directly about the ethics of the media and their own experiences as practitioners. They do not all agree with each other, but they all provide cogent reasons why honesty and accountability to their readers, listeners and viewers are so central to the practice of media ethics. Their voices are joined by those one doesn't normally hear from in books about media ethics – an advertising executive (Jim Moser), a spokeswoman from the sex and porn industry (Fiona Patten), and a best-selling novelist and a trained Sinologist (Linda Jaivin).

ENGAGING INTEREST

Our primary motivation in producing this collection was to stir up and encourage public debate about these issues. Too often, ethics is seen as a scary or arcane topic to be deliberated over by learned professors or opinionated media commentators. Media ethics is presented in dry textbooks for media students to dutifully learn by rote, only to be forgotten or discarded once they are in the thick of the action. We want to make media ethics interesting – to demonstrate that these are vital issues of interest to us all. Reading these essays we hope you will be interested, engaged and entertained. We do not pretend to have all the answers, nor to have covered all the issues. But we do contend that new and popular forms of the media should be taken seriously for what they tell us about ethical engagement and connection, about what's real and what's not, about the types of ethics being practised at the grassroots level, online and in studios and newsrooms; about why honesty and accountability matter to all concerned: journalists, producers, media owners and consumers. In the end, ethics comes down to use it or lose it. We need to practise ethical reflection, to ask and demand more of the public sphere, and to participate as consumers and producers – or else.

NOTES

1   Stuart Hall, 'Encoding/Decoding', in S. Hall, D. Hobson, A. Lowe and P. Willis (eds), *Culture, Media, Language* (London: Hutchison, 1980), 128–40.

2 Real Appeal: The Ethics of Reality TV
CATHARINE LUMBY

IT WAS AN UNSCRIPTED MOMENT WHEN *60 MINUTES* REPORTER CHARLES
Wooley jumped up on stage to perform *Big Brother* housemate Sara-Marie
Fedele's infamous 'bum dance' for the studio audience. The occasion was the
penultimate eviction night in the show's first Australian series and Wooley was
there to document this weird new genre for his viewers. Until he took to the
stage, his approach to the story had been one of amused professional detachment. But as he stared out into a sea of pink bunny ears that were being
sported by hundreds of teenage Fedele fans, you could see the recognition
dawning on his face that *Big Brother* might not be just another flash in the
youth culture pan – that maybe there was something groundbreaking in this
reality TV stuff; that maybe, just maybe, he was staring out at the future of TV.

Despite years of living with the incessant public attention that a TV profile
brings, Wooley was clearly stunned by the fascination generated by a bunch
of 'ordinary' people who'd agreed to live in the *Big Brother* house and have
their lives recorded daily and broadcast nightly to television viewers. 'Why are
they famous?' Wooley kept asking the fans and experts he interviewed. 'What
have any of them done?' The stir Wooley's own presence created amongst the
studio audience lent more than a touch of irony to his remarks. A stream of
young women flocked to him wherever he moved, asking for autographs, and
craning their necks about in the hope of getting their faces on camera.

It's conventional for television journalists to see the fame that goes with
their job as being something incidental – not central – to what they do. It's a
by-product of their skill as a reporter or presenter. The idea that literally
anyone can become famous by appearing on television – and that the viewers

might want to cross over to the other side of the screen – is a confronting one for media practitioners raised on the idea that television is a 'special' medium and that there is an art to television presentation and production. What the *Big Brother* phenomenon has made clear is that viewers no longer regard television as a quasi-mystical phenomenon. They know how it works, they know what it does for people who appear on it, and they want a slice of the action.

Television is a curious medium in this regard. It is, on one hand, a banal medium that increasingly feeds on the everyday, repackaging the rituals, aesthetics and dramas of domestic life. Like the family cat, it sits in the corner of the lounge room and emits a reassuring purr. We are all familiar with its formulas and its production methods – it no longer inspires awe. At the same time, this everydayness coexists with television's extraordinary capacity to influence public perceptions of individuals and events. As our prime source of information and entertainment, broadcast television captures the gaze of millions of Australians every day and it is precisely for this reason that its relationship to the social and political is the locus of so much ethical debate.

Reality television is a genre which, by its very nature, focuses our attention on the ethics of representation. As I'll argue in this chapter, one of the central fascinations the genre holds for viewers is the question of what's real and what's not – or to put it into *Big Brother* housemate terms, who's faking it and who's 'real'. Indeed, one of the reasons that reality television has been the focus of so much ethical concern is that it's a genre that encourages us to actively reflect on media representations – it is television about making television; television which puts 'ordinary' people on the other side of the screen; television that focuses on how the presence of cameras affects people's behaviour.

In popular terms, these ethical concerns have tended to be translated as fears about the propensity of reality to promote voyeurism and to exploit 'ordinary' people and invade their privacy. And certainly there are ethical issues that need to be addressed in a genre which is so reliant on media 'amateurs'. But it's equally important to interrogate the assumptions underlying these concerns – assumptions about the value of privacy, the agency of audiences, and what kinds of bodies, emotions and behaviours are considered acceptable for public consumption. One of the most interesting aspects of reality television is the way in which it invites us to question the very foundations of conventional liberal frameworks for formulating media ethics.

Before scrutinising and responding to some of the common ethical concerns raised by the reality genre, it is worth briefly defining the genre of reality television, mapping its origins and, in particular, asking how it fits in relation to other televisual genres which claim a privileged relationship to the real.

TELEVISING REALITY

While there are many precursors to reality TV, a search of popular media databases reveals that the term 'reality television' or 'real TV' came into currency in the early 1990s in reference to US programs such as *Cops*, a show pioneered by the Fox network that showed dramatic highlights of police work. The term is now used to refer to a broad spectrum of shows, from programs that confront contestants with highly theatrical challenges, such as *Survivor* and *Temptation Island*, to shows that rely on relatively simple editing of footage of everyday life, such as Australia's *RPA*, a program based in a public hospital.

In broad terms, reality television programs exhibit some or all of the following characteristics: the use of ordinary people as opposed to trained actors; editing which emphasises character and narrative; a multi-stranded narrative (normally characteristic of soap opera and drama); gameshow-style competitions and contrived locations; pieces-to-camera delivered by contestants; dramatic tension (the audience sometimes knows things the subjects don't); audience involvement; occasional use of live-to-air footage; and documentary-style voiceovers. What this list of characteristics clearly shows is that reality television programs are a hybrid of conventional information and entertainment programs.

More specifically, reality television genres borrow from an array of familiar genres, blending the elements in a distinctly postmodern manner. With their use of both raw footage of 'ordinary' people and unscripted events and interpretative voiceovers, reality television programs align themselves with news and current affairs. In addition, reality TV shows have something in common with documentaries, in that they often make claims to be analysing human nature – to be engaged in what some commentators have dubbed 'Lab Rat TV'.[1] This claim to be documenting social behaviour was the driving rationale behind early fly-on-the-wall documentaries such as the 1974 UK series titled *The Family*, directed by Paul Watson, which documented the daily life of the Wilkins family. Watson was also behind the highly contentious program, *Sylvania Waters*, which chronicled the troubled life of the Australian Donaher family. The hidden camera technique used so much on current affairs in the 1980s and 1990s has also been extended in reality TV – the camera isn't hidden in the sense that the participants are unaware of it, but they often begin to act as if they have forgotten it's there.

At the same time, reality television owes a large debt to an array of conventional entertainment genres. Many reality shows are part game show, involving some kind of contest such as searching for buried treasure (*Treasure Island*), a large cash prize for surviving the series (*Survivor*), or the opportunity to win a modelling contract (*Search for a Supermodel*). And most employ a structure borrowed from the soap opera genre – the audience has information about the characters that some of the characters don't have, and there is a strong emphasis on relationships, emotions, character and editing, which heighten dramatic tension.

There is also an open-ended narrative, which pulls viewers along with the series from week to week. This combination of documentary and soap is one that the producers of *Sylvania Waters* were quite explicit about. When recruiting a family for their series, they distributed a flyer which asked: 'Any dramas in your house? We are seeking a family whose children cover a wide range of ages and interests. A lively family, with something to say, who are willing to let us into their lives. Let us see how the average Australian family live. Better than a soapie, this is real life.'[2] Needless to say, the resultant family did not consist of a couple of media studies academics and their articulate, bookish children.

The confessional elements of reality television embodied in the 'diary room' sequences of *Big Brother*, the confidential pieces-to-camera that *Survivor* contestants record after voting off team members, and the generalised focus on conventionally private emotions and behaviours also link the genre to the US talk show formats pioneered by Phil Donahue and Oprah Winfrey.

It's this very hybrid nature of reality television – the promiscuous blending of genres drawn from both information and entertainment media – which has, of course, fuelled many of the ethical concerns raised in relation to the genre. But it's also through this very hybridity, in its postmodern cannibalising of other televisual genres, that reality television announces itself as a genre which lays the conventions of television bare for the viewer. Indeed, if reality programs, which span many formats, are linked by any one characteristic, it's their habit of exposing the generic workings of television and inviting the audience – and their surrogates, the contestants – to literally participate in making the program. Shows such as *Popstars* and *Search for a Supermodel* unpack the production of celebrity that drives a host of media formats from music TV to *Neighbours*. Reality game shows like *Survivor* and *The Mole* focus attention on the way that the ability to perform identity (whether for the cameras or for members of a social group) is one of the key survival skills in a mediated society.

REALITY CHECK

Perhaps the most prominent and frequently voiced ethical concern about reality TV is a kind of monstrous eruption in the televisual landscape which tricks viewers into believing that what they see on television is real. Epitomising this view, journalist Paul Sheehan wrote in the *Sydney Morning Herald*: 'The explosive growth of reality broadcasting in all its forms is increasingly blurring the lines between what is news and entertainment, what is real and what is manufactured ...'[3]

Sheehan's criticism is one which has been consistently raised in relation to broader trends in televisual news and current affairs dating back to the 1980s. As Graeme Turner notes in an essay on tabloid journalism, the past two decades have seen a tremendous shift in Western news and current affairs television:

> *[a shift] away from politics and towards crime, away from the daily*
> *news agenda and towards editorially generated items promoted days*
> *in advance, away from information-based treatments of social issues*
> *and towards entertaining stories on lifestyles or celebrities, and an*
> *overwhelming investment in the power of the visual, in the news*
> *as an entertaining spectacle.*[4]

Quite clearly, reality television, as its name suggests, is a genre which attempts to trade off its relationship to real people and events. And certainly many of the pre- and post-production decisions are focused on heightening the 'reality' effect. Sets are often constructed – a whole house, for instance, in *Big Brother* – and there is an attempt to furnish and fit them out in a way that looks 'real'. The selection of participants is also contrived and done with an eye to choosing a spectrum of people who convincingly form a representation of ordinary people. The pieces-to-camera that contestants on *Survivor* deliver establish an intimacy with the audience. Some reality shows favour segments that feature grainy footage and jerky camera movements, which confer the immediacy and 'real' rawness of amateur footage. Reality television, in summary, is constructed on many levels by the selection of participants, the construction of contrived locations and contests, and by editing and voiceovers. Certainly, it is no less 'produced' or 'manufactured' than standard news or current affairs programs, which make equally strong claims of representing reality.

Ethical concerns about the 'reality' quotient of any televisual genre need to be qualified by an acknowledgement that the relationship between the real and the represented is always and already complex, and that all televisual formats, and arguably all cultural products, are implicated in this complexity. But more importantly, they focus us on a critical and hotly contested issue in media ethics: how much agency and understanding should we attribute to viewers? Or to put this in broader terms, how should we understand the relationship between 'ordinary' people (as viewers of or participants in the reality genre) and media producers?

Public debates about journalistic ethics have tended to use a top-down framework for understanding the consumer–producer relationship. Codes of ethics are promoted as tools for protecting 'ordinary' people from media producers and practitioners – even if their application in practice is acknowledged as tenuous. What's rarely questioned in the debate about media ethics is whether media consumers are concerned about the same things as media practitioners or academics commenting on ethics – and if they are, whether these translate into concerns about precisely the same practices.

Writing about media audiences, John Hartley reminds us that audiences are objects of knowledge produced by institutions and experts with an investment in framing the text–viewer relationship in particular ways. Child educators, for instance, may bring a pedagogical focus to their analysis of how children interact with a given television program – a focus which may overlook the way children interact with the fantastical or pleasurable elements of the show.[5] Similarly, some public intellectuals and media commentators may have a rhetorical (and implicitly political) investment in adopting an elevated and paternalistic position when pronouncing on what 'the masses' do with popular culture.

Certainly, the assumption that the audience simply takes reality television's claim to represent real life at face value ignores evidence of the growing media literacy of contemporary viewers. The domestication of audiovisual production equipment once used only by professionals, in the form of handicams and editing software readily available on home computers, has increased awareness of the basic principles of framing and editing – a fact which former director of news and current affairs at Channel Nine, Peter Meakin, readily acknowledges: 'We have to be far more careful,' he claims. 'People understand how television works and they put us in the spotlight and let us know when they think we're trying to manipulate them.'[6]

Certainly it's a trend that has been confirmed in research conducted by myself and Elspeth Probyn into the uses teenage girls make of media culture. We conducted our research into reality television as part of a much larger project titled Girlcultures, which is funded over a three-year period by an Australian Research Council Grant.[7]

KNOWING GIRLS

Teenage girls are routinely figured as the group of consumers most 'at risk' from contact with the media – both from images which are too real or adult (precociously sexual images of young girls in music video clips) and from images that are unreal (extraordinarily thin or beautiful models). In numerous debates, conducted very publicly, teenage girls are often assumed to be so incapable of distinguishing media representations from reality that they are seen to be in constant need of protection by an array of experts (psychologists, educators, sociologists) who are able to discern and repair the damage popular culture has done. Yet, it's an expert knowingness which often fails to ask the simplest and most important question: what do young girls themselves make of particular media products and programs? What do *they* know?

Through extensive focus group interviews with over 200 teenage girls aged between 12 and 18, we discovered that young Australian women had a lot to say about the *Big Brother* phenomenon, and that much of what they did say directly contradicted claims that they are passive or gullible media consumers.

Charles Wooley and other journalists and commentators may have been mystified by the immense appeal of *Big Brother* housemate Sara-Marie Fedele, but young women were very clear about why they liked the gregarious, earthy, size 16 blonde. In focus group after focus group Fedele's popularity was tied to the perception that she is an emotionally honest figure who isn't concerned about appearances – she's 'real'. As one 13-year-old put it: 'She's fat and she's big, but she doesn't care about it and she's even modelled in the magazine *Cosmopolitan*'. An exchange which was frequently cited with approval involved Fedele's response to *Big Brother* host Gretel Killeen. Killeen asked Fedele how she felt about having to sunbathe next to a slimmer, more conventionally 'pretty' contestant, to which Fedele replied: 'We've got the same body, mine's just bigger'.

One of the primary pleasures of *Big Brother* for young women, then, is seeing people who look and act like ordinary people in the media. As one young woman put it: 'It shows that if you go on a TV show and you have a nice personality, you'll shine through and that outside of beauty, what size you are doesn't really count.'

At a deeper level, however, this fascination with Fedele revealed itself to be a fascination with the way a performance of normality and a negotiation of other people's gazes is a central aspect of everyday life. As one focus group participant, a boarder at a private girls' school in country New South Wales, put it: '*Big Brother* is like being at school. You don't get to choose the people you go with – but you have to learn to hang out with them and get on with them, but also be yourself'.

Big Brother, then, was a media text which brought to the foreground a dilemma that is central to young women's identity – the question of how you negotiate the performance of your individual 'self' when you are under the constant scrutiny of others, from friends, to parents, to educators, to a host of anxious experts. Certainly, some media aimed at young women may tend to exacerbate anxieties about body shape and size or what it means to be a desirable woman. But it's true that young women are drawn to media texts that make these anxieties explicit. *Big Brother* performed this function.

Life in a house full of cameras, where the object of the game is to tread a careful line between being yourself and fitting in with the group, is for many young women a metaphor of their own existence – it's life in a mediated world writ large. *Big Brother*, in this sense, was a text that allowed young women to reflect on the ethical dilemmas of life in a mediated and highly self-conscious world – it was a means for thinking about ethical questions, not an end in itself.

THE HUMAN ZOO

One of the more curious aspects of the popular debate about the reality television genre is that it's often the very people who argue most vociferously that young women and other 'vulnerable' categories of media consumer need to be protected from unreal media images, who are most scathing about the 'excessive' realism of a show like *Big Brother*.

Germaine Greer has been an outspoken critic of the damage she believes unrealistic Barbie doll media images of women do to female self-esteem, yet she also disparages the format of reality TV such as the first *Big Brother* series screened in the United Kingdom:

> *[P]eople who like watching torture will tune in to see a table dancer, an air steward, a hairdresser, a medical rep and a web site designer struggling with the contradictions inherent in having simultaneously to bond with and betray perfect strangers.*[8]

In a similar vein, opinion columnist Miranda Devine, commenting on the contestants in the Australian *Big Brother* series, said:

> *[They] are not embarrassed about anything – not the mess in their dormitory bedrooms, the banality of their conversation, their late-night drunken ramblings, their indiscriminate bed-hopping, their liberal use of the f-word. They are the fully evolved embodiment of their vulgar era: people utterly without shame.*[9]

There's no question that reality television requires participants to submit themselves to a high level of public scrutiny and that one of the central appeals of the genre lies in the opportunity it affords viewers to scrutinise the ordinarily private behaviours and responses of others. But the claim that this opening up of the private realm to public surveillance is automatically a degrading process does not necessarily follow. Rather, it's important to see that the boundaries between the public and the private spheres are not, in fact, natural, but political and cultural, and that the relegation of certain issues and behaviours to the domestic realm has not served all social groups equally well.

As Moira Gatens, and a host of other feminist political theorists have argued, the very idea and structure of the modern public sphere relies on the exclusion of women and all things associated with them. The private sphere is the necessary but invisible foundation of the public sphere. She writes: 'The world of the family, infant education, morality and sensuality, is private, domestic, whereas the world of work, citizenship, legality and rationality is public.'[10]

In simple terms, it is women who have traditionally been identified with the private domain of the home, and with emotions and issues considered unsuited for or unworthy of public attention. Childcare, intimate and family relationships, sexuality, mundane matters of the body – all of these things have traditionally been seen as 'women's business'. This separation of the public and private spheres has come under increasing challenge with the growth of grassroots political movements such as feminism and the gay and lesbian rights movement. Over the past three decades, a host of issues once seen as personal or private – from domestic violence and childcare arrangements to sexual preference and the female orgasm – have been brought into the public sphere, both by the media and by the demands of political groups and, thus, politicised. Far from being a sign of the decline of social values, this blurring of the boundaries between the public and the private can equally be interpreted in terms of the ongoing democratisation of political life in Western cultures.

Reality shows frequently focus on dilemmas that confront all of us in everyday life. Dilemmas such as: How far do you go to fit in with a group? Is it unethical or merely pragmatic to align yourself with authority figures in your workplace? Should you marry for romantic love or for money and social status? Is emotional strength more important than physical strength when it comes to survival? Is gender, race or sexuality as big a deal as we think? All of these scenarios and questions have been raised quite explicitly by reality television shows. And in everyday terms, these dilemmas are grounded in key ethical questions – questions that compel us because they are ones we are obliged to negotiate all the time.

Of course, one of the key criticisms of reality television has been that it packages human dilemmas and conflicts up for commercial purposes – pitting humans against each other and exposing their weaknesses for no higher purpose than entertainment.

Certainly, there are potential ethical problems raised by the fact that media 'amateurs' are being produced and directed by media professionals. In a BBC

Panorama documentary, a contestant from the British version of *Big Brother* complained bitterly about the way her image had been edited, resulting in her being stereotyped as a predatory female by the viewing audience. A fellow housemate, who was also one of the least popular contestants on the show, opined that they had all been 'pawns in a game'. In Australia, there was an outcry from the gay community when gay housemate Johnnie Cass was portrayed in edited highlights of the week as being a backstabber – in tabloid parlance, he was dubbed Johnnie Rotten. In an interview immediately after his eviction, Cass admitted he became a little concerned that his cartoon villain image might prompt aggro in the real world. 'But when I saw that people on the street were supportive it was OK', he said. 'In fact, I think it added a little controversy to my image. And while the media tried to make me into something I'm not, I also have to accept responsibility because we knew that was the risk we would take.'[11]

Director of infotainment programming at Channel Seven, Brad Lyons, says that producers of reality shows are extremely conscious of the potential for alienating the public if they openly exploit or manipulate contestants. He also argues that as the genre matures people have become highly conscious of 'what they're going into' and of the opportunities that may be waiting on the other side of the show.

> *People are familiar with the formats. We found that there was a lot more intensity with the second* Popstars *because people who auditioned realised there was something at stake – there really was a future out the back of the TV show.*[12]

Indeed, it's the opportunity for do-it-yourself fame that drives shows such as *Popstars*, or *Search for a Supermodel*. Even contestants who wind up being stereotyped as the program's resident vamp, tramp or meanie, are in a position to collect the rewards of celebrity. It's a perspective that suggests the biggest risk of taking part in a reality show is not receiving too much media exposure, but too little.

But what of the future? Is reality television a genre that demands an upping of the ante? Will media producers be forced, as US academic Stuart Fischoff told the *Panorama* program: 'to escalate the … sex and violence'? The small matter of criminal law aside, will we ever witness the kind of reality television envisaged in the movie *Series 7*, in which people literally compete for their lives. (The opening sequence shows an eight-months pregnant woman shooting a fellow contestant dead in a supermarket and then asking the cashier: 'Have you got any bean dip?')

It's a concern that once again ignores the evidence of the genre itself. In social Darwinian terms, *Survivor* is the show which comes closest to embodying the dog-eat-dog mentality that critics have suggested reality television promotes. And yet, what lesson in survival does the show offer viewers? More specifically, who emerged as the survivor? Despite a plethora of alpha male contestants to overcome, the first series was won by an overweight middle-aged gay guy and the second was won by a grandmother.

On the face of it, *Big Brother* is everything Australian director Peter Weir sought to warn us about in *The Truman Show*, a movie about a man who is unaware that his entire life is the subject of a twenty-four hour live television show. Weir's moral message was clear – spiritual freedom lies outside the unblinking gaze of the television camera. Towards the end of the film we see viewers at home cheering Truman on in his quest to escape from the confines of the large television studio which constitutes his 'home'. It's a tactic which appears to shift the blame for Truman's plight from media consumers to the executive producer of *The Truman Show* – a man with a serious God complex who tells Truman: 'You were real, that's why you were so good to watch'. The final shot in the film, however, unsettles this paradigm. It shows two pizza-chomping security guards facing a blank screen. One turns to the other and says: 'What's on the other channel?' The implication, of course, is that media consumers are equally amoral and that the fascination with reality TV is just an extension of a mindless voyeurism.

At the heart of Weir's movie is a moral claim about the relationship between the real and its representation – a claim which has deep philosophical roots but which also grounds many popular concerns about television – and reality television in particular. It's a claim rooted in a fundamental distrust of the power of images to displace and ultimately replace social reality.

Discussing the advent of reality TV in Britain, prominent television producer Andy Hamilton described the genre as being focused on 'ordinary people improvising around the theme of being themselves'.[13] His remark gestures towards a very different framework for understanding the significance of the reality television phenomenon. Rather than exemplifying the 'dumbing down' of media audiences and the increasingly degraded nature of popular culture, reality television might be understood as a forum in which so-called 'ordinary' people are able to participate, if only partially, in the process of quite literally representing themselves. Certainly, as we've observed, reality television programs are, on the whole, highly contrived and tightly edited. But they do offer media consumers the opportunity to discover life on the other side of the screen – and to watch others like them do so. Indeed, far from presenting the viewer with an amoral or even immoral spectacle, reality television presents us with individuals caught up in the process of negotiating the messy ethics of ordinary existence. They may be placed in contrived situations, but the real challenge for most contestants on reality television lies in managing human relationships, in deciding when to be honest, when to dissemble, where their responsibility to the group lies, and where to draw the line with self-interest. These, after all, are precisely the dilemmas most of us face in the workplace, at school, in family life, and in our broader social existence. Reality television, in this light, might be said to humanise ethical dilemmas, which are too often discussed in abstract terms, and to offer a forum for reflection on the politics of everyday life.

NOTES

1   D. Light, 'Real Appeal', *Bulletin*, 26 September 2000, 64.
2   John Stratton and Ien Ang, 'Sylvania Waters and the spectacular exploding family', in P. Marris and S. Thornham (eds), *Media Studies: A Reader* (Edinburgh University Press, 1999), 614.
3   Paul Sheehan, 'Death by television as audience loses itself in the real world', *Sydney Morning Herald*, 2 August 2000.
4   Graeme Turner, 'Tabloidisation, journalism and the possibility of critique', *International Journal of Cultural Studies* (April 1999), 59.
5   John Hartley, 'Methodological tensions in media research', *Textual Practice* 13:3 (1999).
6   Peter Meakin, personal interview, 25 March 2001.
7   The Girlcultures project is an investigation of what young women aged between 12 and 18 do with popular media, what they like and don't like about the media available to them, how they believe the media affect them, and what media they would like to see produced. We began our research in 2001 and in the first two years of the project we conducted intensive focus group interviews with more than 200 individuals. Focus group participants were sourced from schools across New South Wales and carefully selected to ensure a demographically balanced

sample. In the final year of the project, 2003, we are conducting intensive interview sessions with individual young women to refine the data we have gathered in the first two years of the project.

8   Germaine Greer, 'We are Big Brother', *Australian*, *Media* section, 12–18 July 2001, 6.

9   Miranda Devine, 'Big Brother is watching but who cares?', *Sydney Morning Herald*, 3 May 2001, 12.

10 Moira Gatens, *Feminism and Philosophy* (Cambridge: Polity Press, 1993), 12.

11 Johnnie Cass, personal interview, 18 July 2001.

12 Brad Lyons, personal interview, 24 March 2001.

13 See Graeme Burton, *Talking Television: An introduction to the study of television* (London: Arnold, 2000).

3 Arguing about Ethics*

DUNCAN IVISON

WE LIVE IN A CULTURE SO SATURATED BY THE MEDIA THAT IT SEEMS FAIR to ask sometimes: what is real any more? So much of what we know about ourselves, our communities and our world is shaped by our complex relationship with the media. This results in a kind of paradox. Never before have we had so much access to what is going on around us – the speed and pervasiveness of modern communications are astonishing – and yet many feel even more cut off and unsure of what is, in fact, happening to them. The world seems more interconnected than ever before, and yet ethnic, cultural, social and economic divisions appear to be deepening, not diminishing. 'Reality TV' is more surreal and faked than BBC costume dramas. What is going on?

In this chapter I want to ask how these developments relate to two questions. First, does our postmodern mediasphere mean that because 'reality' seems increasingly inaccessible and diversity so great that just about anything goes? My answer to this is an emphatic *no*. But this raises another question. How should we argue about ethical questions in the public sphere today, given the kinds of dramatic changes that are occurring? Here my answer is more equivocal and indirect. We need to understand why we care about the public sphere in the first place, before moving on to evaluate the effects of various changes – like the increasing pervasiveness of a celebrity-obsessed, commercially-driven media – on our ethical beliefs.

I

When we argue about ethics in the public sphere what are we doing?[1] First of all, we are engaging in *public reasoning*: the exchange of reasons over what

#25

we think of as good or right, or over what we mean by concepts like freedom, equality and justice. Philosophers have offered different visions about what citizens do when they engage with each other in the public sphere. Perhaps the most ambitious vision of all was provided by Plato, in the *Republic*. For Plato, public standards should track the truth, and thus a special class of persons – whom Plato called the Guardians, meaning the philosophers – are charged with discerning the truth and ruling the city in light of it. He drew an analogy between reason governing the soul and reason governing the city: a well-ordered soul is one in which reason rules, and so it should be in the city.

By the seventeenth century, reason was still central to politics, and so was the idea of reason tracking the truth about ethics, but there was much less confidence about 'right reason' being directly applicable to debates over what is good, all things considered, in politics. Instead, some philosophers tried to establish basic ground rules, or 'laws of nature', grounded in quasi-factual claims about the world and man's nature, that could provide a minimal ethical framework for politics. The terrible wars of religion that ravaged Europe for most of the seventeenth century led political philosophers such as Hugo Grotius, Samuel Pufendorf, Thomas Hobbes and John Locke to focus on finding principles that could enable citizens to live together peacefully without necessarily agreeing on the truth about the best way to live. By the eighteenth century, especially following the French Revolution, many philosophers were still looking for a comprehensive ethical vision that could unite society, but at the same time, were increasingly skeptical about the capacity of religion to do so. This was because of the increasing prominence and pre-eminence of science, and also the fact that deeply religious and cultural diversity was here to stay; the wars of religion made that clear. But despite great hopes, science did not seem to entail any obvious solutions for the pressing social and political problems faced by the emerging states in Europe.

In many ways, these doubts remain with us today. We live in ostensibly secular societies, but amazingly diverse ones as well, and also ones in which science is one of the most – if not *the* most – powerful influences on our culture. And yet we still struggle to find a comprehensive and inclusive enough moral language within which to orient our arguments about ethical questions in politics.

I will return to these large themes in a moment. To begin with, however, I want to look more closely at this notion of the 'public sphere' and then show

how it is related to our attitudes towards the media. Philosophers tend to come at these problems rather abstractly, and in some circumstances that can be problematic, but in this case I think there are some benefits. For it is important to know why we even care about the media and the state of our public sphere(s) in the first place. Otherwise, what's the big deal if the media become dominated by one corporate magnate rather than another, or if we have public broadcasters or not? The practical questions facing students of the media are informed by deeper philosophical commitments, or so I will try to show.

II

The idea of the public sphere is central to our thinking about the media. The connections are historical and normative. Thus our attitudes and beliefs about the proper role for the media in a democracy are shaped by our ideas about the nature of the public sphere. If you think the majority of our newspapers, radio, television and web-based programs are just terrible, and that they undermine our grasp of the most important issues of the day, then you have a certain view about the relation between a properly functioning public sphere and democracy. If, on the other hand, you think that tabloid newspapers, shock-jock radio hosts and celebrity-obsessed magazines, web sites and television programs are simply reflecting the reality – the truth – about our culture, and therefore a lament for a lost critical public culture is simply out of place (because it never existed and never will), then you too have a view about the relation between the public sphere and democracy.

I want to explore the deeper philosophical views at stake here. We need to know how our attitudes towards contemporary media are related to these deeper arguments about the role of the public sphere. The conditions of con-temporary democratic life are changing fast. In fact, the speed of change is itself causing problems for our public institutions. Deepening social and cultural pluralism, rapid technological change, and the ever-expanding forces of globalisation, make it difficult for our public institutions to keep pace.

However, just because things are changing so quickly and dramatically it doesn't follow that the values we associate with a democratic public culture should be junked. Just because people can now get massive amounts of infor-mation from television or the Internet, and can exchange their views more rapidly and effectively via instant polls and interactive technology, doesn't necessarily mean these new mechanisms are better from the point of view of democracy. To make that judgement we need a clearer sense of what we mean when we talk about 'the public' in the first place.

Why should we care? Well, first of all, for all of its frivolity and idiocy sometimes, politics is a serious business. States can declare war. In some places, they execute people. Decisions have to be made about the allocation of scarce resources between equally compelling needs and goods. In all of these instances, in liberal democracies at least, *a public view has to be formed* about these things, however transitory, indirect, and imperfect it will be. To make judgements about the plain awfulness (or the exciting multiplicity) of contemporary media, we need to explore these deeper issues first. Otherwise, the media just become a form of entertainment and escapism. They certainly are that sometimes, and there is nothing wrong with that. But entertainment isn't the only role we want our media to play in a liberal-democratic society.

Let's look more closely at these issues. Our idea of the public sphere is actually a very specific one, with a particular history. Perhaps one of the most famous accounts of that history is provided by the German philosopher and social theorist, Jurgen Habermas. In his influential book, entitled *The Structural Transformation of the Public Sphere*,[2] Habermas argued that in the seventeenth and eighteenth centuries there was a fundamental shift in the Western conception of 'the public'. When Louis XIV said 'L'etat, c'est moi', the publicity of the Royal Court was being displayed authoritatively to the people. However, this kind of exclusive and authoritative publicity was soon displaced by a very different idea, one in which 'the public' was now thought of as a collection of private (individual) persons engaging in rational and critical discourse about the state and its power.

This is part of the complicated story of the emergence of representative democracy, and especially the idea that 'the people' are self-governing. So the shift in our specific understanding of 'the public' came about for a variety of cultural and historical reasons. Amongst these included: the rise of newspapers, novels and other forms of new media; the emergence of coffee-houses, salons and other modes of everyday interaction in which views about the issues of the day could be discussed and debated; the rise of critical commentary on music, art and literature; and the development of the modern notion of an economy as a realm quasi-independent from the state.[3] The crucial thing that emerges here, argues Habermas, is the medium in which this interaction occurs – what he calls the 'people's public use of their reason' carried on through the emerging infrastructure of civil society.[4]

What makes the public sphere so important, and not just an interesting historical feature of modern societies, is the *normative* role it is meant to play in liberal societies. That is, the role it plays in helping to legitimate new ideas about the state and the individual's relation to it. There are two important ideas here: first, that people should be able to form their opinions freely, both individually and collectively (as 'a people'). And second, that these opinions should *matter* – that they should have some role in shaping the actions of the state. Remember that these 'opinions' are not meant to be just any old opinion, but ones shaped by critical discourse. They are meant to represent a considered and informed view of some kind. This is the original sense of 'public opinion'. (Notice how far we have moved away from this notion today. Most readers, I take it, would associate 'public opinion' with the slippery and often duplicitous way it is invoked by self-serving politicians and their pollsters. I'll return to this point about the apparent degradation of the public sphere in a moment.)

The formation of 'public opinion' then, in its original and ideal sense, refers to the *active* formation, by citizens, of a common view about the exercise of political power in their society. They don't even have to actually meet or know each other for this kind of conversation to occur. The infrastructure of civil society – the family unit, the economy, the public spaces and institutions, and the various forms of modern media – links citizens in a virtual 'space of discussion'. Of course, infrastructure isn't enough. The right cultural conditions have to be in place too. The public sphere comes to be seen as providing a means of engaging everyone in the process of reflecting critically and informatively on the exercise of power. Moreover, government ought to listen to it, not only because it represents an 'enlightened view', but because it is morally bound to. The people are sovereign, and governments should govern in light of the public views that emerge out of the critical and reflective discourses of its citizens.[5] At least, that was the ideal. In the eighteenth century 'everyone' meant mainly white, property-owning men. Women, the working classes and various racial and ethnic minorities weren't included. These kinds of explicit and implicit exclusions from public discourse have remained an important feature of the concept of the public sphere right up until today, and I shall return to this issue below.

Note that when I talk about the formation of public opinion, or about the formation of a 'common mind' about certain issues, I am not suggesting that everyone *actually* agrees about which ends the state should pursue, or what the best means for achieving those ends are. This point is often misunderstood. There are many different kinds of public conversations going on at any point in time, and more often than not they are characterised by deep disagreement as opposed to consensus. But what is common is the implicit 'backdrop' to these arguments – a belief that they are critical arguments about power, and about issues that affect 'us' as a community or society, and whose institutions and norms we identify with in some way.

What is important here is the way in which the emergence of this specific sense of the public sphere is linked to the promotion of certain valuable liberal goods, and especially individual freedom, self-government and justice. The public sphere is linked to individual freedom because it exists at a distance from the state (though never wholly separate from it), and thus provides a means *limiting* political power. But it also helps us to realise our collective freedom by providing a conduit for making power responsive to collective decision-making.[6] And it promotes justice (when it works well) by ensuring that the public agenda remains open and responsive to the problems and conflicts that emerge between the state and civil society, and between individuals and groups within civil society.

So we have two ways of conceiving of the normative role of the public sphere. First, as an extra-political space that provides a bulwark against invasive state power. And second, as an important aspect of the ideal of self-government.

III

I've painted an ideal picture up to now, as philosophers often do. The 'structural transformation' of the public sphere that Habermas maps in the eighteenth century is essentially an idealistic one. Most liberal societies today barely come close to this ideal. What went wrong? The bulk of Habermas' book, in fact, is taken up with showing how the emancipatory potential of this new idea was quickly betrayed and abandoned. He even suggests that contemporary economic and social conditions make it even *more* unlikely that the ideal can be redeemed in any meaningful way. In particular, he worries that powerful actors (such as states, but also multinational corporations and other non-governmental actors) are much more capable of dominating and 'colonising' public space – and thus of manipulating public conversations – than ever before. This is in part due to what he calls the 'interpenetration' of the state and civil society, that is, the closing of the gap between the state and the public sphere. This is crucial, remember, because without it public opinion loses its critical edge. It no longer acts as a limitation on power, or generates ideas for the shaping of power, but instead simply becomes an extension of it. In these conditions, argues Habermas, the public sphere doesn't challenge power but instead becomes a place of empty rhetoric, manipulation, and 'benign acclamation'.[7] All the various elements of modern liberal-democratic states – including the role and function of legislatures, political parties, social movements and other actors in civil society – are affected by these developments. When we add to this the forces of economic globalisation at work in the world today, the prospects for a robust and critically engaged democratic public sphere look pretty bleak indeed.

Why should we care? The philosopher Charles Taylor has suggested some of the worrying consequences of these developments. If the ideal of self-rule is one we genuinely value, then if it atrophies too much – if we become too cynical and thus complacent about the possibilities for freedom and our capacity for self-government – the stability of liberal society, and thus the goods it provides, is threatened.[8] Not only does the state become loosened from the discipline of critical public opinion, but a vicious circle seeps into place, something the nineteenth-century French observer of American political life, Alexis de Tocqueville, brilliantly analysed.[9] He argued that a sense of powerlessness causes people to disconnect from the political process, which in turn serves to concentrate power even more in the hands of a few, which in turn engenders more apathy. For Taylor, fragmentation is a very real danger in modern democratic societies that lack a vital public sphere, not necessarily because they will become totalitarian (as de Tocqueville warned), but because citizens lose a sense of a common purpose and common empathy with others, something required in order to support broadly based social programs such as universal health care or public education. And this means societies become more atomistic and potentially less just. Of course, people disagree profoundly about the best means of realising these goods, as well as about the interpretation of the goods themselves, but Taylor argues we still need to feel that decisions about them form a common space of concern, and that what we think and say about them will have some impact on how the goods are to be distributed.[10]

At this stage you might think that I've presupposed precisely what is at issue; namely, that the public sphere is an ideal worth hanging onto at all. But it is striking, as Taylor points out, that even in societies where the values associated with it are being blatantly suppressed or manipulated, it is often faked.[11] So the real debate, I think, is over the nature of the public sphere we have, and ideas about the one (or many) we would like to have.

Sometimes critics of liberal conceptions of the public sphere, and of Habermas in particular, claim that his vision (and that of other liberals) is too rationalistic and intellectualised, and as a result, rules out all kinds of important public speech and behaviour that don't fit the model of 'rational–critical' discourse. It's important for theorists to be reminded that the kind of arguments we have in politics are not akin to those in the seminar room. So the criticism is important but often overstated. There is some confusion over what people mean by 'rational' speech or behaviour. Leaving aside Habermas for now (since he complicates things by going on to develop a complex and highly idealised account of the nature of 'communicative action'), there is nothing inherently wrong with the idea of the public sphere being associated with 'rational' discourse. It all depends on what you mean by 'rational'. At a minimum, acting rationally simply means doing what you most have reason to do. But different people will have different reasons for acting and pursuing the ends they do. There is nothing in the concept of rationality itself that necessarily picks out *the* right way for people to live. Of course, there will be ways of living that are clearly irrational for me or for you to pursue. I wanted to play ice hockey for the Montreal Canadians, but given my abilities on the ice as compared to those in the classroom, it would have been irrational for me to pursue that goal instead of finishing high school and going on to university. Note that this doesn't show that there is, in fact, a *single* life-plan that it would have been rational for me to pursue. I could have been a stockbroker, scriptwriter or taxi driver instead of an academic. We don't need to assume that there is a one way of life, and thus a single set of goods, that it is rational for everyone to pursue (or even for one person to pursue). Seeing this takes the sting out of the charge that the concept of the rational itself, applied to public debate, excludes and limits the kinds of goods or arguments that can be appealed to.

Where the criticism is onto something, I think, is when it is tied to the historical and cultural features of particular public spheres. Interestingly, much of the critical energy directed at the ideal of the public sphere has emerged from the margins of that sphere itself. It is true that liberals in the nineteenth century, such as de Tocqueville and John Stuart Mill, worried about the effects of the expansion of public discussion (through the expansion of the franchise) on the quality of deliberation. And variations of these concerns can still be found today when people talk about the dangers of the rise of 'mass publics' and popular culture. But what is striking is that those originally excluded from the public sphere – such as workers, women, and members of various ethnic and national minorities – have used the very same conditions that enabled its emergence to make the case for their inclusion.

As Habermas makes clear, the public sphere is almost always in danger of being subverted and co-opted by powerful actors. But the process is also more complicated and less clear-cut than he suggests. A wide array of recent theorists have pointed out that 'the' public sphere is, in fact, composed of a multiplicity of spheres – spaces in which individuals and groups attempt to contest and re-shape the dominant idioms and norms governing more mainstream public discourses and institutions. And this deepens, broadens and improves deliberation, as opposed to undermining it.

A good example of this is the way various social movements organised around race, gender and sexuality have emerged in recent years in countries like Australia and the United States. Lesbians and gay men have been challenging not only the formal means of discrimination embodied in workplace relations, family law and the criminal code, for example, but also some of the embodied and unspoken norms and habits that govern everyday social relations. A similar story could be told with regard to the women's movement, the environmental movement and campaigns focused on ending various forms of racial discrimination.

These movements challenged not only the formal structures of the public sphere, but also their customary ones: not only the content of public arguments about sexuality or race, but the habits and dispositions that have become entrenched in the interactions between different individuals and groups (and often reflected in stereotypical representations in the media). In this sense they do indeed challenge what counts as a rational or 'reasonable' move in public discourse. And critics are right to suggest that we often ice how these customary norms work, and how they need to be ....d as much as the formal means of discrimination entrenched in law.

Let me try to summarise the discussion up until now. I haven't attempted to answer the question as to whether or not today the public sphere is so saturated by powerful and manipulative actors that its democratic potential has been irreversibly lost. Or whether 'popular culture', aided by the emerging new media and their new technologies and formats, is capable of redeeming that potential. Others in this book are more able to address those questions than I am. Rather, my focus has been on the philosophical backdrop to this debate, and on the ideas and values that inform our thinking about the public sphere in general. We still care about the role that the public sphere plays in our societies because our individual and collective freedom are still linked to it in various ways, however difficult the challenges we face.[12]

This leads us to another set of issues that I mentioned above and promised to return to. How can the public sphere be inclusive enough to give everyone a genuine stake in its outcomes, and yet critical enough to shape power?

IV

It's tempting when looking at modern societies to think that since religion no longer provides the comprehensive framework (if it ever did) within which to think about ethics, and that people's worldviews are so diverse, there is no point in talking about common values at all. I think this is premature, but we do have to proceed cautiously. One thing we shouldn't do is infer that, given pluralism about ethics, anything goes.[13] This is the kind of mistake that first-year undergraduates are often tempted to make. (I know, because I teach first-year philosophy at Sydney.) Simple-minded relativism is often accompanied by an even more simple-minded subjectivism.[14]

But good students make another, more thoughtful move. OK, they admit, it doesn't follow from pluralism that *anything* goes – since, amongst other things, the tolerance they usually suppose relativism entails would lack any basis of support – but surely cultural diversity and moral disagreement create deep problems for identifying genuinely universal or objective values in ethics? Surely there are all kinds of moral judgements that we make that have presuppositions relative to particular social, cultural and political norms that are not universal, and hence shape what we think of as good or right?

In fact, I think this is right, and it connects up with our earlier discussion of rationality. What it is rational for someone to value or pursue, remember, will often vary from person to person and indeed within a single person's life. Cultural and social norms play a crucial role here, and these vary across time and space. There will be forms of life or particular goods that one society will value highly and that another won't; or that will be valued at one point in time but not in another. And the same value or principle, or sets of values, might be understood very differently according to local norms and customs (for example, the way rights are understood in the United States as compared to Canada or Australia).

The relativity of norms, then, is relevant to moral judgements in all kinds of significant ways. But it doesn't follow, therefore, that moral judgements are *in general* relative, especially given our practice of critically evaluating those norms that shape our judgements about what is good or right or virtuous (a practice we find in human societies everywhere).[15]

There is another kind of deep skepticism about our capacity to respond to the world in an ethically coherent way that I mentioned at the very beginning, and which is linked to the emergence of the 'new media' and to our media-obsessed age. This is, that our culture is so media-saturated, that we perceive the world and all its glories and ills so completely through the prism of the infrastructure of the (post)modern media, that ethics is essentially an illusion and that reality or 'the truth' doesn't exist any more. Instead, there is only layer upon layer of representation, all the way down. We have all become spectators, in other words, and have the beliefs about the world we do as a result of becoming enmeshed in the self-referential world created by 'the media' – by what we read in the papers, see on television, or imbibe from surfing the Web. Hence the 'compassion fatigue' generated by constant TV pictures of famine or bombing victims, and the lack of empathy for the sufferings of those whose plight never makes the evening news. We only seem to act ethically went prompted by the right combination of descriptions and images on TV, and then only for the sake of those who are lucky enough to have caught the attention of our media masters.

This argument is a variation on the cynical view of the public sphere mentioned above, with an added philosophical claim about the disappearance, so to speak, of reality and truth. I think it is confused. If it is a variation on the argument about the manipulation of the public sphere by powerful interests, then it is appealing to an alternative view of the public sphere that is more inclusive, critical and democratic, and thus to certain values we have reason to endorse. If the philosophical claim is meant to be taken seriously – that reality doesn't exist any more, that real suffering and harm are not being endured by anyone, but are merely 'simulacra' created within a virtual media world – then I think this is just patently false. Our beliefs about what is good or right, or about what our duties to our fellow citizens and others should be, are undoubtedly shaped by the complex ways in which the modern media circulate images and descriptions of the world around us and draw out various responses in relation to them. But we aren't trapped in that virtual world. We have the capacity to step back, evaluate and argue with each other about the things that are being put to us, and to test what we see, hear or read with our own considered judgements, and indeed, with reality. A vibrant, diverse, inclusive and critically engaged public sphere can help us do this.

Having said this, there are still tremendous challenges that we face. I've already mentioned the economic forces of globalisation. These penetrate just about every aspect of our public life. But I want to discuss another problem that touches on the discussion in the previous paragraph. Call this the 'fragmentation of value'.[16] As we've already seen, the extraordinary diversity of modern societies will shape our thinking about ethics. It's not just that there are lots of different views about how to live well, but that there are lots of different views about important ethical questions which are entirely reasonable, and yet there is no obviously independent way of ranking between them. (We've already seen that invoking the concept of rationality won't get us very far.) So it's not simply the diversity of views that matter, but the kind of diversity involved.[17] If we value individual and collective freedom, then how are we supposed to justify the exercise of political power to each other?

My argument so far has been that there is a danger in thinking we don't need any sense of the public at all, because if we value living in liberal-democratic societies, then it is hard to maintain the goods they provide without *some sense* of a common commitment to the basic institutions that link us together. But there is also the danger of what we might call 'false community'; of nostalgic appeals to apparently cohesive communities of the past, or to comprehensive religious or moral doctrines presumed to be accessible to all. We need to guard against the facile and often manipulative use of claims about, for example, what the 'Australian community' thinks about complex issues like immigration, multiculturalism or family law.

For these and other reasons, some philosophers have been tempted to argue for the possibility of a more neutral or 'free-standing' form of public reason that could transcend – or at least side-step – the deep moral controversies and differences that exist between people.[18] It's not that Christians or Muslims can't still appeal to their deepest beliefs in public discourse, but that they shouldn't expect those appeals to carry weight with non-believers when it comes to justifying the use of state power. Instead, arguments will have to be found that appeal across a wider spectrum of society, which means appealing to notions of equality and freedom. 'Thus sayeth the Lord' is not an appropriate way of justifying the exercise of political power in Australia today.

Although the problem is properly diagnosed, I believe this particular strategy has its problems.[19] It is very difficult to imagine just how arguments about basic constitutional matters – for example, whether to have a Bill of Rights, or whether to legalise euthanasia, or how best to acknowledge Aboriginal land and political claims – could be made without drawing on deeper normative and philosophical views that would violate the strictures of neutrality, even the sophisticated version defended by the American philosopher John Rawls. Some critics are suspicious, suggesting that liberal values are allowed to pass into the public sphere as legitimate forms of public reason while other views are blocked, despite there supposedly being no independent basis upon which to justify such a move.[20] Other liberals think the strategy involves too much pussy-footing around. Liberal norms trump non-liberal norms when it comes to basic political arrangements because they are the necessary pre-condition for sustaining the kind of society in which people who disagree about the best way to live can live together freely and peacefully.[21]

This debate will not be resolved here. (My own view, for what it's worth, is probably closer to the second.) But in thinking about the nature of the public sphere we need to acknowledge the centrality and persistence of disagreement, and yet at the same time, the role it plays in promoting the kind of goods we associate with liberal societies – individual freedom, self-rule and distributive justice. Finding ways of making disagreement more bearable, and indeed even more fruitful for democratic life is as important, I think, as focusing on the conditions required for consensus.

V

Philosophers are prone to give us models and images of public reason that mirror distinctly ideal conditions. Plato gives us the image of a city-state ruled by philosophers who love only the good and the true; Rawls, the model of Supreme Court judges explaining and justifying their decisions by sticking to arguments and terms laid down in the Constitution; and Habermas, a highly abstract story about the necessary presuppositions of communicative action in general. My own view is that we should see the public sphere as something much more diverse and less ordered than these standard views suppose. And our philosophical orientation should be less towards consensus and more towards how we can live with the disagreements we have with each other. Since there is no standpoint outside of the conversations and arguments of the actual interlocutors that is rationally or morally authoritative on its own, we have to begin with the premises and beliefs that are brought to these arguments and work from there.

The way this works practically in democratic societies today is that the party-electoral system is supplemented, if we're lucky, by the energy and urgency of advocacy groups and social movements that emerge from the broader public sphere (including, increasingly, cross-national and international movements and actors). These movements and groups often challenge common norms and policies, and help to keep the public agenda open and ever-shifting.

Sometimes political parties listen and respond, and sometimes they are bypassed entirely. And sometimes the whole thing freezes up and atrophies. Political parties cut themselves off from the dynamic forces emerging from the broader public sphere, and particular groups are unable to build new coalitions across social and cultural difference.

We need to work to keep the possibilities for new arrangements and new coalitions that emerge out of our arguments about ethics from being foreclosed too quickly. And yet, at the same time, we need to guard against the tendency to infer that just because our public spheres are teeming with ethical arguments and disagreements, then just about anything goes. There are arguments to be had, but also goods well worth defending.

NOTES

* This chapter was written while I was a Laurance S. Rockefeller Visiting Fellow at the University Center for Human Values, Princeton University in 2002–03. I am grateful to the Center for providing such a wonderful environment in which to

work. Thanks also to Catharine Lumby and Elspeth Probyn for their comments on an earlier draft.

1   For my purposes, 'ethics' means pretty much the same thing as 'morality'. Some philosophers like to distinguish between the two, but I won't go into that here. Ethics involves the study of concepts like 'good', 'right', 'duty', 'obligation', 'freedom' and 'responsibility', and how they relate to what we should do. Ethics also involves what philosophers call 'second-order' problems, to do with questions about objectivity, subjectivity, relativity and skepticism. I'll discuss some of these terms in a moment.

2   Jurgen Habermas, *The Structural Transformation of the Public Sphere: An inquiry into a category of bourgeois society*, trans. Thomas Burger (Cambridge, Massachusetts: MIT Press, 1962); see also M. Warner, *The Letters of the Republic; Publication and the Public Sphere in Eighteenth Century America* (Cambridge, Massachusetts: Harvard University Press, 1990).

3   Habermas, *The Structural Transformation*; see also Charles Taylor, 'Liberal politics and the public sphere' in *Philosophical Arguments* (Cambridge, Massachusetts: Harvard University Press, 1995).

4   Habermas, *The Structural Transformation*, 27.

5   Taylor, 'Liberal politics and the public sphere', 263.

6   This normative role was stressed by writers such as John Locke and John Stuart Mill, as well as by Taylor, 'Liberal politics and the public sphere', and Habermas, *Structural Transformation*.

7   The phrase is from M. Warner, *Publics and Counterpublics* (New York: Zone Books, 2002), 50. Warner provides an excellent survey of the voluminous debates surrounding Habermas' argument (21–63).

8   Taylor, 'Liberal politics and the public sphere', especially 279–87.

9   Alexis Tocqueville, in J.P. Mayer (ed.), *Democracy in America*, trans. George Lawrence (London: Fontana Press, 1994).

10 Taylor, 'Liberal politics and the public sphere'. Concerns about the concentration of media ownership are relevant here. If too much of the mainstream media is controlled by just a few, then a genuinely inclusive and open debate about alternatives is less likely to occur, which (aside from contributing to bad decision-making) can increase people's sense of alienation from and frustration with political institutions.

11 Taylor, 'Liberal politics and the public sphere', 259: 'Editorials appear in the party newspapers, purporting to express the opinions of the writers, offered for the consideration of their fellow citizens; mass demonstrations are organised, purporting to give vent to the felt indignation of large numbers of people. All this takes place as if a genuine process were in train of forming a common mind through exchange, even though the result is carefully controlled from the beginning.'

12 My argument does suggest that a diverse, inclusive and critically engaged public sphere is a genuine public good, and one that we (as citizens) have good reasons

to support and encourage. Although I can't argue for it here, I think this does entail an important role for publicly subsidised and less commercially-driven forms of public media – such as the ABC and SBS in Australia, the CBC in Canada, PBS in the United States and the BBC in the United Kingdom. But this leaves open the question of what the precise *mix* should be between publicly funded and more commercially-driven media. Nor should we presuppose that only publicly funded media are capable of providing the critically engaged and inclusive (i.e. 'rational') forms of conversations I've been arguing we need to have. Maybe Oprah has as much to contribute to our thinking about race as does a discussion on Philip Adams' radio program *Late Night Live* … or a Sri Lankan movie on SBS. All three present different kinds of potentially valuable contributions to public conversations and arguments about race. But left to its own devices, the market is not able to generate a minimally fair and inclusive representation of views about the important issues of the day. And that is not healthy for a democracy.

13 An extreme version of this view is that morality is simply an illusion and that nothing is ever right or good, or just or unjust. This is nihilism – the view that there are no moral constraints whatsoever and that everything is permitted. (I'll be touching on this view again in a moment.) Very few people are comfortable defending this kind of argument. We use sentences like 'it's *not right* to torture people', or 'we *should* tolerate or recognise cultural difference' all the time. This doesn't refute nihilism, of course, and especially milder forms of moral relativism, but it suggests that a much richer argument will have to be given to show why we should abandon these beliefs.

14 By 'subjectivism' I mean the belief that moral judgements are ultimately subjec-tive, that is, variable according to one's subjective constitution and situation, and thus incapable of being considered objective in any foundational sense. There are sophisticated discussions of both relativism and subjectivism in ethics which are well worth thinking about. See footnote 15 below.

15 For one of the best introductory discussions of relativism in ethics see B. Williams, *Morality: An introduction to ethics* (Cambridge: Cambridge University Press, 1972); see also G. Harman, *The Nature of Morality: An introduction to ethics* (New York: Oxford University Press, 1977); and R. Rorty, *Objectivity, Relativism and Truth* (Cambridge: Cambridge University Press, 1991). For a particularly clear and lucid discussion of some of the themes in this paragraph see Waldron, 'How to argue for a universal claim', *Columbia Human Rights Law Journal* 30:2 (1999), 305–14.

16 The phrase is from Nagel's *Mortal Questions* (New York: Cambridge University Press, 1979), but he should not be held responsible for what I go on to say here.

17 As John Rawls has pointed out, it is one of the consequences of people exercising their freedom to think for themselves. See his *Political Liberalism* (New York: Columbia University Press, 1993).

18 ibid.

19 For further discussion see Duncan Ivison, *Postcolonial Liberalism* (Cambridge: Cambridge University Press, 2002).

20 For an entertaining and robust version of this argument see S. Fish, *The Trouble With Principle* (Cambridge, Massachusetts: Harvard University Press, 1999).

21 B. Barry, *Justice as Impartiality* (Oxford: Oxford University Press, 1995) and *Culture and Equality: An egalitarian critique of multiculturalism* (Cambridge: Polity Press, 2001).

4 'Their own media in their own language'

JOHN HARTLEY

Part A – Journalism and the Indigenous polity

Indigenous peoples have the right to establish their own media in their own language. They also have the right to equal access to all forms of non-Indigenous media.

States shall take effective measures to ensure that State-owned media duly reflect Indigenous cultural diversity.

United Nations Draft Declaration on the Rights of Indigenous Peoples, Part IV, Article 17, 1994 (still not ratified).

IN THE COURSE OF RESEARCHING OUR BOOK ON THE REPORTING AND reception of Indigenous issues in the Australian media, Alan McKee and I became keenly aware of a standard liberal approach to the subject of Aboriginal people, ethics and the media.[1] It goes like this: you round up the 'usual suspects', which comprise hostile reporting, racial prejudice, the stereotyping of Aboriginal people, and their sacrifice at the altar of a good story (also known as a fast buck). You offer a quick critique of the corporate greed and insensitivity that drive the media. And you make a plea for ethical behaviour by individual journalists. Everyone then goes home, none the wiser.

Our own three-year study, which was supported by an Australian Research Council Large Grant, was an attempt to broaden the framework for thinking

#42

about the way Aboriginal affairs are reported in the media and how Indigenous people are represented both as media professionals and as subjects in the media. Where previous work in this field has concentrated on finding examples of racist and 'negative' coverage, we set out to put questions of media, racist and Indigenous representation into a larger context. In concrete terms, this meant studying a much broader range of media coverage than is normally included in research of this kind – we looked beyond news and current affairs reporting to entertainment and life-style media. We were also very concerned to bring as many Indigenous voices into our research as possible and, to this end, we convened a series of state-based and national media forums which brought media organisations, journalists and regulators into direct contact with Aboriginal people and organisations.

One of the first things we discovered in our work was that, in proportional terms, Aboriginal people are over-represented, not under-represented in the Australian media, and that they attract an equally disproportionate amount of interest in international coverage too. The reason for this is not only the actual circumstances of Aboriginal life, whether understood as culturally exotic, constitutionally unresolved, or as fourth-world scandal, but also the way these are made to stand for – to represent – major conflicts in the symbolic domain of our national identity. Indigeneity, in other words, has become central to Australia's status as a nation. It is the point around which many political debates about social justice, fairness and the adequacy of social structure in Australia take place.[2]

Another key insight was that much of the contemporary media coverage, which is often criticised for presenting racist or negative views of Indigenous people, is merely conforming to generic type – to an established mode of *news* narration that emphasises conflict and favours 'bad' news stories over 'good'. When we looked at the representation of Indigenous people across the media – not just in news and current affairs – we found a preponderance of positive images of Aboriginal people, exemplified by Indigenous celebrities such as Cathy Freeman.

The time has long gone when it was accurate to think of the media as opposed to and acting (malevolently) upon Indigenous people. And it's important to acknowledge that Indigenous people aren't just the objects of media representation – they too are journalists, reporters, presenters, editors, producers, as well as readers, viewers and listeners. But even with maximum

Indigenous involvement, a discussion of Indigenous Australia and journalism ethics would still be deficient, conceptually. This is because, at root, the problem of journalism that deals with Indigenous affairs is not an ethical one. It is not about the 'rule-governed comportment or moral principles of an individual or group', nor about 'good and bad or right and wrong actions and motives' (these being common definitions of ethics). In the end, as I argue below, the problem is political – it arises from the condition of the Aboriginal polity, not from the conduct of individual journalists.

WHOSE ETHICS? – THE JOURNALISM OF INDIFFERENCE

There's an inherent problem for journalists who wish to behave ethically towards Indigenous people. *Good* journalism requires fearless critique, impartial treatment and no allegiance to party or faction – it requires professional *indifference*. But this is exactly what looks like *unethical* journalism to people in an outsider group whose organisations and leaders are dragged over the coals on what seems like a routine basis. To them, such journalism looks like part of the control strategies of a regime in which they have no independent stake. Fearless reporting isn't experienced as a cleansing agent in 'our' body politic, but as a toxic weapon in 'their' arsenal. It is not simply unethical but destructive.

To avoid that, a journalist with ethical sensitivities might decide to take on the stance of the group under investigation. But that results in *bad* journalism, if the sense of solidarity entails the pulling of investigative punches. If good journalism is the very thing that comes across as *unethical* to an outsider group like Indigenous people, then taking up a stance that belongs to the ethics of such a group will inevitably result in bad journalism.

For example, skeptical, adversarial, investigative journalism, using the 'but surely' line of questioning, works well if the people being grilled are high-status members of one's own group's business or government: Paul Barry dogging the footsteps of Alan Bond, perhaps; or *Four Corners* tracking those responsible for black deaths in custody. But it can come across as harassment or worse if a journalist belonging to a powerful media corporation pursues the same tactics against people who perceive themselves as powerless.

Similarly, people in an 'outsider' group who aspire to the practice of good journalism will have their allegiances to their group and even their own identity severely tested. Can you report for the Australian media and remain true to Aboriginal ethics? Although Indigenous people are indeed passionate, talented and successful in various branches of media and journalism practice, there remains a constant sense that they are caught uneasily between cultures, if not nations – between a 'we' and a 'they' group.

Good journalists are supposed to be professionally 'indifferent' to party or cause. They don't take sides; they report 'both sides of a story'. Their ethics are professional, not a matter of individual belief or choice. It shouldn't even matter if they are racists, since they're paid for their ability to record accurately what someone else is saying or doing, not for their personal views. Similarly, a journalist with strong sympathies for Indigenous people is still regarded as having an ethical duty to report unpleasant truths about the Indigenous community. Certainly, it's a view which was encapsulated in the decision to award the 2001 Walkley award to *Age* journalist Andrew Rule for his investigations into allegations that ATSIC chairman, Geoff Clark, had sexually assaulted several women.

But an Indigenous journalist can't be 'indifferent' in the same way, without appearing to abandon some of the very morals, principles and modes of conduct – in short, some of the ethics – that attach to Indigenous identity in the first place. No one wants to be represented by corrupt organisations or criminal individuals. But for Aboriginal journalists to pursue Aboriginal wrongdoing with the enthusiasm displayed by some mainstream media could seem destructive and prejudicial; acting against the interests of one's own people, and perpetuating the 'business as usual' model of prejudicial reporting of Indigenous affairs.

So it is just this professional *indifference* that makes journalism such an easy target when you look at the outcomes from the point of view of people who are not wholly within the 'we' community, but who are constantly treated as a problem that it has to worry about, for one reason or another. In journalistic terms, Indigenous people occupy just such a place. They're treated in much the same way as are youth. Newspapers have traditionally treated young people as a problem. Adolescent boys need 'correction'; girls need 'protection'. For decades, news media have been stern about what should happen to those who err. The press was never shy about recommending the harshest regimes of 'correction and protection' imaginable. But sooner or later those who survive that regime grow up, stop being young, and become members of the 'we' community – they become ordinary citizens. In the realm of journalism, Aboriginal people simply never make it to that comfort zone. They remain a problem. They never 'graduate' from 'correction and protection' – custody and welfare, police courts and family courts. Of course, real Aboriginal people do grow up. But journalism doesn't have a place for them to go. If they're just 'Australians' then they're the same as everyone else – an identity that is historically (decidedly) not Aboriginal. If they remain Aboriginal, then they don't really fit into the grown-up polity once they get past the 'problem' age.

AN INDIGENOUS PUBLIC SPHERE?

An Indigenous public sphere is, on the face of it, a contradictory notion. In conventional terms, the very idea of a public sphere assumes a nation and a citizenry who are authorised to come together as equals and make decisions on their own behalf. Yet, Indigenous people have no representation which is separate from the political institutions that developed under European colonisation. But there's another way of thinking about public spheres in late modern culture – one that emphasises the way communities can come together, define identities and 'represent' themselves in a virtual sense, in and through the media. This kind of model of an Indigenous public sphere suggests that the media are not merely a place where Indigenous peoples are reported on in a passive sense – but a forum where self-representation and community building actively occurs.

It's certainly a way of understanding Indigeneity which is at odds with conventional journalistic understanding of the media's function. Journalism is classically the place where government and business (freedom and com-fort) can be discussed and contested. Journalism's *function* is to scrutinise the nooks and crannies of daily life, to find anomalies and test decisions.[3] It is most interested in ordinary people as the beneficiaries or victims of policy decisions made by government and business. How will the budget, price-hike, profit forecast (etc.) affect the citizen?

Journalism is the only representative sphere that Indigenous people have access to in Australia, but it hasn't asked itself what an *Indigenous* polity might comprise. Australian journalism doesn't recognise Indigenous government. It wouldn't know the Indigenous economy if it fell over it. So the 'anomalies' and 'decisions' that are its stock in trade are focused on the human, personal, social and cultural levels. Aboriginal people figure historically as objects of public policy: correction and protection. You can read about them as perpetrators or victims of crime, but not about Aboriginal enterprise (Aboriginal people as perpetrators or victims of profit!); you find them in sports where clash and contestation are legitimised, but not on the Business or Political pages of the newspaper, where adversarial conflict may result in economic or political outcomes.

Meanwhile, matters that affect Indigenous people deeply and disproportionately – health, welfare, policing, custody – don't seem to be under their control, but are aspects of what government does *to* or *for* them, not what they decide for themselves.

So the image of Indigenous people in Australian journalism concentrates on culture, correction, protection and identity. They don't figure in politics, business or decision-making. This is not an 'ethical' matter, but a fundamentally *political* one (i.e. relating to the polity, not just to party politics). It is about the polity – or rather, the fact that Aboriginal and Islander people don't have one.[4]

Imagine a world where there was an Aboriginal nation (a federation certainly!), and a Torres Strait Islander confederated nation too. And imagine you're a citizen of it. Ask yourself a few basic questions. What is the mode and conduct of our government? Who are our leaders? What are our freedoms? Which bastards ought we to be keeping honest? What is the size and composition of our economy? How do we conduct business amongst ourselves and with the world? How well are we doing this year? Where are we in the economic cycle? Upon what is our wealth founded? What aspirations do we have for our populations? Who are our inventors, entrepreneurs, scholars? Who are our giants, tall poppies, heroes? What problems and difficulties must we overcome? What struggles and deficits impede our progress? What cultural and traditional values help or hinder our women, children, immigrants, emigrants? What is our refugee policy? our stance towards Iraq; the United States?

While we're at it, what are our people like beyond the realm of government and business? In other words, how do we appear in what might be called 'non-news journalism' – life-style, fashion, travel, shelter, hobbies, technologies (cars and computers), entertainment, etc.? And how do we figure in the wider world of fiction and storytelling, where relationships, identity, communal values and 'lore' are formed and communicated? In short, where are our faces and our follies in soap opera, action drama, comedy, music, and games?

We'll never know. Journalism can't *imagine* how to ask such questions, let alone answer them, because it is dedicated to the nineteenth-century modernist concept of the nation-state, which cannot 'recognise' nations such as these, and is therefore blind to 'people without a polity'. And as a result, the right that the United Nations wants to recognise, namely that first peoples require 'their own media in their own language', cannot suffice, since 'their own media' are embedded in the mainstream Australian public sphere, and 'their own language' includes the journalistic language of indifference, which seems so often to be indifferent to the Aboriginal community as a whole, rather than to any vested interests within it. In such circumstances, where the national status of Indigenous people is not resolved, fundamentally political issues remain to be dealt with on a daily basis. They pose ethical problems for those who tread that track, some of which are discussed in the next section by Indigenous reporters and editors. But it ought to be remembered that everyone treads that track. The 'ethics of journalism' reside as much in the reader or viewer as in the journalist. When we all go home and watch the news, it's up to each one of us to resist remaining 'none the wiser'.

Part B – Ethics and the Indigenous public sphere
How do Indigenous people cope with the only public sphere they've got? How do they operate within the polity that governs them? How do they see issues of journalism ethics? We asked some of them (in this case, 'we' refers to research fellow Elinor Rennie and I). With one exception our interviewees were active as journalists at the time of the interview, although all have had varied careers. They are:

Todd Condie: Editor, *Koori Mail*
Todd Condie has worked at the *Koori Mail* since 1998 in various capacities including as a cadet, journalist, photographer, and now editor. He is a descendant of the Yidinji people of the Atherton Tablelands in far north Queensland. The *Koori Mail* is a fortnightly publication that is 100 per cent Aboriginal-owned and 100 per cent self-funded.

Craig Egert: News editor, 4AAA Brisbane
Craig Egert was working part-time at 4AAA and studying journalism at Queensland University of Technology when he was asked to cover the Sydney

Olympics in 2000. He is now the full-time news editor for 4AAA. Craig is of the Coenpul people from Stradbroke Island.

Gary Foley: Senior curator, Museum Victoria
Gary Foley is the senior curator in the Indigenous Cultures Department at Museum Victoria. He has been at the centre of many major political activities including the Aboriginal Tent Embassy and the Bicentennial protests. He has been involved in, amongst other things, the establishment of Redfern's Aboriginal Legal Service, the Aboriginal Medical Service in Melbourne and the Aboriginal Arts Board and the Royal Commission into Black Deaths in Custody Inquiry. His acting portfolio includes *A Country Practice*, *Dogs in Space* and *The Flying Doctors*. He was born in Grafton, Northern New South Wales, of Gumbainggir descent.

Kerry Klimm: News director, NIRS
Kerry Klimm is the news director of the National Indigenous Radio Service. She holds a BA in journalism and Asian Studies and is currently completing a BSS in Australian politics and history. She has worked as a journalist and news producer at WIN television and Imparja as well as freelancing for Channel Seven and Sunshine TV. She has also worked as a consultant on the Apunipima Cape York Health Council's Oral History Project. She is of the Koko Lama Lama people of Princess Charlotte Bay and the Koko Jelandji of the Daintree.

Rhoda Roberts: Presenter/journalist, *Awaye!* (ABC Radio National)
Rhoda Roberts came to prominence in the media in 1989 as the first Aboriginal person to host a national primetime current affairs program, SBS TV's *First in Line*. In 1997 she was the artistic director of the 'Festival of the Dreaming', the first of four Olympic arts festivals. She was also appointed as Indigenous cultural advisor to SOCOG and a creative director responsible for devising a component of the Sydney 2000 opening ceremony. She currently presents *Awaye!* on ABC Radio National. She is a member of the Bundjalung nation, Wiyebal clan of Northern New South Wales and South-East Queensland.

The questions were divided into three sections. The first section was intended to explore the usefulness of mainstream media for Indigenous people; the second looked at Indigenous media; the third raised the question of ethics directly. Our respondents' minimally edited replies are recorded below.

I INDIGENOUS PEOPLE'S INTERESTS IN MAINSTREAM JOURNALISM

The coverage of Indigenous issues in the news often comes across as hostile, partial or prejudicial. But the news media are also a means for Indigenous issues to be conveyed to a wider public. Can you comment on the value of news media for Indigenous Australians, both positive and negative?

Rhoda Roberts: The opinions of Indigenous people on issues that are not specifically Indigenous are never heard. For example, on the refugee issue, there has been a lack of reporting on the views of Indigenous leaders or of the traditional owners of the Woomera area. It's the same thing with Australia's involvement in overseas warfare or industrial disputes. White leaders and celebrities are asked to comment on national issues but Indigenous leaders and celebrities are only asked to comment if the issue is considered a specifically Indigenous one. If Indigenous people are left out of national debates they are left out of Australian culture, resulting in an 'us' and 'them' divide. For me, becoming part of Australian culture is a true indication of equality – the Indigenising of Australianness. This requires involvement in all aspects of debate and creativity. Indigenous people should participate on an equal level with non-Indigenous commentators, leaders or cultural representatives. [On the day we spoke to her in February 2002, Roberts' program *Awaye!* on Radio National featured a story on Aboriginal and Torres Strait Islander perspectives on the war on Iraq.]

Todd Condie: It is a fact that Indigenous people still suffer disproportionate levels of dysfunction in this country; however, mainstream coverage continually focusing on Aborigines and Islanders as a 'problem' can lead Indigenous people, particularly the youth – who make up a large part of this population – to see themselves as 'other' or 'alien' in their own country. Therefore, the value of news media to Indigenous Australians can be both positive and negative;

positive, in the sense that every citizen should have the right to up-to-date, accurate and factual information about current events, and that Indigenous Australians can use the mainstream media to lobby the wider community for support for a particular campaign. On the other hand, it can be negative if the reporting and coverage of Indigenous people and issues predominantly focus on negative issues. As a result, the situation can arise where Indigenous people in Australia are demonised unnecessarily and seen as scapegoats for many of the woes facing society, even though as a group they are consistently at the bottom end of socioeconomic indicators.

Kerry Klimm: The problem with *negative* reporting on Indigenous issues is that it's become an unshakeable 'bad habit' of mainstream media – and it continues because the majority white audience keeps tuning in. However, one cannot ignore the fact that negative reporting can also be the most powerful catalyst for positive change. A perfect example is the mass coverage of late on the high levels of domestic violence in Indigenous communities – coverage which has forced these communities, governments and wider society to face the truth about an ugly issue, and look at solutions.

My other point is how many women abused not only physically but psychologically find it hard to leave such a relationship. How often have we heard that these women have been humiliated for so long by their partners, they begin to believe there is truth in comments like they are useless, dumb, etc. Why is it that we sympathise with these battered wives and not, it seems, with the troubled Indigenous communities who are in some part products of 'media degradation'?

However, too often the media gloat at their ability to highlight the 'wrongs', and fail to provide enough 'rights'. Over a long period of time this can do more harm than good for Indigenous people. As a child growing up in Cairns, I recall the constant media coverage on the 'park people'. After weeks – possibly months – of seeing images of Aboriginal people getting drunk in the park, I told my mother I didn't want that to happen to me because I thought that's what happened to all adult Aboriginal people. Almost two decades later the Queensland government has embarked on a program to try to address the concerns and needs of the 'park people'. The media's barrage of coverage obviously did little more than to create another stereotype about Indigenous people.

Can mainstream journalism, which is produced largely by non-Indigenous people and often follows familiar story-lines, ever be of strategic and political use to the Indigenous community?

Rhoda Roberts: There's a need for positive reporting on Indigenous issues, a need to avoid casting Indigenous people as victims. We have a moral obligation to stop perpetuating associations of welfare and helplessness.

Todd Condie: Increasingly, Indigenous people are becoming 'media savvy', which means mainstream media will always be looked at to further a particular message or viewpoint. This is where relationships between journalists and Indigenous people, communities and organisations are crucial in establishing trust between interviewee and interviewer. This might only happen over time, if at all. Campaigns related to issues such as the Jabiluka uranium mine protest in the Northern Territory, the Kupa Piti nuclear waste dump protest in South Australia, the whole ten-year native title process in Australia, the Stolen Generation's healing process and the proposal for a treaty between Indigenous and non-Indigenous Australians have all, at one stage or another, targeted mainstream media for coverage of their particular cause. To be fully effective, media-savvy Aborigines know to use both the mainstream and Indigenous media networks to state their case.

Kerry Klimm: Yes, we've already seen the likes of Noel Pearson, Aden Ridgeway and Lowitja O'Donohue, who often use their experience in the media to their advantage, to push for improved conditions in communities.

Craig Egert: There's a town in Queensland just outside of Mt Isa where they hadn't had proper drinking water or sewerage for the past two months. *Four Corners* got on to them. If that story hadn't run, the problem wouldn't have been treated immediately as it was. Government bureaucracies seemed to respond and money has been promised now. Yes, to get their message out there – particularly remote communities – the media seem to get governments into action.

Are there any news outlets that Indigenous Australians trust, or regard as their own?

Todd Condie: For radio listeners, the National Indigenous Radio Service (NIRS), which has extensive links to many other Aboriginal radio stations in remote Australia, is one service that many Indigenous Australians tap into. For print, I would like to think that the *Koori Mail* has covered many issues of particular interest to its readers that are not found in the mainstream press – such as the complexity of Aboriginal identity, and all the issues surrounding various skin colours, or the effects of being a stolen child. The strengths of these two services, I believe, are that both have the capacity for 'talkback' or 'feedback' from their audience, largely black Australians. It is rare that Indigenous people get the opportunity to defend themselves in the mainstream media when they are attacked, due in part to factors such as feelings of hopelessness, vulnerability as a poorly resourced group of people, health factors restricting quick responses, cultural factors such as shame (which affects the ability of Indigenous people to be in the spotlight, especially in a conflictive situation), and simply in many cases they are not asked for their side of the story.

Kerry Klimm: Any outlet that employs Indigenous people, such as the community radio stations, the *Koori Mail* and Indigenous programs on the ABC and SBS such as *ICAM*.

Craig Egert: From an urban perspective, lots of people use the *Koori Mail* and the *Aboriginal Independent Newspaper* (the new one). They are widely distributed throughout most Aboriginal organisations. They are used for advertising and to report stories on the organisations. I think a lot of Aboriginal people take to the *Koori Mail* and the *Aboriginal Independent Newspaper* and really like reading them. There is a trust there, because they have Indigenous reporters going out there and making stories and taking photos. They know more of the community, which sources to tap into. You get more of an actual picture.

> **What improvements would peak Indigenous leaders, especially those with a national profile, like to see in the reporting of their own affairs?**

Rhoda Roberts: Although arts and sports help to promote positive images of Indigenous Australia, there is an absence of stories about Indigenous people working in other areas, such as academia or medicine. This means that Aboriginal children are not provided with role models to encourage them to enter such professions. Broadening the representation of Indigenous Australians in all issues and stories is a priority. Furthermore, Indigenous programs developed by the ABC and SBS are predominantly in magazine-style formats and current affairs. For instance, there's no Aboriginal drama. But the work of actors like Deborah Mailman and Ernie Dingo is important, as they have made their way into Australia's everyday cultural texts.

Todd Condie: I would like to see more cross-cultural awareness workshops held for mainstream journalists and editors, so that when (not if) they are asked to report or write an article on an Indigenous issue they have more of an awareness of the dynamics of Aboriginal culture. The basics of journalism still apply – balance, accuracy, relevance – when reporting on Indigenous issues. However, extra consideration needs to be applied. Simple things such as ensuring tribal, language, and clan affiliations are recognised in the report-ing; being respectful of elder interviewees; being mindful that many Indigenous people in remote communities run their lives on 'Aboriginal time', which means that 'things happen when they happen', not necessarily when you want them to (this can seriously affect working to deadlines); and not assuming that Indigenous Australians are one homogeneous mass with one set of beliefs.

Kerry Klimm: If media do continue to chase the 'hard news', focusing on alcoholism, domestic violence, etc., then journalists should be more creative and tackle the whys and hows.

Can non-Indigenous journalists perform a useful role in criticising and investigating Indigenous people and organisations?

Todd Condie: Sometimes it takes a mainstream story to spark debate and discussion amongst Indigenous leaders and communities, so the story can be a catalyst for social change. Indigenous people themselves want to know if organisations set up to better their situation are operating as they should, especially if the funding for the service comes from the public purse.

Tasmanian Aboriginal leader Michael Mansell raised an interesting point recently in regard to the mainstream media coverage of the 2002 Aboriginal and Torres Strait Islander Commission (ATSIC) regional council elections. He said that in its coverage of potential candidates for ATSIC chairperson, one national newspaper influenced the result by being highly critical of the incumbents, Geoff Clark and Ray Robinson. 'But one lesson white journalists need to heed is that the public running down of any Aborigine usually attracts Aboriginal support for that person', Mansell said. 'In its blind haste to be rid of Geoff Clark, the mainstream media practically guaranteed Clark's re-election.'[5]

Kerry Klimm: It depends on what they're criticising. There is no question of the importance of uncovering issues such as misappropriation of government or public funds, or questioning a person's character *if* the outcome means Indigenous and non-Indigenous people have greater faith in Indigenous organisations and leaders. What non-Indigenous journalists seemingly revel in, however, is challenging Indigenous culture.

Craig Egert: If it's done correctly they can, but my experience from the newspapers I read up here (such as the *Courier-Mail*), there's been a lot on the investigations into ATSIC and they sensationalise a lot of the stories. A lot of the positives of the Indigenous stories aren't told and the negative stories are the lead, more or less.

Can they perform a useful role in explaining Indigenous issues to a wider audience?

Todd Condie: In many cases the answer would have to be a resounding 'no'. With modern news cycles, the time to explain the background history to complex contemporary issues is just not there. Many issues are extremely legalistic in nature, e.g. native title, stolen generations, and deaths in custody, which can make it difficult even for journalists to grasp a simple reading of the story. It is common knowledge that many Australians simply do not want to know about Indigenous issues. To sell more papers or achieve higher ratings the Indigenous stories that are most readily considered for inclusion in the news mix relate to conflict, scandal, corruption, mismanagement, black-on-black crime and violence.

What is your own 'best' and 'worst' experience of journalism in Australia?

Todd Condie: At the Sydney Olympics I was part of a team reporting on the Games from an Indigenous perspective. During the lead-up to the Opening Ceremony I was fortunate to cover a protest by Kupa Piti women from Maralinga in South Australia. They were voicing their concern that having personally witnessed the atomic tests by the British at Maralinga in the 1950s – one of the women was actually blinded by the initial flash – they had a right to say 'no' to a proposed nuclear waste dump on their recently 'rehabilitated' lands. I cite this example as the group of women held a press conference with some Sydney media, international media, and members of the Indigenous team. I had the privilege of sitting in on an interview by Indigenous radio broadcaster Keith Lethbridge who, after all the English speakers finished their questions, proceeded to speak to the old women in their own language. Their responses to English questions were quite brief, limited and guarded. However, when Keith interviewed them they became animated and spoke to him for at least thirty minutes about what it really felt like, as Aboriginal people, to witness such an act. Knowing that the interviewer and interviewees were remote Indigenous people, speaking in their language, and that the subsequent broadcast would be heard by remote Indigenous people, it really struck me that this is what journalism is all about.

I think the worst, in recent times, has been the 'trial by media' of ATSIC leader Geoff Clark. To me this represented the worst type of journalism as it appears that the concept of 'innocent until proven guilty' did not apply. But ironically enough, the allegations and subsequent coverage have raised the issue of domestic and sexual violence by Aboriginal men on their partners and children.

Craig Egert: My own personal experience as a journalist: I covered the Sydney Olympics where NIRS got twenty Indigenous reporters from Aboriginal radio stations throughout Australia and we did Olympic coverage – not only of the sport but also of the Tent Embassy and the protest marches. We covered a re-enactment that was done of Botany Bay, where Aboriginal protesters 're-enacted' the right way and the wrong way of how Captain Cook should have discovered Australia. That was one of my best experiences.

Another one for me would be when I interviewed the Prime Minister. That was in tribute to the 1868 Aboriginal Eleven cricket team that went to England. I asked him if there was enough awareness out there about that and if they should be acknowledged as Australia's first cricket touring team. Now Ian Chapell is calling for them to be recognised as Australia's first touring team. The Prime Minister didn't think there was enough awareness of the cricket team and that it should be the theme of the cricket match to give more awareness about that. He was overawed because one of the grandsons of one of the actual players was in the crowd. He thought that it was great to see that they were there and he said that down the track they should be recognised as Australia's first cricket team.

A bad experience for me, because I was shocked at the story I heard, was when I did a series of interviews with an elder from up north and she spoke about her son who'd been killed – a death in custody incident – and they were campaigning up there to get the message across. They were trying to get a group together to highlight what atrocities they'd been through. She told me that one of the ladies up there went to see her son after she'd just found out that he'd died in a hanging incident, and she went to the cell and he still had the noose around him. That was one of the most shocking experiences in an interview that I've ever done. So I suppose just finding the reality out there of what some of these Indigenous issues mean is hard.

II INDIGENOUS PEOPLE'S OWN INVOLVEMENT IN THE CREATION OF MEDIA

Indigenous people are passionate and active creators of media content, although mostly not in 'hard news'. Can you comment on the production of media by Indigenous people, both within mainstream organisations like the ABC or SBS, and in Indigenous media from the *Koori Mail* to Goolarri Media, CAAMA to NIRS?

Todd Condie: I can only comment on the Indigenous media sector. Indigenous media cover difficult and sensitive news on a daily basis. However, few Indigenous organisations have the considerable resources necessary for investigative reporting or defamation lawyers.

The coverage of some Indigenous media practitioners can be constrained by family and community allegiances, which is much more prevalent amongst Indigenous reporters as the Aboriginal population is considerably smaller.

Indigenous media organisations were initially set up (CAAMA in Central Australia) as a response to the surge of US programming about to hit Central Australia in the 1970s through the introduction of Aussat. So for these groups the use of media can be quite different from Western uses. For example, while the production of local news bulletins is not to be denied, the primary achievement of these services has been cultural maintenance, and more importantly the ability of local people to broadcast and receive information in their own languages.

Kerry Klimm: Indigenous media seek to swing the pendulum back to the middle to provide a greater balance of stories. For instance, mainstream media became caught up with claims that Lowitja O'Donohue was not part of the Stolen Generation because she was not physically 'stolen' by government authorities from her family. Indigenous media highlighted the fact that Professor O'Donohue's childhood and culture were 'stolen' because of the government's poor treatment of Indigenous people at that time.

Are Indigenous people's interests adequately served by their own media?

Rhoda Roberts: There's a need for Indigenous media workers in the area of reviews and cultural critique. There is a tendency for non-Indigenous reviewers to be less critical of Indigenous creative product than of non-Indigenous works, most likely motivated out of caution – not to be seen as racist. In instances where you or I can plainly see something is not that good, a favourable review lowers the standard of what Indigenous producers set out to achieve. In the same circumstance the reviewer would crucify a white artist. Employing Indigenous people to fill that role would overcome the propagation of false standards.

Todd Condie: I think the only restriction to the progress and development of Indigenous media is its apparent lack of resources, and ability to generate income through its service. As far as I am aware, there are few self-funded

Indigenous media organisations, with the majority being radio stations funded by regional ATSIC councils, or the Community Broadcasters of Australia Association. Therein lies the problem. Indigenous media will only get as big as their recurrent funding, and with ATSIC itself fighting for its very existence, Aboriginal radio stations tend to be overlooked in the struggle for funding priorities such as health, education and housing priorities.

Do you support the establishment of a National Indigenous Broadcasting Service (NIBS)?

Craig Egert: I've done a lot of travelling, been out in the community and been involved in media. There's a sense of some Aboriginal people not seeing the Aboriginal media as serious. We're not Channel Seven or Channel Nine. And people think that if they want to get their message across, 'We'll go to the mainstream media'. I don't know if it's just because of the misconception out there ... But if we can establish a NIBS, then we can contend with the mainstream media organisations and we'll get some kind of credibility out there. That's what seems to be lacking in some Aboriginal communities. That's the main thing about NIBS – you want national mainstream coverage to be a competitor.

Todd Condie: I am extremely supportive of the proposal to establish a National Indigenous Broadcasting Service to better serve the interests of Aborigines and Torres Strait Island people.

Kerry Klimm: Yes.

Does the concentration of Indigenous production in non-news areas (culture, creativity, identity) serve to disadvantage the political and social interests of Indigenous people?

Rhoda Roberts: I would like to see a broader range of issues reported in Indigenous media publications.

Todd Condie: The work of Indigenous people in the media who perform 'non-news' roles is, I think, consistent and complementary with the political and social interests of Indigenous people – in many cases all these strands are intertwined. This enables Indigenous people to make a statement through a song, to send a message through a painting, teach Australians their own history through a play, or highlight an issue through a photograph.

Kerry Klimm: Indigenous people are becoming more savvy about harnessing culture, creativity and identity to improve their social status and, in turn, political standing. Political messages in the form of music, theatre, art and text are powerful tools with the potential to reach a wide cross-section of the Australian and international community. If there was greater coverage of these issues in mainstream media, then non-Indigenous Australia could better appreciate the rarely reported fact of how strong Indigenous people are. The fact that despite the tragic effects of colonisation – such as poor health, education, etc.; the basics of our society – 'culture' continues through adaptation.

Craig Egert: I interviewed a young bloke who was the first Aboriginal person to have been invited to talk in Greece – it was for the Olympic movement – and his seminar was on how Aboriginal people can use sport as an outlet to get away from their disadvantages and things like that. He told me that because there were the Cathy Freemans – there were always stories on the big achievers in sport – they were taking the spotlight away from the average person who tried to achieve. Sometimes I tend to agree with that.

Are there Indigenous ways of seeing that can be communicated to non-Indigenous people through the media?

Todd Condie: The biggest hurdle for Indigenous people has been applying a Western media form, in this case the printed word, developed and refined for centuries since the invention of the Gutenberg press, to the oldest form of communication, oral transmission of cultural and generational information. To this end, the print form is fairly limited in being able to capture the true essence of Aboriginal life-style and culture, without the requisite language, dance, ceremony, ritual and storytelling aspects available to the reader.

Craig Egert: I think so. Shows like *Message Stick* have that Indigenous perspective, and if that message is put out there in a positive way it can change the thoughts of non-Indigenous people on some Indigenous issues.

What is your own favourite Indigenous media show or publication?

Todd Condie: The *Koori Mail*, of course, but also *Land Rights News*. Electronically, it is *Message Stick* (ABC), the *Awaye!* radio show (ABC), Lola Forester's national radio show on SBS, and the National Indigenous Radio Service (NIRS).

Kerry Klimm: *Bush Mechanics* (SBS-TV) – it really shows how resourceful and adaptable Indigenous people are.

Craig Egert: *Message Stick*.

Gary Foley: While I am looking at and pondering your questions, you might take the time to check out one of the best Indigenous information outlets in the country; my web site: http://www.kooriweb.org/foley/indexb.html

III PRACTICAL ADVICE FOR PROFESSIONALS AND READERS/ VIEWERS ABOUT ETHICAL REPORTING OF INDIGENOUS ISSUES

What practical advice do you have for journalists wanting to report Indigenous affairs in an ethical way?

Todd Condie: Use your commonsense.
- Follow protocols if visiting or invited to an Indigenous community.
- Recognise that there are many different language groups and Aboriginal nations in Australia – applying one area's protocols to another could cause offence.
- Effective two-way communication with Indigenous people requires most of all the ability to listen.
- Indigenous concepts of time should be adhered to as trying to work to Western deadlines or timeframes could be seen as disrespectful.
- Establish trust through interpersonal relationships – learn who the respective leaders are in a particular community.
- Do not lump all Indigenous Australians together – there are many differences between groups, languages, ceremonies and physical features.

- For many Indigenous peoples it is often impolite to ask too many questions, while direct questioning may cause offence, so keep this in mind.
- It is important to seek input but listen carefully to replies to see whether your questions have already been answered in the earlier responses.
- If at all possible, provide interviewees with the opportunity to look at material before it goes to air or to print – not always possible in modern communication, I know, but highly desirable when trying to establish trust with Indigenous people.

Kerry Klimm: If you don't understand some of the protocols, that does not mean you can ignore them. If you have spoken to one Indigenous 'leader' it does not mean that person represents the views of all Indigenous people. Indigenous Australia is not a political party – where one person speaks for all and everyone is agreed on that 'policy'.

Craig Egert: I think the best way is not to find the sensational highlight. Get behind the real story, examine the underlying factors that contribute to it, and go on that.

A lot of Indigenous stories are complex and there is always a positive angle there if you're looking for it and too many times the negative stereotypical sensationalist angle is taken.

Too many times in the mainstream media you hear of crime stories where someone is described as being 'of Aboriginal appearance'. That's too broad a description as there are a lot of dark-skinned people out there. They're quick to say 'Aboriginal appearance' when down the line you find out it wasn't an Aboriginal person. That's a stereotype, a prejudice and that 'rough and ready' news timeframe is a part of why they do that. It's not being sensitive to a specific culture. You never hear stories where 'he was of a New Zealander appearance'.

If there's a TV story about an Aboriginal community or specifically about an Aboriginal issue, too often you see Aboriginal people standing around in the park drinking or something like that. There are negative background pictures that also portray negativeness that does not always relate to the story.

How can respect for Indigenous culture and difference be accommodated to the rough-and-tumble news culture of deadlines, negative news, conflict, and a good story?

Rhoda Roberts: While the achievements of Indigenous journalists working on the reporting of Indigenous issues are often celebrated, the achievements of Indigenous journalists working within the mainstream media on issues *not* specific to Indigenous issues generally go unnoticed. Les Kennedy has been working for the *Sydney Morning Herald* for twenty-three years, doing the police rounds and other stories that are not Indigenous. Recognising Indigenous people's achievements that are not in direct reference to Indigenous politics is one means of promoting an idea of Indigeneity as being part of mainstream culture.

Todd Condie: I think in many respects it can't be accommodated because of the time factor of meeting increasingly shorter and shorter deadlines, leaving little room for in-depth research or even background information into Indigenous stories. For some stories where different Indigenous languages are spoken, translators may have to be used, and consultation with community elders carried out, which can take days, even weeks in some remote areas.

What for you would count as 'ethical' and 'unethical' treatment?

Todd Condie: Ethical treatment by journalists when reporting on Indigenous affairs would have to include qualities such as: respect for the interviewee and his/her culture; having good background knowledge of the people, group or organisation that is to be focused on; attentive listening skills; and an empathetic attitude.

Unethical treatment would include: having a paternalistic attitude; talking over people or finishing their sentences; visiting an Aboriginal community uninvited; using pidgin English to quote an Indigenous person whose second language is English, instead of using a translator; having a hidden agenda or angle unknown to the interviewee; and, quick 'blow in, blow out' visits by journalists, where local people have not had a chance to tell the full story because of time constraints and in many cases don't even actually see or read what is being broadcast or printed about them.

Kerry Klimm: A recurring theme in the unethical treatment of Indigenous issues is commercial television's use of pictures to accompany a story. The well-worn vision of sick Aboriginal children, drunken people and fly-ridden camps is all too predictable. The file footage is probably twenty years old, some of these communities are now probably much cleaner, the sick children could now be teachers and other professionals, and these drunken people may now be clean. Worse still, some could now be deceased and the use of the vision highly offensive to their community.

> **What would you advise the interested reader/viewer to look out for when they see Indigenous issues being reported in the press or in the media?**

Todd Condie: Things I look out for include:

- whether Aboriginal people are actually identified in a story. For instance, when Aboriginal trackers were finally called in to search for missing tourist Peter Falconio at Barrow Creek in the Northern Territory in 2002, they were not identified by name, language group or their role in the search. It was just assumed that these old men came in from the bush like fauna to help the investigation.
- whether more than one Indigenous representative or leader is interviewed in relation to a particular issue. The tendency has been for the mainstream media to look for one recognised representative to speak for all Aboriginal peoples, which is acceptable when the spokesperson is talking about their local area, but can be inappropriate when the issue is a national one.
- the predominance of coverage of high-profile Indigenous athletes, politicians, performers and artists to the detriment of coverage of community events or the people of remote and rural communities. A cartoon that highlights this point appeared in one of the metropolitan dailies around the time of the Sydney Olympics, showing a white Australian leaning out of his 4WD which had just driven into an obviously remote Aboriginal community, yelling out: 'Why can't you all be like Cathy Freeman?' And the answer is 'We can't'. Journalists have to reflect what is really happening in the lives of Aboriginal people, no matter how challenging it is to get the information, instead of applying non-Indigenous values to their subjects.

Kerry Klimm: Just think about how they feel after they've read or watched the story. What is their first reaction? Then question why they're angry, surprised, not surprised or happy? And finally do they feel any guilt about that reaction? The power of the consumer can be just as powerful as the media. If you accept or don't accept what you've seen or read – make it known.

ABBREVIATIONS AND LINKS

ABC   Australian Broadcasting Corporation – the 'national broadcaster' for settler Australia; its Indigenous Programs Unit produces *Message Stick* (http://www.abc.net.au/message/tv/ipuabout.htm) and *Awaye!* (http://www.abc.net.au/message/radio/awaye/)

ATSIC   Aboriginal & Torres Strait Islander Commission – the government department responsible for Indigenous affairs: at time of writing its elected Chairperson is Geoff Clark; the minister is Philip Ruddock; it produces its own news products; see http://www.atsic.gov.au/news_room/default.asp)

Aussat   Australia's national satellite company – the first Aussat satellites were launched in 1985 and 1987 to provide broadcasting services to remote Australia (http://www.skyrocket.de/space/index_frame.htm?http://www.skyrocket.de/space/doc_sdat/aussat-a.htm)

CAAMA Central Australian Aboriginal Media Association – Aboriginal-owned, operated and controlled group including Imparja TV, 8KIN-FM, and various music, production and retail ventures (http://www.caama.com.au/)

ICAM   *Indigenous Cultural Affairs Magazine*, broadcast on SBS-TV (http://www.sbs.com.au/icam/icam_set.html)

NIBS   National Indigenous Broadcasting Service – a proposed 'national broadcaster' for Indigenous Australia (http://www.atsic.gov.au/programs/Social_and_Cultural/Broadcasting/National_Indigenous_Broadcasting Service/default.asp)

NIRS   National Indigenous Radio Service (http://www.nirs.org.au/index.php3?home+aboutNirs). NIRS also runs NINS – the National Indigenous News Service (http://www.nirs.org.au/index.php3?home+aboutNins)

SBS   Special Broadcasting Service – the 'national broadcaster' for multicultural Australia. SBS broadcasts on TV (Channel 28) and radio, with Indigenous programming on both (http://www.sbs.com.au/sbs_front/index.html; see its code of practice: http://www.sbs.com.au/sbsi/cop.pdf; and guidelines for Indigenous production: http://www.sbs.com.au/sbs_booklet.pdf)

I would like to acknowledge with gratitude the assistance of Elinor Rennie, post-doctoral fellow at CIRAC, in the preparation of this chapter, and thanks to Todd Condie, Craig Egert, Gary Foley, Kerry Klimm and Rhoda Roberts for their contributions.

NOTES

1   John Hartley and Alan McKee, *The Indigenous Public Sphere: The reporting and reception of Aboriginal issues in the Australian media* (Oxford: Oxford University Press, 2000).

2   For detailed data on the representation of Indigenous people in our media see Hartley and McKee, 207–40.

3   John Hartley, *Popular Reality: Journalism: Modernity: Popular Culture* (London: Arnold, 1996).

4   For further discussion, see Hartley and McKee.

5   For further discussion, see http://www.greenleft.org.au/back/2001/453/453p11.htm

INTERVIEW WITH MAXINE McKEW

BEYOND THE DISCONNECT: PRACTICAL ETHICS

(ABC JOURNALIST AND SENIOR WRITER AT THE *BULLETIN*)

I want to begin by asking you about the role of the current affairs interviewer. In conventional print media terms the news journalist is objective and the opinion writer is subjective. Where does the interviewer sit on that spectrum?

I think in newspapers those two roles are blurred. To give a recent example, we had Paul Kelly on the front page [of the *Australian*] with a news story based on an interview with the Prime Minister. It was about the prospect of war with Iraq. But Kelly's commentary was in there as well. We have a lot of that in Australian journalism. Certainly, when it comes to the role of the TV interviewer, I'd say absolutely both those roles are crunched.

You are always looking to get a news line out of it – I am anyway. What I find far more problematic is the tedious sort of formulaic posture of inter-viewer as almost feral aggressor, which results in the interviewee becoming defensive and saying nothing. I think the more productive middle ground is the interviewer as information seeker, prepared to be combative and who will come back, with alternate views, or press for a direct response. I find that much more likely to yield fresh information which the viewer can take away, and say: 'Yes, I got something out of the ten minutes'. A lot of radio interviews irritate me because it's a case of: 'We're now going to have X who is going to interrupt Minister Y for the next seven and a half minutes' and not a shred of information comes out of that.

#67

Do you ever think it's your responsibility as an interviewer to bring the sub-text of political language to the surface? Let's say, for instance, that you believed there was a racist sub-text to political rhetoric being employed by politicians to win votes?

The short answer is yes. But we have to ask why politicians who've played the race card in recent years in Australia have been so successful. We've been through this decade-long and very dreary debate about political correctness. It's caught on to the extent that it has because there's a germ of truth in what the neo-conservatives have been arguing. I'll give you an example from my own background. Years ago when I first started working as a young cadet in Brisbane in the mid-1970s, I did one story after another on Aboriginal missions in North Queensland. This was the height of the repressive Bjelke-Petersen regime and the old policies of protection still held sway. At the same time, you also had the beginnings of a self-determination movement by Indigenous people. My sympathies were with the latter – and at the time it was pretty hard for them to get much of a representation in the media. So I felt it was my God-given duty to be sympathetic and give them as much airtime as I could. If you were to look at my reports from those days they would hardly be balanced.

When I look back now, where I think I spectacularly erred was in the area of self-censorship. I can remember my earliest trips to remote communities in far north Queensland and a typical scenario would begin with the male elders gathering around to debate whether in fact they would bother to talk to a *female* journalist. So there was a sexist sub-text that had to be dealt with. The discussions would take up to half a day, and half your precious crew time. Now, did I ever tell my audience that? That to add to all the other issues, there was some pretty aggressive sexism underlying Aboriginal society? And worse, as we now know, this underpinned decades of passive acceptance of a shocking level of violence towards Indigenous women. It was a huge issue, and most of us turned a blind eye.

Thirty years later I can say it was wrong and that we should have found a way to talk about some of these things. I understand absolutely why I didn't, and I'm sure most of my colleagues in the same situation would say exactly the same thing. How could you possibly seek to muddy the waters by creating another layer of complexity about a people who were so wretchedly oppressed to begin with – politically, socially, and every other way? We wanted to present a nice clear picture where you had Bjelke-Petersen the baddie, versus the oppressed Indigenous Queenslanders who were fighting for self-determination. It was a noble goal, and, to me, Bjelke-Petersen was a wretch; however, there was a much more layered story there. There were corrosive elements within Aboriginal society that needed to be talked about.

If we fast forward to what we've had in the 1990s and are still experiencing – an equally corrosive debate based on what we call dog-whistle politics – where the demonising of particular groups is par for the course amongst certain shock jocks and others – I can certainly see where this has come from. It's in part a reaction against what many of us were doing, attempting to present issues in a good versus bad manner, when in fact things were much less clear-cut.

What about some of the current coverage of Muslim Australians? Do you believe politicians and other forces in public debate have scapegoated them and do you think journalists have an obligation to draw attention to some of the sub-texts behind the attacks on this community?

Over the past couple of years or so the Islamic communities in western Sydney have been hit with the triple whammy of Tampa, of 9/11, and of the Lebanese rapes [sexual assaults by multiple assailants carried out on Anglo-Australian women]. They feel utterly besieged. They believe they have been targeted as a community and certainly feel that a huge section of the media has gone along with this. Equally, as many in the Islamic community have seen it, they've also had the interesting situation whereby a conservative Prime Minister and a Labor Premier [Bob Carr] have been singing from the same songbook, on some of those issues.

But there's another layer here. Why has it been so hard for journalists to say: 'Look, this is a lot of rubbish'? Well, for a couple of reasons, I think. It seems to me there's a problem of leadership within the Islamic communities themselves. They are not well served by religious leaders who, despite long-term residence in Australia, simply don't speak English. Public pronouncements from the leaders, certainly in Sydney, are always via interpreters; not that satisfactory when you're trying to mount a defensive case.

This gives you a clue as to another issue. A lot of us in the media have been in denial about problems of social integration; particularly in places such as Lakemba. There are problems, and a lot of us haven't wanted to talk about them. We've all wanted to believe what is mostly true about Australian society – that we are a successfully integrated multicultural society. But where I'll admit to errors is that in wanting to believe this, I've probably on occasions fallen over the line, and propagandised on behalf of the notion. In so doing I've been guilty of not telling the full story. Hence the situation we had in the mid-1990s, where the media elite was pushing out one line, and Pauline Hanson quite another.

My own approach is certainly different now. A recent example was a profile of two marvellous Islamic women who are battling to fill the leadership vacuum in their communities. They talked about why they choose to dress in the traditional hijab [veil] and defended their faith against many of the contemporary myths. Equally, I wasn't coy about pointing out their reluctance to address some of the contradictions – why they won't condemn more forcefully and publicly the extremes such as the Taliban.

That's a long way of answering your question, but I think journalists would have had more success with countering the political offensive, the scapegoating, if we'd been regularly readjusting our social antennae.

> **There is quite a famous interview that you did with Pauline Hanson in which you asked her questions which exposed her total ignorance of the kinds of statistics politicians are supposed to know about. Would you have done that differently in hindsight? Is there any truth that journalists – particularly journalists in the quality end of the media spectrum – are part of an elite?**

After I did that interview I was a hero to my colleagues for at least a week because I was the woman who had humiliated Hanson on television. Well, in fact, I didn't humiliate her at all. The penny only dropped for me a while later, when we conducted a wider discussion with key rural constituents and the whole Hanson agenda came up. I remember one particular farmer came up to me afterwards, and he'd been a very worthwhile member of this panel – he'd made some good points – and he said: 'You just don't get the whole

Hanson thing, do you? The more you people attack her and ridicule her, the more we warm to her. We don't all think she's a genius, but the point is, she's been a lightning rod for a lot of our frustrations and you guys don't get it.' Well finally I did start to get it.

But to go back to the interview with Hanson. My view was that if she was going to say yes to a show like *Lateline*, she wasn't going to get away with what she got away with on *A Current Affair*. She was going to sit there for fifteen minutes, and she needed to take some decent questions on exactly what the trade figures were, or what the state of the national debt was, or what real immigration figures were. She was clearly found wanting. I make no apologies for that.

But it's the other stuff you see and hear on television, apart from the words, that also matters. It's the woman in the suit with the clipboard, looking as if she's running the show, versus someone who is actually trying to say: 'Look, there's a whole lot of stuff out there that you people just aren't concentrating on, and we think this country's going off the rails a bit and it's about time you paid attention to us.' No wonder then, that everyone's favourite whipping boy in recent years has been the 'media elite'.

What we're really talking about here is an ethics of engagement. So in the light of that, let me ask you, to what extent do you owe someone whose views you find deeply offensive, basic respect and civility?

It's always my starting point that everyone is owed a basic level of courtesy. But it hasn't got me very far with some hard-line ministers. In recent years, with people such as Immigration Minister Philip Ruddock, I feel I've comprehensively failed. There was a point in time where almost every other week there was an issue of riots or fires at detention centres [for asylum seekers]. I always felt my primary obligation was to keep asking: 'What is it that justifies such draconian measures?', especially as it seemed obvious to me and many others that, in policy terms, we were using a hammer to crack a nut. So I saw my primary obligation as continuing to ask the question: 'What justifies this lack of proportionality in the application of public policy?' But Ruddock is someone who seems to have a stock set of answers. It's eye glazing to listen to them and he always responds in a highly technical, legalistic way. Going back a few years, Industrial Relations Minister Peter Reith took exactly the same approach when it came to the waterfront dispute.

I always try to keep in mind that what offends me about someone's position doesn't necessarily offend the audience (clearly the detention policy satisfied an overwhelming majority), so the basic rules are that the interviewee has the right to finish a sentence without being interrupted. Most of the time!

> **What about the media's role in broader terms? Do you think the media is still the kind of fourth pillar of democracy – the watchdog? the fourth estate?**

Is the media still an independent prosecutor of cases? Do they have the power to expose political issues and sway opinion? It's interesting that politicians always whip themselves up into a frenzy about the line a particular paper has taken. And yet if you think about what came out in the *Australian* just before the 2002 election, they were on the cusp of cracking the Children Overboard story. [The revelation that photographs which purported to show asylum seekers throwing their children into the water so they would be rescued did not depict this and that senior bureaucrats and at least one government minister knew.] They had a critical story on the Thursday before the election, which pretty much nailed the government for perpetrating a fraud. But it didn't result in community outrage – some would argue the very raising of the issue helped polarise opinion even more.

And I'd add to that that, Tony Jones [host of *Lateline*] put the Prime Minister under huge pressure on this issue. The PM was clearly extremely uncomfortable with the line of questioning because that day the head of the navy kept changing his story. It was a mess – the whole story was unravelling at a rate of knots. The Labor Party was delighted that the media were doing their job for them. But at the end of the day it didn't change a single vote. People's views on this were locked in.

> **So we have circled back to the issue we began talking about – the question of whether the quality media's idea of what is an issue really is the issue. In broader ethical terms, are journalists performing their function of engaging with the community and honestly serving their needs?**

Well, I don't know that it raises ethical issues. I think it raises the practical issue that many journalists have commented on and that's that we've just got to get out there more. This whole business of just working the screen and the phone, from an air-conditioned office in the middle of the CBD – there's a limit to where that can get you. That's fine for the business pages, but when it comes to the social pulse of the community, then we've just got to be out there.

We know what the story is now. We know that journalists live in certain postcodes, and that a lot of interesting stories are in postcodes that most of us never go anywhere near. That's the big disconnect – it's geography, it's a mind-set, and I think we've got to get back to a bit of pounding the beat. It's a cliché – but ultimately it's about being in touch with those communities.

5

A Viable Ethics: Journalists and the 'Ethnic Question'

GHASSAN HAGE

INTRODUCTION

BECAUSE SOCIAL ETHICS IS ALWAYS CONCERNED WITH THE WAY individuals relate to and interact with each other, the question of 'the other', the one we are interacting with, is always at the heart of all social ethical concerns. Indeed, if there is one question that encapsulates the essential concerns of all social ethical investigations, it is this one: when we human beings interact with each other, how should we regulate our conduct so as to sustain each other's viability as human beings? This means a recognition that other people are, like us, engaged in a struggle to make their lives as human beings worth living. To try and sustain the human viability of others is to help them in this struggle.

In this essay, I will reflect on the significance of this question for White journalists writing and talking about Third-World-looking Australians, or as they are more popularly referred to, 'ethnic' Australians.[1] I want to know, how could White journalists report or comment on 'ethnic' people in a way that sustains their human viability? I hope it will become clear that such ethical questions are not about 'being nice to people'. They are about treating people as human beings. 'Being nice' to some people does not mean you are treating them as human beings. You can be very nice to animals without necessarily humanising them and, likewise, you can be very nice to humans and animalise them.

Dealing with ethical questions entails hypothesising about the impact of a specific way of acting in the world. Yet, at the same time, ethical questions cannot be primarily about impact. A journalist can't control the effect of what they say or write about people. A journalist's capacity to act ethically is always

#74

dependent on the situation they find themselves in. So what is the point of ethical considerations? Mainly they are to encourage journalists to be *disposed* to think and act ethically. For example, it's safe to say that most people consider it unethical for a journalist to make readers or viewers feel that their lives are not worth living: to encourage them on the road to social, if not physical, suicide. According to this definition, an ethical journalist is one who strives to be aware of the impact they are having on others – and to avoid having a negative impact on others. In theory, this approach should guarantee that the overall impact of their work will have an ethical rather than an unethical impact.

THE ETHICS OF INCLUSION: *KHIDNA B HEL'MAK*!

'Khidna b hel'mak!' is an everyday Lebanese exclamation that people use when someone accidentally bumps into them without noticing their presence or takes no notice of what they are saying in a meeting. It literally means: 'Hey! Include me in your dreams!' Dreams here mean something like the symbolic or conceptual space that people imagine themselves to be in as they are engaging in a specific action in the world. In a meeting, the conceptual space of the person addressing the meeting is often the space made up of all the people the speaker imagines to be his or her audience. When a person feels that the speaker is not taking their position into account, they might say 'khidna b hel'mak' as a way of asking that their views be considered. The expression is also useful if a person feels their interests are not being considered. So when someone suggests a course of action that might be detrimental to the interest of another, the latter can interject with 'khidna b hel'mak'. In this sense, the exclamation is nothing but the expression of one of the most discussed questions in the history of philosophy: the desire for recognition.

If, as we have argued above, social ethics deals with the question of 'how to sustain the human viability of the other', this act of sustenance cannot happen without 'the recognition of the humanity of the other' as its pre-condition. Such a recognition not only involves the recognition of the mere existence of the other, it fundamentally involves a recognition of their humanity. This is why, when the Lebanese exclaim: 'Khidna b hel'mak', they often add, 'Are you mistaking me for a chair?' or, 'Are you mistaking me for an electric pole?' meaning: have you missed the subtle fact that I should be a human being for you and not just an object?

In the introduction above, I specified that my object of reflection is the interaction between White journalists and Third-World-looking Australians that occurs when the former write or comment on the latter. But this definition contains an optimistic assumption that the journalist reporting about Third-World-looking Australians is actually interacting with them; that in the process of commenting on them the journalist *recognises* their existence. And yet, in Australia today, many Lebanese read the paper or watch television and feel like telling journalists: 'Hey! Khidna b hel'mak!'. I am sure many Indigenous people and many Asians also have their own way of saying the same thing.

As Teun van Dijk, a Dutch researcher on racism and the media, pointed out long ago, ever since migrants have become news in the Western world, they have become present in the form of 'they'. That is, journalists talk *about* them – not *to* them.[2] This has also been a longstanding problem in the reporting of colonised racial minorities. This difference between 'talking about' and 'talking to' constitutes the demarcation line between the ethical and the non-ethical reporting of 'others'; between the journalism of recognition and the journalism of non-recognition. But this division is only theoretical. In practice, it is hard for every journalist reporting about some 'other' to simply talk to them and ignore the rest of their audience. From a practical perspective, the ethical art of recognition is to know how to talk *to* another, even when you're talking *about* them. It means never losing perspective of the fact that 'they' are also listening, reading and viewing the media at the same time that they appear in it as objects of concern. In popular terms, it means recognising that 'they' are not from Mars – they are fellow human beings and fellow nationals.

It is important to stress that the recognition of others does not simply mean 'noticing' their existence. The whole point of recognition is the interactive nature of the 'noticing'. As such, it is an act of inclusion – this is why the ethics of recognition *is* the ethics of inclusion. From a journalistic point of view, talking about 'ethnics' constitutes an obvious recognition that 'ethnics' exist. But the problem with this equation is that noticing someone does not necessarily entail recognition. Noticing the 'ethnic' is not the same thing as recognising that they are not just an object of contemplation but a human subject of interaction; someone with whom we are bound in an inter-subjective relation.

This is why the German philosopher Hegel, who has provided us with one of the most thorough investigations of the logic of recognition, sees recognition as a dialectic of desire in which we recognise the other's basic humanity by recognising them as desiring human beings: they want something from me. Accordingly, a White journalist writing about Asians who does not begin by asking, 'What do Asians want from me?', cannot claim an ethical disposition towards them. The White journalist is excluding them from his or her imaginary sphere of humanity.

Every journalist imagines an audience in his or her head when they are writing or speaking. Clearly, this imagined audience will always have a sociological specificity. Depending on the personal history of the journalist, and on which paper, radio, or television station they work for, the image will have particular class, regional and ethnic characteristics. According to most critics, while the class, gender and regional basis of this imaginary audience changes from one journalist to another, and from one media workplace to another, it remains relatively unchanged with regards to ethnicity: The audience is invariably imagined as White.[3]

For example, in the case of the 'Muslim Lebanese rapes' controversy, from which I will be taking some examples later, White journalists rarely even begin to think about what the Australian Lebanese they are writing about think of what they have written, let alone ask the question: 'What do my Lebanese readers want?' They merely imagine themselves as having a conversation between White Australians about 'the Lebanese problem'. The analysis of racism in the media is often about the content of how journalists portray the 'other' they are talking about. Yet, approaching reporting in terms of recognition allows us to understand that the imaginary audience is the key to understanding the national and the racial nature of the spatial imaginary of the majority of White journalists. Who is more racist – the White journalist telling a Lebanese readership that they should get their act together because they have rapists in their midst, or the White journalist telling an imagined White audience that the Lebanese are really OK after all, while ignoring their status as readers or viewers?

When journalists use or think the phrase 'we Australians', what is the content of their imagined 'we'? Is it White mono-racial, mono-cultural, or is it multicultural? If it is multicultural, then the question still remains: how is multiculturalism imagined? As I have argued in *White Nation*, there are two main modes of imagining 'ourselves' multicultural. One is based on the verb 'to have': we *have* a multicultural society. The other is based on the verb to be: we *are* a multicultural society. In the first, the verb 'to have' works to distance the national 'we' from 'multiculturalism' in the way 'I have an umbrella' works to distance me from the umbrella: I am not an umbrella. I just *have* one. It is useful and I like it, but please, even though I might have it with me every day, I don't want you to start thinking that I *am* an umbrella! On the other hand, multiculturalism structured around the verb 'to be' invites the person to think: we *are* multicultural. Cultural diversity is what we are, not what we have. That is, our 'we' is not an appreciator of difference; it is constituted in difference, made out of various cultures. This is different from the idea that 'we have cultural diversity', where the we can remain mono-cultural even if it has, and loves, 'cultural diversity'.

In Australia today, I have no problems asserting that the journalists who still operate with an imaginary mono-cultural 'we', or a multicultural 'we have', are simply unethical. For when they are excluding a very large number of Australians from their imaginary of the nation they are, more often than not, excluding them from their imaginary idea of what constitutes 'humanity'. Anthropologists have long shown that there is a relation between one's conception of 'humanity' and one's conception of 'community' – whether this community is perceived as a village, a tribe or a nation. The anthropologist Claude Lévi-Strauss points out that:

> *[F]or huge portions of the human species, and during tens of millennia, the notion [of humanity] seems to have been totally lacking. Mankind stops at the frontiers of the tribe, of the linguistic group, and sometimes even of the village, to the extent that a great many of the peoples called primitive call themselves by a name which means 'men' … thus implying that the other tribes, groups and villages have no part in human virtues or even human nature.*[4]

Though modernity has seen the prevalence of a general category of 'humanity', the colonial experience encouraged the European 'tribes' of colonial capitalism to construct themselves as the ideal type of what it means to be a 'human being'. What the history of the rise of European colonialism showed was how this 'being the best type of human being' became associated with being White European, while other 'Third-World-looking types' were at best perceived as a lesser kind of humanity. In fact, excluding people from

'humanity' or considering them as 'less human' than we are is the best definition of colonial racism there is.

In the encounter between White journalists and 'ethnic' Australians, it is
the reproduction of this colonial form of racial exclusion that one sees. And
this exclusionary colonial gaze is a fundamentally unethical gaze, whichever
way one looks at it. The journalist seriously interested in developing an ethical disposition in their practice will have to engage in a long-term project of
modifying their conception of their imaginary audience. This is no easy task
for it involves reminding oneself every second of the day that 'they' are part of
'us', with human desires and wishes that need to be taken into account. Only
when this culturally plural conception of their imaginary audience becomes
instinctive will they have succeeded in setting themselves up on the road
towards an ethical journalism when dealing with 'the ethnic question'.

But as I have argued above, the recognition of the humanity of the other is
only the founding step towards such ethical journalistic practice. It involves
not only the recognition, but the sustenance of the other's humanity. I will
now move to explain what this 'sustaining of the other's human viability',
mentioned in the introduction, actually entails for journalists.

ON IDENTIFICATION: SELF-REPRESENTING OUR HUMAN VIABILITY

When philosophers and social scientists speak of human viability they often
perceive it as a struggle. This flows from a very basic idea: in this life, there is
no guarantee that our life is worth living, that it has a meaning. We are constantly struggling to ensure it has. It follows that there is no such thing as a
person with an intrinsically meaningful and satisfying life. There are people
who are more or less successful in making their lives meaningful and satisfying. The viability of our lives is dependent on the extent to which we are
involved in 'life projects' such that we can subconsciously say to ourselves 'my
life is worth living'.

For the sociologist Pierre Bourdieu, for instance, it is society that is the
prime distributor of meaningful lives. Society, however, as Bourdieu is quick to
point out, does not distribute meaningful lives equally. Some of us receive a
very meaningful life to begin with and have to struggle to maintain it, and
some of us receive so little that we literally go begging for a meaningful life.[5]
But for all of us, those of us who have plenty and those of us who have little,
the meaningfulness of our lives, and the satisfaction we derive from it, is

always precarious and dependent on the support and the recognition that others give us along the way.

There are many ways in which we can support and sustain the other's struggle for viability. Here I want to concentrate on the processes of identification that are part of this struggle, for they are of particular importance in the practice of journalism. I will examine the significance of self-identification in the way we construct our viable selves and its relationship to the way others identify us. It is around this question of the 'identification of the other' that I want to discuss the ethical disposition in the media's approaches to the ethnic question. This is a question often discussed from a different perspective under the label of 'ethnic labelling' and the question of 'negative stereotyping'.

The process of self-identification, the identities we adhere to or give ourselves, is the way we represent to ourselves and to others our relationship to our life pursuits. And the significance of each of our many identities to ourselves is often linked to the significance of the life pursuit they help us represent. It is in this sense that our mode of self-identification reflects the way we define our human viability to ourselves and to others.

But because our human viability is a struggle, it embodies the constant fear of failure and we experience it affectively, not just rationally. Human viability is a carrier of wild emotions, because it embodies the threat of what Bourdieu calls 'social death': the fear of having nothing to live for, when we feel that our life is no longer a viable life.

The French psychoanalyst, Jacques Lacan, has shown that in every process of identification the statement 'I am this or that' is only, at best, a comforting illusion. We can say, in light of his work, that there is no such thing as 'being' this or that, there is only a 'trying to be'. When people declare themselves to have an identity, to *be* something, even when that identity is as general as being human, the statement 'I am human' simply hides an anxious struggle. It really means, 'I am struggling to be what I think a human should be'. Consequently, for Lacan, to be a human is only an ideal. The feeling of being a viable 'human' derives from how 'successfully' we feel we are trying to be human. That is, we are viable insofar as we feel we are successfully trying to be viable, or, to use Lacan's language, insofar as we can sustain a *fantasy* of viability. It is because of the fragility of this fantasy that the way others identify us generates so much affect – and can have such a dramatic effect on how we experience our own viability.

It follows that the common critiques of ethnic stereotyping based on the idea that 'they do not correctly reflect reality' miss the point. People's identities are all 'stereotypes', and none of them 'reflects' reality. Indeed, the first thing we can learn from the above is that identification has nothing to do with who people are; it reflects the fantasies they create about themselves.

To clarify this concept, let us briefly examine the two processes that constitute identification: the choosing of a category of identification and the choosing of its meaning. We can call these the process of category selection, and the process of articulation of meanings. Category selection describes the way we end up giving some of our identities more importance than others. As a person I can be Catholic, Lebanese, a woman and a social worker – and all of these identities are ways in which I relate to something that I am or do in the world. Not all of them are identities I have chosen. Some I have inherited. Some are imposed on me by others. Already, even at this point, the process of selection is a struggle: I struggle to be only what I want to be even though others might try to make me what they want me to be.

Clearly, for each person, some identities are more meaningful than others. Some are inherited as important. This is the case with national identities. But even if one inherits an 'important' identity, one can grow to experience it as less important. We can be born Catholics, and continue to see ourselves as Catholics without Catholicism being an identity that affects ourselves one way or another.

There will be other identities to which we relate more affectively. These are usually the identities which reflect who it is we would like to see ourselves as being. Usually such identities are trans-situational: they constitute our identity wherever we are. For instance, someone might feel themselves to be a social worker only at work, but Australian everywhere they go. Others can feel that their identity as a social worker is far more important than their identity as an Australian.

Increasingly today people have a 'hybrid identity'. They fuse two or several identities together, such as Tiger Woods describing himself as 'Cablinaisian', a fusion of his Caucasian, Black, Indian and Asian identities.[6] People who have hybrid identities are no more 'fragmented' than people with mono-identities. In fact, people often use hybrid identities to stop themselves from fragmenting. What is important to remember is that in all these pluralities of categories of identification people are struggling to select the one or many identities which can come to signify to them and to others what they consider significant about themselves socially and affectively.

But this selection is not only a selection of a mere category. It is a choice of the meaning and significance associated with this category. This is what the process of articulation entails. These socially and historically specific meanings that become attached to a category of identification are what we refer to as the 'articulated meaning', after the concept of articulation developed by the English theorist Stuart Hall.[7] The more articulated meanings are attached to a category of identification, the more it is likely to be socially and affectively important in defining a person's fantasies of viability. It is because they are often the bearers of so many articulations that communal identities (ethnic or national) acquire such importance for so many individuals. But again, it is important to remember that articulation is a struggle. People identifying as Catholics in Northern Ireland might struggle to articulate the meaning 'freedom fighters' has to the Catholic identity, while others might like to articulate it to 'murderers'. Identification at all levels of selection and articulation is an endless struggle to put yourself in the best possible light in relation to others who might want to put you in a different light – or even in the worst possible light.

Usually, the more people feel unthreatened about their communal identity the more capable they are of articulating negative things to it: 'We Australians are impossible, etc …' If people feel they are under siege, any attempt to associate negativity to an identity that matters to them becomes experienced as an attempt to disintegrate their viability. This is the case with Australians who reject any hint of an articulation such as 'Australians murdered Indigenous people in the past' and experience it as threatening to their whole well-being.

Consequently, the journalist who enters this field of identification unaware that it is basically an arena of struggle, and thinking that an identity is merely a 'description' is very naïve indeed. In the journalist's use of ethnic identification, they become a participant in people's struggles to construct viable fantasies of themselves. The journalist can do so in various ways: by trying to adhere to their own identification of themselves, for instance, or through imposing on others categories they do not wish to identify with – or even through articulating to their identities meanings they do not wish to articulate to them. The journalist does not always choose the way of intervention, but they should always try to be as aware as possible that they are. Nor is there a 'best way' to intervene. Sometimes people's fantasies of viability involve the puncturing of the fantasies of others and it might be necessary to challenge them. So it is not clear-cut what one should *do* about it. What is clear is that whatever one does, one should always be ethically predisposed and knowledgeable so as to maximise wherever possible the struggle of others to sustain their viable identities.

I think that more than ever, this fostering of an ethical disposition is of prime importance today for reporting about the very difficult Arab/Muslim/Lebanese arena of identification which is crisscrossed by issues like 'gang rapes', 'refugees', 'terrorism' and 'war on Iraq'. The complexity of the situation suggests that 'behaviourist guidelines' in the form of 'this is what a journalist should do' are profoundly unhelpful. Whatever journalists *do*, whether they are being critical or supportive, if they lack awareness that Lebanese/Arab/Muslim Australians are part of the 'national sphere of humanity', and they have an obligation to try whatever possible to maximise their viability, then they will be failing ethically, and gratuitously, harming other human beings. Most probably, they will also be harming the well-being of Australian society.

Journalists might not think much of writing 'the murderer, a man of Lebanese descent ...', but today they cannot avoid thinking about the impact this actually has, and how useful it is to Lebanese Australians reading it. They have to think about the inter-subjective dramas their mode of interaction with the 'ethnic question' can lead to. The journalist using this combination is not necessarily stereotyping or being empirically incorrect. But they need to train themselves to be aware that there is a large number of Lebanese/Muslim/Arab Australians who feel understandably fragile about their struggle for a viable life. This is especially so for people who have no compensatory class or educational power to immunise them against the unprecedented barrage of negative media coverage. These days, there is an article every second day which contains phrases like 'the rapist, a Muslim Lebanese ...' or 'the defendant, a man of Lebanese background ...' or 'Following the murder, the man escaped to Lebanon'. In facing the negative stereotyping of their own identities, people who feel targeted in this way begin to develop their own stereotype of the 'Australian' reader – a stereotype that suits their fragile state. Suddenly, they imagine thousands, if not millions, of gullible readers or viewers thinking for the nth time and thanks to yet another article or news item: 'Lebanese ... killer'. They see the White Australian gaze falling on them, penetrating them and even disintegrating them. Or they might mentally displace themselves into the body of a Muslim woman if they are not one: She is vulnerable, she is being attacked! Or into the body of a Lebanese youth if they are not one. He is now being attacked. Everyone is pointing the finger: 'Lebanese killer'. What gain do we have in making other fellow nationals feel this way unless we are really treating them not as fellow nationals/humans but as sub-humans/enemies?

I have before me an article by Paul Sheehan.[8] It argues that: 'It cannot be a coincidence that the least cost-effective immigration/refugee stream in the past fifteen years, in terms of high unemployment, high welfare dependence and high crime, has come from the Middle East, particularly Lebanon'. And it immediately goes on to say:

> A 1998 article, 'Sydney's Ethnic Underclass', by demographers Bob Birrell and Byung-Soo Seol, measured the incomes of men aged 25 to 44 and found that a very high percentage of those born in Lebanon, 40.7 per cent, earned less than $15,000 a year. This was compared with 14.7 per cent among Australian-born males. 'The community that stood out as the poorest and most welfare-dependent was the Lebanese,' says Dr Birrell.

What interests me in this piece is not the correctness of the statistics that are being used – though they could be disputed – but the total lack of sympathy that oozes out of the article. Sheehan is talking about his fellow human beings and his fellow nationals here. They might be adopted nationals, and he might not have had a say in their adoption, but they are his national 'brothers and sisters', even if he thinks they are 'physically handicapped' as a community. Yet what is Sheehan's attitude to them? Sheehan epitomises the journalist as rightwing worrier,[9] in which the attempt to obliterate 'the other' is justified because the other is not perceived as 'us' at all; even when this other is Australian for all practical purposes. Such journalism does not like itself to be labelled as 'racist' and maybe it is not. But, in taking human beings that are part of the nation and treating them as enemies whose presence is a nuisance, it seems to me to be unethical.

As I have argued above, it is not the question of being critical or uncritical that separates the ethical from the unethical. It is the distinction between 'being critical with' rather than 'being critical against'. We can criticise to elevate, and we can criticise to obliterate. We can criticise 'in the family', so to speak, and we can criticise by creating barricades.

An article by Rosemary Neil questioning the uncritical support that scarfed Muslim women were given on Headscarf Day is a good example of an inclusive critique.[10] Here, although there is a questioning of the cultural signification of the Muslim headscarf in terms of inter-Muslim gender domination, the critique is not animated by a divisive spirit. Regardless of whether one agrees with Neil or not, it's clear she believes that Muslims belong in the same human and national boat. And it is precisely this attitude – that 'we' and Muslim Australians are in the same boat despite the storms brought about by terrorism, rape and war – that an ethical disposition towards sustaining the viability of the other ought to foster. I don't think I am exaggerating if I say that without this ethical disposition, and not just by journalists, and given the anti-Arab/Islamic storms that loom ahead, Australia, as the *still* relatively relaxed and comfortable kind of place we know, will be lost to us all.

NOTES

1   There are a number of reasons why I am specifying that the object of my reflection is the relation between White journalists and Third-World-looking Australians. First, in dealing with issues of 'journalism and racism' or 'journalism and ethnicity' it is important to specify exactly what kind of journalists and what kind of readership, audience or viewers we are talking about. The critiques and studies which place 'journalists' on one side and 'audience' on the other without any further clarification fail to see the complexities that each specific combination brings with it. This is the case, for example, with the commonsense critiques of 'media representation' and of 'ethnic stereotyping'. While it might be made explicit or implicit that the journalists being talked about are White journalists, the audience/readership is somehow nondescript and homogenised. Furthermore, it is important to note that I am using the concept of White not as skin colour but as the descriptive of a relation to the dominant culture in Australia. This is because there are many people who are not White in terms of skin colour but who are White in terms of identification. For a development of this point see Ghassan Hage, *White Nation* (Sydney: Pluto Press, 1998).

2   Teun van Dijk, *Racism and the Press* (London: Routledge, 1991).

3   This is largely implied, for example, in Andrew Jakubowicz et. al., *Racism, Ethnicity and the Media* (Sydney: Allen & Unwin, 1994).

4   Claude Lévi-Strauss, *Structural Anthropology*, Vol. 2 (New York: Basic Books, 1976), 329.

5   Pierre Bourdieu, *Pascalian Meditations* (Oxford: Polity Press, 2000), 76–7.

6   John Gabriel, *Whitewash: Racialised politics and the media* (London and New York: Routledge, 1998), 2.

7   Stuart Hall, 'Religious ideologies and social movements in Jamaica' in R. Bobock and K. Thompson (eds), *Religion and Ideology* (Manchester University Press, 1985).

8   *Sydney Morning Herald*, 5 September 2001.

9   A similar animosity towards fellow Australians can be seen in the writings of even more straightforwardly self-declared rightwing worriers like Miranda Devine and Janet Albrechtsen.

10   *Australian*, 14 November 2002.

6 Ethics, Entertainment and the Tabloid: The Case of Talkback Radio in Australia

GRAEME TURNER

IN AUSTRALIA IN 1999, A GROUP OF CONSERVATIVE AND COMMERCIALLY dominant talkback radio hosts – pretty much the epitome of 'the tabloid' in its local incarnation – were involved in a scandal which exposed widespread exploitation of their market power through secret paid endorsements for products, companies and political positions. The consequent official inquiry found it difficult to locate just what was the ethical principle being transgressed, partly because these were not (ethically bound) journalists but (ethically free) 'entertainers', and partly because of the general evacuation of such principles from the industry codes of practice. The privileging of commercial responsibilities and the gradual displacement of community responsibilities which have occurred over the last decade have, in effect, reduced the possibility that an ethical or democratic critique of mass media practice could now be effectively elaborated and understood.

What we now know as the 'Cash for Comment' scandal presents us with a case where, in my view, the media's successful and unregulated pursuit of a mass audience took it beyond the reach of ethical appeal against its specific practices. Tellingly, in its defence, the media organisation concerned barely even pretended to acknowledge its responsibility to any broader community interests than those of the mass audience. The contest between commercial and community/democratic imperatives is at its most naked here; and ultimately at issue is the very relevance of an ethical regime within an entertainment-based, rather than an information-based, 'tabloid' media.

The following argument examines the role played by ethics, and by alternative or complementary considerations, within the regulation of an

#87

entertainment industry employing the kind of journalism we see in the media today. My starting point is the Cash for Comment scandal and the subsequent Australian Broadcasting Authority (ABA) inquiry. To recap, this centred on radio talkback hosts, John Laws and Alan Jones, as a result of an ABC-TV *Media Watch* story which revealed that hidden commissions had been paid to the broadcasters in order to secure their on-air editorial support for the political and commercial interests of the companies concerned.[1] Rumours about the existence of such contracts and the payment of large amounts of money had been around for years without generating much media coverage, but the breaking of this particular story provoked broad and intense media scrutiny. The reason, perhaps, is that in this instance Laws' agent had approached the Australian Bankers' Association himself, offering to change the editorial line the broadcaster was currently taking on their members' activities in exchange for a substantial payment. More conventional versions of 'payola' (that is, positive treatment for sponsors in return for cash or other rewards) seem to have been tacitly accepted and tolerated by the organisations concerned. However, this approach looked sufficiently like blackmail and constituted a sufficiently clear abuse of market power to raise the level of media interest.

From one point of view, the Cash for Comment scandal could be understood as a story about the decline in the relevance of ethical standards for media practice in Australia. It is possible to regard this decline as a consequence of increased and unregulated competition between broadcasting organisations since the deregulation of the radio industry formalised in the *Broadcasting Services Act (1992)*. The Act understood the media more as a business than a cultural industry and the media have behaved increasingly unequivocally like a business ever since. Issues of media ethics dropped off the regulatory agenda as a result of the so-called co-regulation arrangements that effectively allowed the industry to police its own ethical standards. The expectation of civic responsibility that underpins a commitment to media ethics also, necessarily, dropped off the agenda as regulatory environments were increasingly designed to ensure the profitable operation of commercial media companies rather than to serve the interests of citizens (or even consumers). So, from July through to November 1999, it was something of a novelty to find media ethics a daily presence on the front page of every newspaper, and debated with implausible sobriety by the hosts of commercial television current affairs programs.

As a result of this revived attention, a number of ethical issues emerged which were regarded, fairly generally, as being worth closer examination and possibly independent regulation. First, it was noted that the line between advertising and editorial content had been deliberately blurred, misleading listeners in order to benefit those paying for the broadcaster's services. This was amongst the few things expressly forbidden by the codes of practice for the commercial radio industry. Second, while the status of talkback as information rather than entertainment programming is hotly contested (let alone whether it counts as news and current affairs, which is how the ABA presently sees it), it was argued that the standards used to guarantee accuracy, objectivity and independence in news and current affairs should also apply to talkback – whether or not the host is a journalist. Third, the political objectives addressed by the Cash for Comment arrangements were seen to constitute a deliberate abuse of media power, employing secret commissions to influence public debate. Jones' and Laws' sponsors all had specific political objectives in mind; none was simply concerned with maintaining a market image or a commercial competitive advantage.[2] Fourth, and perhaps most worrying of all, the controversy revealed the inadequacy of the existing codes of practice and the system of co-regulation. Industry suggestions that media-specific codes of practice should be replaced by a commercial code of practice did not convince many observers. Robert Manne, on the ABC's *Lateline* program (20 July 1999), even suggested that this might be the opportunity for the community to properly investigate business ethics as well, if this was how large and influential business organisations thought they should treat their public.

One of the most significant factors in this story is that it was actually quite difficult to establish – given the nature of the current codes and standards, and given changes in the kinds of practice tolerated over recent years – exactly what ethical standards had been breached. The issues did not emerge easily. Not only was it difficult to specify a formal breach, but there was also disagreement about what currently constituted legitimate media practice. What some industry observers saw as fundamentally unacceptable, others regarded as totally unexceptionable.

Within the regulatory authority, at first, there seemed to be genuine puzzlement as to whether there had been a breach of the codes or standards and, if so, precisely what it was. This was the first inquiry of its kind since the ABA was established. Hence, while the New South Wales Director of Public Prosecutions was trying to determine whether or not a crime had been committed, Professor David Flint was saying on the ABC's *Lateline* program (20 July 1999) that he didn't know if the Broadcasting Services Act did prohibit such activities, but that he was trying to find out.

On the same edition of *Lateline*, celebrity manager Max Markson and (Sydney radio station) 2GB broadcaster Mike Gibson argued about whether the Laws contracts were in fact normal (and thus acceptable) commercial practice. Max Markson maintained that this kind of thing happened all the time and why not, but Mike Gibson likened the Laws/Jones activities to prostitution and repudiated them as acceptable practice for a reputable broadcaster: 'I sell my voice but I don't sell my backside', he said. In the *vox pops* around the industry which accompanied most of the early print media stories, broadcasters were divided over the issue. Some (Wendy Harmer, for instance) deplored the activity, while others (such as Mike Carlton) simply saw it as part of the business of commercial radio.

Given such a split within the industry, it was not entirely disingenuous for Laws to maintain his innocence. Jones simply denied everything despite the evidence placed in front of him, or else maintained he neither remembered what he had said on air nor the detail of his contracts. I find it hard to determine any kind of principled stand behind what he had to say. But Laws adopted a more substantial defence. He noted that the broadcasting code of ethics was a code for journalists. Since he was not a journalist but an entertainer, he was not bound by the code ('There is no hook for ethics', he famously remarked).[3] As an entertainer using the media, he was not subject to any ethical appeal. This view was not just a convenient fiction invented to protect him at the inquiry. According to evidence given to the inquiry, when 2UE station manager John Conde had issued a warning to his on-air staff about entering into such agreements in breach of the code of practice, Laws told Conde he believed the warning did not apply to him.

Finally, the decline of ethics as a regulatory discourse over the 1990s came home to roost in arguments made by, amongst others, former journalist and editor Max Suich at the inquiry. Drawing attention to the fact that stories similar to the *Media Watch* report had been circulated previously, and that the industry was generally aware of the kinds of arrangements now under attack, Suich pointed out that the ABA had not expressed any official interest at all on these previous occasions. As a result, he argued, broadcasters were entitled to believe that they were operating within the ABA's understanding of the code.[4]

While some of the origins of this drama lie in specific policy decisions made by the then Labor government, concern about the declining relevance of ethical standards on commercial media practice is not confined to Australia. Indeed, what could be seen as something of a moral panic around tabloidisation has been provoked by what is usually regarded as a trend that affects the Western media as a whole, to a greater or lesser extent. In a recent article that focuses on arguments about tabloidisation and journalism ethics, Christopher Pieper argues that the current rules for professional behaviour in the United States are 'obsolete'. The specific performance of the news media in the United States is now, he argues, totally incompatible with the kinds of truth claims customarily made for the press, as well as with the principles of objectivity routinely invoked by members of the news media when defending themselves or attacking their competitors.[5]

Nevertheless, Pieper contests the narrative of decline and contagion usually attached to accounts of tabloidisation. First, he argues that it is difficult to find evidence to support the proposition of clear differences between the content and practices employed by mainstream or quality media and the tabloids. While both sectors of the industry claim the status of 'news' for what they do (as distinct from gossip or entertainment), almost all the available promotional tactics are used by almost all the outlets. The only area immune from the so-called contagion of the tabloid in terms of their content and news-gathering practices, according to Pieper, lies outside the commercial domain in the United States: National Public Radio and *The News Hour* with Jim Lehrer. Pieper concludes that the so-called disease of tabloidisation is simply the consequence of unregulated market competition. The problem with the practice of contemporary journalism, he says, is the 'confounding factor' of the profit motive:

> *[T]he mainstream media have not been 'infected' in any real sense by the rampaging virus called sensationalism, placing the media in the role of the passive victim and tabloids as the aggressor, but they instead gradually poached techniques from the tabloid side, as needed, to supply what they discerned to be public tastes.*[6]

Pieper suggests that what is most often discussed as an issue of standards, and represented through metaphors of disease and decline, is actually a structural issue. The commercial media, shorn of any checks and balances to exert a public policy influence over their activities, behave increasingly like a business. As the mainstream media in the United States are finding out, this may actually endanger their survival because it constitutes a partial misrecognition of what the media are: that is, they are a cultural as well as a commercial industry, and many of the normal commercial rules about product development and investment do not apply. As the title of Julianne Schultz's 1994 book says, it is not 'just another business'.[7] Nevertheless, in the United States, where competition has increased and the regulatory hand has never been strong, the media sphere has become a thoroughly commercial domain.

There are other angles we could take on this debate which credit the commercial media with more diverse and positive outcomes. John Hartley's *Uses of Television* argues that the media in contemporary culture serve more than the profit motive – perhaps far more than they might realise. For a start, the media provide us with the means of constructing a modern citizenship. Not only that, but it may well be an increasingly progressive form of citizenship. According to Hartley's argument, the Western mass media are tightly implicated in what has been a relatively recent move away from addressing what was conventionally thought of as a 'mass', modern but undifferentiated, citizen.

The mass media now seek a highly differentiated, what Hartley calls a 'DIY', postmodern citizen. They do this through the specialised address we might associate with cult television, fanzines, or slash comics, but it is also implicated in the market success of mainstream television programs such as *The Panel*, and talkback radio hosts such as John Laws. Hartley argues in relation to television, in particular, that while it may well aim at something different as its commercial objective, its by-product is in fact a citizenship of the future:

> [D]ecentralised, post-adversarial, international, based on self-
> determination not state coercion, right down to the details of identity
> and selfhood. Its model is the 'remote control' exercised by television
> audiences, and its manifestations include fan cultures, youth cultures,
> taste constituencies, consumer-sovereignty movements and those
> privatisations of previously 'public' cultures that succeed in

democratisation without politicisation: extending to everyone
membership of the republic of letters that was once reserved for
literate/clerical elites.[8]

This has occurred in the context of an increasingly commercialised, deregulated, and ethically relaxed media. The great irony for Hartley is that what was once thought of as a homogenising 'mass media' is now actively producing multiple, fragmented, highly differentiated identities – all claiming 'difference' as a right.[9] Far from accidental, it would seem, this is a result of the new focus of the media. A centralised and highly selective location for information and entertainment has become a proliferating source for the distribution of information, entertainment and identities, as news and journalism move from operating as a 'discourse of power' to operating as a 'discourse of identity'. We can see the result in our programming, argues Hartley: the 'object of news was once the decision-maker' but is now 'the celebrity'[10] – which is why some decision-makers try to become celebrities.

Hartley's position is elaborated within a characteristically optimistic and anti-statist account of the cultural function of the media – an account encapsulated in the neologism he employs throughout *Uses of Television* to label certain aspects of the relationship between the media and the citizen. By using the term 'democratainment', Hartley locates the media as a site of both pleasure and pedagogy, privileging the primacy of entertainment while still reminding us that it is nevertheless through the media that citizens participate in public debate.[11] One doesn't have to accept the full range of implications of this neologism, and I should admit here that I do not, to respond to the notion that a primary cultural function for the media is the construction of personal and public identities. Nor is it difficult to accept that amongst the effects of the highly commercialised and expanded mediascape of today is the proliferation of new, hitherto marginalised, personal identities, and disrespectful, hitherto silenced, public voices. Their presence is probably reflected, in fact, in the prevalence of the rhetoric of declining standards which is so often used to support the critique of tabloidisation.

There is no doubt, I would agree, that the media's size and structure have changed in recent decades. Some of the changes are beneficial, and probably involve what Hartley refers to as 'transmodern teaching', the 'gathering of audiences' and the creation of 'cultural literacies', which are just as important as those traditionally associated with what he refers to as the literate/clerical elite. There is enough evidence to suggest that, as observers or students of the media, we must continue to revise some of the more traditional assumptions about how the media operate, in what configuration of interests they can work, and what kinds of democratic potential they carry.

If there is substance to Hartley's view, then, how seriously should we take the ethical failings that occur along the way to this DIY citizenship? If we are witnessing the democratisation of the media sphere, should it matter that certain ethical constraints will give way in the face of unregulated commercial competition? Does it really matter that the commercialisation of the public sphere, and its realignment with the provision of entertainment, effectively side-steps the traditional claims of journalism ethics – claims still implicitly based on the provision of information to the citizenry? What, precisely, is the problem if the media disinvest in the culture of public service in order to maximise the benefits of a culture of business?

First of all, it is important to accept that there need not be a categoric answer to this. Certainly, in the specific case we are looking at here, I think it does matter. In this instance, there is clear evidence that the manipulation of public opinion on important matters carries effects that are the reverse of democratic. The connection between the media format and the formation of public opinion has been articulated to private and secret interests. As a result, rather than public opinion being what David Chaney calls 'the creative fiction of a new political order [i.e. democracy]' – and therefore a good thing – the formation of public opinion becomes the 'rhetorical fiction of institutionalised elites' – definitely a bad thing. The very media structures which ought to *enable* democratic participation work against such an end when 'public opinion … is conjured into being by interested groups' through the media 'to rationalise and legitimate the play of institutionalised politics'.[12]

That said, when we move beyond the specific case, there is a comprehensiveness about the claims of an ethical critique that seems insufficiently contingent for our current needs. We need to ask to what extent are ethical issues still relevant for media analysis as well as for media practice? Of course, a code of ethical practice has been a favoured means of protecting the interests of individual members of the national public, as well as those of the nation, in more than the media industries. It had a particular point, though, in its relation to the media industries. The media participated in the cultural formation of the modern citizen and thus carried out a civic responsibility that could be framed in fundamentally democratic terms.

However, the citizen looks a little different to us now. Ideally, today, cultural identity is offered up as the object of choice, DIY, through active identification rather than some form of designation or attribution. The consensual momentum invested in the idea of the nation has lost some of its power. At the same time, the idea of the modern nation is losing some of its democratic furniture as more and more of its operations are privatised, deregulated and turned over to the market. This has not been such a difficult transaction. The categories of the citizen and the consumer are easily, even unproblematically, merged through the liberal-democratic rhetorics of choice and cultural identity preferred by most Western democracies today.

This makes many of us uncomfortable. It is difficult to reconcile a view of the media that, on the one hand, sees their expansion and plurality as a positively democratising force with, on the other hand, a political economy of the media which charts the increasingly concentrated pattern of media influence and ownership around the world. These two principles work against each other. One welcomes the proliferation of voices, access and diversity, while the other is intent on controlling and reducing participation to those elements which are profitable for a very small number of beneficiaries.

This conflict requires some managing through a regulatory structure which will privilege 'where necessary' (and this is a minefield I will leave alone in this argument) the interests of the national citizen over those of the commercial consumer. Here, an ethical regulatory regime is still required. The recent Productivity Commission Report on Broadcasting pointed out the need for guarantees of ethical media practice within a number of areas: these included the respect for privacy, issues of access, right of reply and redress, and accuracy of reporting.[13] Crucially, they suggested such guarantees should be obligatory conditions of media licences, not just codes of professional practice. Significantly, also, the Productivity Commission returned to some implicit invocation of the ethical/democratic responsibilities of the media by suggesting that, in addition, an outline of what they called 'general conditions' should be incorporated into the broadcaster's licence.[14]

In the past we have had such general codes – variously articulated as an independently scrutinised regime of 'standards' (which was a taste-based means of policing a particular version of 'quality' as operated by the old Australian Broadcasting Control Board) or the current 'code of ethics' (which effectively established the professional codes of journalism as the only ethical regime required). What the Productivity Commission proposes is a charter of fundamental social responsibilities to the citizen and the nation, guaranteed in return for the commercial privilege of ownership of public space. This represents a significant revival of a less market-oriented construction of the relationship between the media and the nation-state.

Ethics here operates as a means of framing certain aspects of the contract between the media licensee and the licensing state. But it assumes a model of media practice that is still based on journalism or on the provision of information. What kind of regime – if any – do we institute for a media industry primarily concerned with providing entertainment? As someone working within cultural studies, that is now a pressing question. An ethical regulatory structure is neither enough nor, on its own, appropriate for managing our relation to this kind of media.

The media are supplying quite varied needs now; and much media criticism routinely devalues those needs it does not share. We should not forget that ethics are not only tied to issues of citizenship, but also to issues of class. It is not too long ago that the role of the metropolitan intellectual (or Hartley's literate/clerical elite) was explicitly to shape both opinion and taste: to 'civilise' an emerging class by educating them in the values of an elite. Cultural studies has been amongst the forefront of movements exposing the interests embedded in that role for the intellectual. Previous comfortable agreements about what is an appropriate ethical position or what are acceptable tastes have fallen apart. As a result of the turning of critical attention onto cultural forms based on the experience of women, people of colour, gays and lesbians, what were once considered disinterested ethical positions look a lot more like interested political positions. What was once, according to Andrew Ross, 'exclusively [and unproblematically] thought of as the education of taste', now has to draw upon 'many different schools of ethical action, informed not by "universal" (i.e. Western) humanist values, but by the specific agendas of the new social movements against racism, sexism, homophobia, pollution, and militarism'.[15]

Just as in the case of the critiques of tabloidisation, these movements have 'run up against the same reactionary consensus of left and right, each unswervingly loyal to their respective narratives of decline',[16] and each of them grounded in an explicit ethics.

We need to accept that even the discourse of ethics is not innocent. This is not to claim that we don't need it, but to argue that we need more than that.

As has been found in the Cash for Comment instance, a code of ethics has not been enough to protect us from the effects of the market. However, an obvious alternative, or complementary angle of inspection, involves a regime of content regulation based upon a particular consensus around assumptions of 'quality' – much like that exercised by the old Broadcasting Control Board. This kind of regime still operates in the United Kingdom. In June 2000, a storm blew up over the fact that the UK television content regulator (the ITC) intervened on two occasions. It first warned Channel Five that the populist character of its programming was an object of concern (a naked game show was the provocation here). Then it tested the limits of its powers by instructing ITN to move its News at Eleven back to the previously traditional slot of News at Ten in order to provide access to the news for a larger proportion of the population.[17] I am not recommending this kind of regime at this point, but it is a possibility that deserves revisiting for public debate. Furthermore, it is worth pointing out that such a regime effectively operates in relation to the ABC through the influence of the government of the day (particularly frequent under Minister Richard Alston), while the commercial networks are free from such kinds of scrutiny.

At this point, I am arguing for a much less institutionalised form of cultural criticism of media output that interposes itself against the forces of the market. There has to be a more active and watchful context of consumption – something the Cash for Comment inquiry has helped to create, even if only temporarily. This story was broken by the ABC's *Media Watch*, taken up by the Fairfax press, debated on *Lateline* and *A Current Affair*, and prosecuted as a public policy issue by the Communications Law Centre. That, it seems to me, is how it *should* happen – only more often. And it should involve people from within media and cultural studies more often. Talkback radio has been virtually ignored by the academy, even though it constitutes one of the major influences on the media's shaping of public opinion. There are important modes of critique which do not carry the universalising assumptions built into the concept of ethics, which will be explicitly motivated and contingent, and which will be mounted on a case-by-case basis.[18] Such modes of critique are amongst the potential contributions to be made by media and cultural studies to this context of consumption.

The distribution of capital is largely left to the market but few of us are happy with the results. The distribution of cultural capital seems to me far too important to leave to the market, but its regulation is a thorny problem because even the most principled intervention will serve specific interests. On the other hand, of course, we know that the market is not in fact left to its own devices. The Cash for Comment scandal is a perfect example where the possibility of effective political participation was restricted by those who had access to influencing media content. That access was provided by their market power. The power of access can be understood as a significant form of cultural capital in itself. As Chaney says,

> *[It is] not only markedly unevenly distributed, but has also proved to be easily appropriated by dominant organisations. The meaning of the public sphere in different social formations must be continually inspected, unless its failures are to persistently rob the concept of citizenship of effective meaning.*[19]

I have suggested elsewhere that this has proved difficult for cultural studies over recent years, in that reactionary or populist media forms – indeed, entertainment genres overall – no longer provoke enough attention from a cultural studies perspective, which thinks of itself as having left ideology critique behind.[20] With the revival of a context that might encourage informed and case-based critical scrutiny, one would hope to see an expansion in the critical field. This is a context in which there is now a lexicon of ethics as well as commerce, some revival of discussion of what might be the specific point of a culturally regulatory regime over the commercial media, and wider understanding of the fact that media content may no longer have much to do with the provision of information. Now, more than ever, certainly in relation to Australian talkback radio, there are opportunities to 'contest, reconstruct and redefine existing terms and relations of power'[21] in the media through direct critical engagement. That means more specific studies – not necessarily exemplary, nor theoretically clarifying or programmatic, just inspections of media content in its own right, because it matters.

NOTES

1   I present an account of this in 'Talkback, advertising and journalism', *International Journal of Cultural Studies* 3:2 (2000), 247–55; a book-length account of the subsequent inquiry is Rob Johnson's *Cash for Comment: The seduction of journo culture* (Sydney: Pluto, 2000).

2 Caroline Overington goes through the political connections in her piece in the *Age*, 'Talk bank radio', *News Extra*, 23 October 1999, 6.

3 This was reported throughout the media, on 30 October 1999.

4 This was reported and discussed at length, for instance, in the *Australian*, 27 October 1999, 3.

5 Christopher Pieper, 'Use your illusion: Televised discourse on journalism ethics in the United States 1992–98', *Social Semiotics* 10:1 (2000), 61–79.

6 ibid., 74.

7 Julianne Schultz, *Not Just Another Business: Journalists, citizens and the media* (Sydney: Pluto, 1994).

8 John Hartley, *Uses of Television* (London: Routledge, 1999), 161.

9 ibid., 164.

10 ibid., 159

11 As Liz Jacka pointed out when this paper was presented to the 2000 ANZCA conference, the use of 'democracy' in this formulation is not at all precise. Rather than an increasing 'democratisation' of media content, she suggested, what Hartley describes is the increasingly *demotic* content of mainstream media in the Western world. To inscribe this with a democratic politics requires another level of argument and demonstration. I am grateful to her for this observation.

12 David Chaney, *The Cultural Turn: Scene-setting essays on contemporary cultural history* (London: Routledge, 1994), 108.

13 Productivity Commission 2000 *Broadcasting*, Report No. 11 (Canberra: Ausinfo, 2000), 455

14 ibid., 455–62.

15 Andrew Ross, *No Respect: Intellectuals and popular culture* (New York: Routledge, 1989), 211.

16 ibid.

17 At the time of writing, this ruling was to be tested in the courts. For a sample of the debate in the press, see Damian Tambini, 'One watchdog that needs teeth', and (no byline) 'Bring back News at Ten, or else (er, or else what?)', *Media, Guardian*, 26 June 2000, 5. An academic account can be found in Howard Tumber, '10pm and all that: The battle over UK TV news', in Michael Bromley (ed.), *No News is Bad News: Radio, television and the public* (London: Longman, 2001).

18 An elaboration of what this might mean in practice is contained in Graeme Turner, 'Tabloidisation, journalism and the possibility of critique', *International Journal of Cultural Studies* 2:1 (1999).

19 Chaney, *The Cultural Turn*, 112.

20 See 'Tabloidisation, journalism and the possibility of critique' as above. See also Graeme Turner, 'Reshaping Australian institutions: Popular culture, the market and the public sphere', in Tony Bennett and David Carter (eds), *Culture in Australia: Policies, Publics and Programs* (Melbourne: Cambridge University Press, 2001).

21 Ross, *No Respect*, 213.

INTERVIEW WITH MIKE CARLTON

MONEY **VERSUS ETHICS**

(COLUMNIST WITH THE *SYDNEY MORNING HERALD* AND RADIO BROADCASTER WITH 2UE)

At the time of the Cash for Comment affair you said you felt sorry for John Laws, and I'm curious about that.

I still do in a way, because I don't think Laws has ever made any secret of the fact that he is a salesman, he's a voice for hire, he advertises things, he flogs things, and I think he was probably stunned at the tonne of bricks that fell on him. He actively promotes himself as a super salesman.

Do you think that most of his listeners understand him that way?

I think to a great degree they know that Laws will spruik anything. He's as obvious about it as the demonstrator standing in Coles frying little sausages and handing them to you on toothpicks. He's never made any secret about it.

What about the argument that he was presenting his own opinion?

I think that was really badly handled. He probably can see that now too. It should have been made much clearer that this was verging into editorial, well not verging – that it was editorial.

#100

Let me ask you then about Alan Jones. Do you look on Alan Jones' role in the Cash for Comment affair in the same way?

No, I look at it in a very different way because the Australian Broadcasting Authority (ABA) inquiry showed that Jones was also paid *not* to say things. I think that's a significant difference. Jones claims he never read any of his contracts. He actually said to the ABA, 'I never read the contract'. But it seems plain that he obeyed the contracts to the letter, and that in some cases he read editorial stuff directly provided for him by various companies, and passed it off as his own comment. Although he claimed his opinions couldn't be bought, the ABA inquiry clearly didn't believe him and said so.

Could we say that we have different expectations of Jones – that he promotes himself as a different kind of person?

Laws and Jones promote themselves as different people. Laws is unashamedly the bloke standing outside the tent saying, 'Roll up, roll up, two a penny', and Jones promotes himself as a serious current affairs commentator who can shift events and move prime ministers.

In the case of Laws, he said there was no hook for ethics on the basis that he is an entertainer, not a journalist. Can media professionals be divided into journalists and entertainers, and what are the implications for applying the code of ethics?

Yes, they can be divided into journalists and entertainers. The trouble is that the punters don't always know, and can't always tell. Jones is, above all, an entertainer. He's a tap dancer but the public doesn't know that. The public sees him as a serious commentator. This is where it can get very sinister.

Well, then the question comes back, if we use John Laws' simple distinction that he's an entertainer and so the code of ethics doesn't apply, it's a bit problematic isn't it?

It's very problematic. A code of ethics does apply, even though it mightn't be the journalist. Basically you've got to be honest with the audience whether you're a journalist or an entertainer. You owe your audience a duty of honesty and candour. In Jones' case, he drove a tank through it, and in Laws' case, I think he probably blew a few things, but not as badly.

> **Of course to focus on just Cash for Comment is to miss the much broader trend towards the collapse of information entertainment, often quite explicitly on TV. Can you comment more broadly on the implications of this for the old-fashioned, ABC/ BBC idea that there's this code of ethics and you stick to it?**

Not just an ABC/BBC idea, it's also a *Sydney Morning Herald*, and even occasionally it's a News Limited idea; but it is going out the window. It's not just happening in Sydney radio, or in Australia, it's happening worldwide, where, for example, in the war against the Taliban, in Afghanistan, after September 11, Rupert Murdoch's Sky News channel in the United States sent along an afternoon talk show host, Geraldo Rivera, who turned up with a pair of pearl handle pistols and announced he was 'going huntin' for Saddam Hussein himself, for 'Osama Bin Laden himself'. Throughout his broadcast he referred to him as 'that asshole'. That's not reporting, that's vaudeville. Increasingly the American television networks – and we'll copy it here – have thrown the switch to vaudeville. They don't want reporting, they don't want facts, they want victories, fanfares and triumphs. One of the American TV networks tried to hire Major James Hewitt – Princess Diana's bonk – to cover this coming war on Iraq because he'd been a tank officer in the first Gulf War. They don't want it reported, they want a circus.

> **You've been in this game for a very long time, and you've occupied many roles. Are you just being a grumpy senior journalist? You're not just saying, 'Oh it was better in the old days'?**

I am saying it was better in the old days, because it bloody well was better in the old days. There were ethical standards drummed into us.

> **And you always followed them? It wasn't something that you kind of felt was a bit abstract?**

I don't think every journalist has always followed them. I don't think any journalist has always followed them. You try to be honest with your audience, and honest with your employer, sometimes at considerable cost. Particularly in the work I'm in you may have to take an unpopular line, because you happen to believe it's right – as with the refugee boats, or the asylum seekers.

And you think that's an unpopular line?

Damn right. I got crucified for criticising what the Howard government and Ruddock were doing to asylum seekers. But I did it because I believe it's the right thing to say.

Crucified by listeners or …?

Yeah, by listeners. Ratings died in the bum. That then puts pressure on you from your employers who say, 'Couldn't you just agree with them?'

Thinking back across your career, is there a situation in which you really did have to go back to the code of ethics and think about it and take a stand?

By and large, a code of ethics should be operating every day – that you deal with your interviewees honestly, and that you should be honest with your audience. That's what you're there for. Now employers think you're there for the advertisers, and the ratings and so on. But basically I am there for the audience.

When the Cash for Comment affair broke, you were critical of some at the ABC. Do you think there might be a false distinction made by the quality media between themselves and other forms of media?

There was a great deal of sanctimonious claptrap going on at the ABC which I pointed out at the time and didn't get thanked for. They had a radio host who I considered was taking large sums of money from practically the fortuned

500 in Australia, the top 100 companies in Australia, that also was not disclosed to the audience. The ABC made a great song and dance about how he separated himself but who was he working for – the corporations or the ABC?

Have you made that a point of principle yourself, working at 2UE or in commercial radio generally?

I have never done a Cash for Comment deal. I don't do them. I have been paid money by sponsors, on occasions, to read commercials, but they're very clearly commercials. I have never once been paid to shut up about something, or been paid to take any political or commercial line.

These days the broadsheets are also full of supplements. Are these distinctions between quality/commercial/tabloid splits really relevant any more when it comes to the behaviour of journalists?

There used to be a clear dividing line, and now the whole thing is blurred. The broadsheet newspapers are full of advotainment, infomercials, call it what you like. There's some very high quality tabloid journalism around as well, so the split isn't nearly as discernible as it was.

And in an intense competitive environment, is it at all pragmatic or realistic to expect young journalists to just stand their ground?

I think it's vital to expect them to do that and I think many of them do. It's drummed into them at journalism school, and they emerge with the most lofty ideas, which is fine. It's exactly as it should be. In the cold hard light of day, when they get their first job, they find it doesn't always work that way. But at least they're imbued with the idea of ethics. If we abandon it totally, we might as well abandon journalism.

So you're saying it never works perfectly?

Of course it doesn't. It's an imperfect idea. Journalists are subject to all sorts of commercial and political pressures. There are fudges and compromises that happen every day, but you've still got to keep the main goal in sight.

So would you say that the system we have in place, the code of ethics and the various forms of self-regulation that operate are adequate?

They're probably not adequate. You could always make them better. I think that peer pressure, the opinion that other journalists have of you, can be important. I know that when I write I have a list of about ten journalists, friends and critics, and I wonder what they would think of what I'm writing. That can be dangerous – writing for other journalists and not for your reader-ship or your audience – but it's not a bad system of checks and balances, thinking about journalists who you respect and who are honourable.

To go back to Cash for Comment, do you think the inquiry has had much impact on the commercial talkback radio sector?

Yes, it has. Everyone's a helluva lot more careful about it now, and you've got to be because a radio station can lose its licence. We've all got to declare interests and that sort of stuff. But there are ways around it. Jones, for example, doesn't do any deals at all any more, but he has a financial interest in 2GB, which does do deals. It's all perfectly legal, and I'm not saying otherwise, but where do you go from there?

That's the other issue, isn't it, that there are forms of power and influence that go well beyond these kind of narrow ethical issues, but arguably raise larger questions for democracy or the health of public debate.

Yes, in Britain if you are a designated current affairs or news commentator on radio or a person on radio, you're not allowed to do ads. You are simply not allowed to read an advertisement or lend your name to a commercial enterprise on air. That makes for a much tougher regime. Radio stations would hate it here, because they like the idea of their much-loved personalities selling things, from condoms to Holdens.

A final question. Of late, has anything piqued your interest in media and ethics?

I am probably more frightened of what's going on in the boardrooms of the media industry, whether it's the boardroom of the ABC, or Fairfax, or News Limited or Channel Seven, or whatever. Increasingly the pressures will be to get into entertainment and less into journalism, and a journalistic code of ethics often gets in the way of an employer's desire to make money. I think that's increasingly happening and that's a huge worry.

7 Eating into Ethics: Passion, Food and Journalism

ELSPETH PROBYN

FOOD AND MEDIA – THE COMBINATION IMMEDIATELY CONJURES UP THE luscious curves of Nigella Lawson as she flirts with the camera, looking straight at us, the wide-eyed, open-mouthed and hungry viewer. For those with other tastes, there's Jamie Oliver, whose 'mockney' expressions became part of our vocabulary – 'pukka', 'scrumbly-bubbly'; cool ways and cool food made him the young woman's favoured piece of crumpet. His dishes are simple, and in fact rarely require a recipe – a list of ingredients would do – but he managed to do the unthinkable when he bumped Delia Smith from her position as queen of the kitchen. Delia taught us how to boil an egg and if her turn-on appeal was limited to those with a penchant for schoolmarms, at least no one starved from lack of instruction. In between Delia and Nigella came Nigel Slater, of 'real food' fame.[1] Slater was one of the first TV chefs to get down and dirty. He licked and sucked and made eating alone look sexy, if messy. Welcome to the world of food porn.

I've been hooked on food TV ever since *The Two Fat Ladies* roared onto the screen. Once television food moved out of daytime programming and into the glossy values of primetime I've been watching, feet up on the sofa, glass of wine nearby, and pen and paper in hand. I take notes. I buy the cookbooks. Even stranger, I also cook from the recipes. If the commentary in the media is to be believed, it seems that I'm a lone cook amongst the watchers. The received opinion is that people who watch food porn don't cook. In the words of an American food writer, Adina Hoffman, this type of food media is nothing more than 'a self-absorbed and shameless promotion for the Good Life'.[2]

#107

The tag of food porn isn't innocent – it brings to mind an image of losers who can't get it, so they watch it. Or in Hoffman's estimation, they are a bunch of self-obsessed wankers. Apart from real porn, or reality TV, or girls' magazines, there are few areas of the media where it is seen as totally acceptable for critics or for non-fans to be completely dismissive of other people's enjoyment. Condemnation and disdain are summed up in that age-old complaint about popular culture – it's nothing but escapism. In terms of food media, the pleasures of watching become deeply suspect if watching doesn't turn into cooking – if you watch and read about the preparation of food with no intention of ever putting pot to stove.

This is an interesting twist on an old argument about what popular forms of media offer, and what their audiences do with them. It's a prejudice underpinned by a barely concealed contempt for the types of people who make up the targeted audience. It's still not that uncommon to hear a middle-aged man deplore, for example, 'those *addicted* to soap operas'. Of course, soaps' main audiences have been women in the home, and increasingly students. The comment about addiction and escapism is, funnily enough, never made in regards to those who obsessively watch and read about cricket. The perception of the food media tends to be even worse than soap opera, which has been elevated by countless academic studies (and perhaps because of the changing gender profile of its audience). The analogy between food and soaps is useful because traditionally it has been thought that food media are directed at the same demographics – women in the home, conventionally figured as bored, frustrated housewives. And like soaps, until very recently food was never primetime TV or a legitimate part of the print media.

However, the analogy breaks down when one remembers that writing about food has a long and noble history. It is the subject of a wealth of books on the history, sociology and anthropology of food. It has produced writers like Elizabeth David and M.F.K. Fisher, who are regarded as fine writers, sometimes despite their subject matter. More generally, across history and cultures, food is good to think with. In other words, it has long been accepted that writing about food practices is a good way to understand cultures and societies. Following in this vein, in this chapter I argue that the food media offer us fodder for rethinking ethics – an ethics that is perforce, and by the very nature of the food media, located and practised in our everyday lives.

If it's respectable to write about food in a scholarly manner, why is it that food on television or in magazines and newspapers is so often referred to in condescending ways? As I've hinted, some of the disdain is because of the presumed passivity and gender of its audience. It's also because it overtly has to do with the personal, the domestic, the private and the home. But this is precisely why the ethics of eating has become so important. Questions about the ethics of eating have also become mainstream. As fewer people identify with overtly ideological categories – for instance, being a feminist, or a socialist – increasingly eating is seen as political, in a good sense. Especially amongst young adults, there is a clear rejection of any identity label except that of vegetarian. For many, the decisions about what and how to eat are performed within and as an everyday ethics. Then there's the popularity of organic food, which has become big business – every major supermarket chain now has its organic sections of meats, vegetables and a wide array of assorted organic or humane items. In part, this is the direct result of food writing and journalism. And yet, while we wouldn't question the ethical impulse to buy organic or to only eat, say, 'dolphin-friendly tuna', there is little public acknowledgement that it is in large part the food media that have produced this important shift in how we practise ethics through eating.

However, from my research,[3] there seems to be a split between the ethics of eating and the ethics associated with writing about eating. If the importance of the former is firmly established in the public sphere, the latter is still largely ignored. While I've written at length on the connections between eating and identity,[4] I'm now interested in the effects of the food media. Over the last couple of years I've interviewed food journalists about their professional practices – about what it's like to eat for a living. I've talked to leading food writers in Australia, Canada and the United Kingdom to get a sense of how they perceive their relationships to their topic, to their readers and to a wider ethics of eating. Together with my researchers, we have also interviewed so-called ordinary people about their perception of the influence of the food media. As I'll describe further, food journalists tend to be articulate about their mandate. By and large, they are sensitive about the ethics of food journalism, and a wider ethics of eating. In terms of the ordinary public, the opinion about food journalism is mixed. Apart from 'foodies', while many are committed to an ethics of eating, they also tend to regard food journalism as either a frivolous or a guilty pleasure.[5] Much like the stereotypical dismissal of other 'soft' or popular genres – reality TV, quiz shows or soaps – and because the mainstream media propagate a disdain for them, people do not readily own up to being influenced by the food media.

This disjuncture is fascinating. On the one hand, eating is a major site for individual ethics, and on the other, there is little consideration given to the role of food journalism in propagating modes of eating and living. Part of the problem is that food journalism hasn't been considered worthy of serious attention. There is little or no academic research about food journalism. Within the media themselves, there is a distinct lack of regard for food journalism. Especially amongst hard journalists – those seen as serious – food journalists are considered 'soft'. In fact, they're not really journalists at all. After all, they don't report facts, they give opinions. As such, few people outside of food journalism would even think to apply journalistic ethical standards to a branch of the media that trades in opinion. Amongst media practitioners, and I think for the general public, objectivity is still the measure of how media ethics is understood.

As we'll see, the question of objectivity has special resonance for food journalists. However, the ways in which they confront and are confronted by notions of objectivity provide a cogent argument against understanding ethics in these terms. In a more positive vein, the practices of food journalism may also provide inspiration for a different understanding of ethics, one attuned to intimate and convivial forms of media. Perhaps in breaking down some of the misconceptions about the food media, we can begin to understand the impact of their role, and the ethical questions raised both within and by food journalism. Media ethics in this way is not a specialised domain to be deliberated upon by experts. It is, and especially in the case of the ethics of food journalism, something that is central to our lives and that needs to be engaged with widely.

EATING INTO OBJECTIVITY

As other essays in this book explore in more depth, codes of ethics exist for nearly every area of the media. Especially in print journalism, objectivity is the golden rule. In countries as diverse as Belarus, Australia, Croatia and the United States, codes of ethics place objectivity as the first point of principle. Objectivity is understood as journalistic detachment and distance – the presentation of unadulterated facts. For instance, in the Croatian Journalist Union's Code of Ethics, it's stated that 'a journalist must not be involved in activities threatening his independence of judgment which would limit his objectivity in publishing true facts and undermine his journalistic dignity'.[6]

If objectivity is understood as not being influenced by others, it's clear that food journalism is in an awkward situation. For instance, the practice of accepting freebies is accepted as a fact of life within the trade, at the same time that it is deplored by some. Offers of free trips and bottles of wine apparently happen frequently. These attempts to influence journalists are explicitly ruled out by various ethics codes, to which, of course, food journalists – like any other journalist – are subject. The International Food, Wine and Travel Writers Association (IFWTWA) Code of Professional Conduct states as its first principle that 'food and travel journalism must be accurate and free of unwarranted prejudice'. This is immediately linked with the policy on 'comps': 'Members shall use the most severe efforts to avoid compromising recognized journalistic ethics in the area of receiving complimentary food, travel, lodging or related items'.[7]

In Australia, the food scene tends to be quite intimate. Given our small population, as well as the recent phenomenon of an established food scene, food journalists tend to know each other and the chefs and food producers they write about. One of my interviewees, John Newton,[8] reported a joke aimed at a particular critic. The critic in question has said that he has no friends as chefs. To which his colleagues respond that he has no friends at all.

It is impossible to work as a food journalist in this country without knowing who you are writing about. In recent years, and in part because of the media interest in food, food has become big business. Public relations (PR) firms are not shy in bombarding food journalists with all sorts of enticements to get them to write about their products. One US Internet site, 101 PublicRelations.com, is devoted to advising PR firms on what they can get away with. One of its lead questions is: 'If you're hosting a media tour for travel writers at your new resort ... do you automatically assume that if they accept your invitation, you will pay for everything?' They seem to have no problem with the idea of paying, and the advice is clearly directed at how to get around those tricky 'ethics policies that dictate what reporters can and cannot accept'. In their opinion, broadcast journalists 'routinely EXPECT free lunches and gifts of food' (original emphasis).

The journalists I've interviewed agree that these PR practices aimed at currying favour are widespread and pernicious. They also tend to say that they are not influenced by these practices but that they constitute a type of harassment. This seeming contradiction – can you be harassed by something that doesn't bother you? – raises questions about how deeply rooted such behaviour is, and whether it cannot fail but impinge on journalistic objectivity.

A few food journalists have publicly voiced their criticism of the food industry's attempts to influence journalists. Joe Crea, an American food editor, describes the situation as 'the gravy train open to those who carry a culinary byline'.[9] In his estimation, many of his food journalist colleagues consider their job as 'a banquet sans cover charge'.[10] This is perhaps an overly harsh description and it is mostly directed at restaurant reviewing. But the rare news stories that circulate about questionable journalistic behaviour tend to focus on restaurant reviewers.

Recently there was a bit of a controversy about the food editor for the *Boston Magazine*. Annie Copps came to the job with no journalism training and straight from the kitchens of Boston's finest. The magazine publishes a 'Best of Boston', which is described as 'the holy grail for many restaurateurs'. As reported in the Boston *Daily Globe*, Copps' closeness to the restaurant scene and her power have led to some discussion. The reporter, Mark Jurkowitz describes the situation:

> *It is that web of relationships – as well as the magazine's role as a crucial publicity vehicle – that has made Copps a controversial figure in Boston's high-profile, high-stakes, and high-strung food world. Her critics, those who think her connections to people featured on Boston's food pages represent a conflict of interest and affect coverage, are, frankly, too nervous to speak for the record.*[11]

Highly connected, high-strung, and high stakes – it's a good description of any number of food scenes, including Sydney. While it is only a small part of food journalism, restaurant reviewing tends to have the highest profile, and it's where the most obvious ethical problems arise for journalists. It's also where the public has the greatest interest in food media ethics. If you are about to shell out big bucks because of a favourable review you've read, you do not want to find out that the restaurant had paid for the reviewer's meal – or worse, she had been paid by the restaurant to review it. In the past at least, it was common practice for restaurants to pay for the reviewer's meal.

As Cherry Ripe points out in her interview, it is still not unusual for newspapers to allow this practice, either because of small budgets or because they have so little regard for restaurant reviewing as a legitimate form of journalism. In Australia, Fairfax and News Corp Ltd stipulate that journalists must acknowledge when they have been paid guests, although this practice is more evident in the travel pages than in the food pages. Elsewhere it seems that the rules are less stringent. Jürgen Goth, one of the most well-known Canadian food journalists, comments on the subtle and not so subtle attempts to influence him in his reviews. He is frequently contacted by restaurants inviting him to visit their establishment. Clearly implicit is the fact that they are going to buy him dinner. In response to queries about how this affects his objectivity, his response is: 'Listen, if you want to bribe me, buy me a Porsche. But if you're going to pick up a seventy dollar dinner bill ... well my standards are a bit higher than that.'[12] Goth also points out that the newspapers conjoin in a dubious practice whereby their advertising department will phone the restaurant under review to ask if they want to take out an ad, which then runs next to the review.

From the research I've done comparing Australian and Canadian food cultures, Australia emerges as definitely more developed. All of the Canadian food writers we interviewed were enthusiastic about Australia's food media and their impact in furthering a general food culture. As Don Genova, another established and prominent food journalist, comments: 'Australia just seems to be far ahead of us in the quantity and quality of their food media. They have many more magazines, radio and television shows. They have more star chefs, broadcasters, everyday names there.'[13] In this way, it seems that the more developed and established a food media scene is, the more likely it is that ethical guidelines will be adhered to, and that practices such as restaurants paying for the reviewer's meal will not be allowed.

SOFT MEDIA, SOFT ETHICS?

This begins to suggest the importance of taking food journalism seriously. However, even if Australian food journalists are well regarded in the eyes of their Canadian counterparts, here they still have to contend with the perception that they are not real journalists. In the eyes of their hard colleagues, many would not be considered journalists at all – they are 'life-style', not much up from gossip columnists in the estimation of other journalists. News purists would argue that the rot set into journalism when newspapers started turning out supplements about food, living, real estate, health, etc.

Increasingly, even the broadsheets are composed of more supplement than not. The accusations of being soft can bleed into a perception that food writers are also soft on ethics. Few established food journalists in Australia were trained as such. But then there's a whole generation of journalists who in general did not go to journalism school, and who sneer at the idea of a university course in journalism. Food journalists would argue that they bring to food a complex set of knowledge that goes beyond journalistic expertise: scientific facts about food; the intricate world of the restaurant industry; the economics of food production and distribution; and a feel for aesthetics. They might argue, and in many cases with good cause, that their passion for food is the result of years of interest, study and practice.

The combination of passion and journalism is problematic and interesting. Ruth Reichl, the noted restaurant critic for the *Los Angeles Times* and then the *New York Times*, recounts her first attempts at journalism. Reichl had run a successful restaurant in San Francisco before being wooed down to Los Angeles to write restaurant reviews. After one attempt to jolly up a review of a rather dreary restaurant by imagining that Gloria Swanson, already long dead, was her dinner guest, the editor called her into his office. The editor, 'Looked into my eyes, cleared his throat, and said, "Ruth, this is a newspaper"'. Told in no uncertain terms that she could not bring Gloria Swanson back to life, Reichl replies: 'Haven't you noticed that food all by itself is really boring to read about? It's everything around the food that makes it interesting. The sociology. The politics. The history'. To which her editor replied, 'In journalism you have to tell the truth'.[14]

Reichl's anecdote raises a central quandary. How do you report the truth of the experience of food? Certainly in some newspapers a great deal is made of a points system in restaurant reviews. The *Good Living* section of the Fairfax *Sydney Morning Herald* is a prime example of trying to make the reporting of a meal into 'the truth'. The main restaurant review 'Good Eating', now written by Matthew Evans, is accompanied by an explanation of how points are awarded. The 'scoresheet' on the side of the review states that 'ten points are for food, five for service and three for ambience, with an extra two points possible for a sprinkling of magic, whether it be the warmth of the welcome, the excitement of the plate, or a spectacular setting'. It's hard to say whether the quasi-scientific wording is tongue-in-cheek, or just affectation. It's probably a bit of both. *Good Living* has set itself up as the word on dining in

New South Wales, which it often suggests is the state of culinary excellence in Australia – much to the fury of Melbourne. When we interviewed readers they often commented that the *Herald's* food pages are elitist. One interviewee compared the Sydney food scene and the Sydney obsession with real estate, describing them both 'as things particular to Sydney-siders'.[15] Sydney-based writer John Newton agrees: 'Sydney is about fashion, Melbourne is about gastronomy ... Sydney tends to take food much more frivolously, and they are more interested in the chefs, where they eat and what underpants they wear'.[16]

Frivolous or not, it is undeniable that the *Sydney Morning Herald Good Living* supplement (published every Tuesday) and the *Sydney Morning Herald Good Food Guide* take themselves very seriously. The Guide began in the early 1980s following in the steps of Leo Schofield's *Guide to Eating Out in Sydney*. Each year the *Good Food Guide* provides a distillation of the year-long restaurant reviews. Over several months, reviewers scour the restaurant offerings and award points of merit, called 'hats', to different categories. Like the Oscars, the most coveted is the category of best restaurant, which gets three hats. The system is both self-perpetuating and self-promoting. The *Guide* and *Good Living* both belong to the same closed and self-referencing system: it is considered 'news' when a restaurant loses a 'hat' or gets a bad review. It is, of course, often only news in the pages of *Good Living*.

Occasionally scandals from the food realm are also covered in other sections of the paper. Several years ago, Terry Durack, who was then the head reviewer, took away one of Neil Perry's hats for Rockpool. Durack and his wife Jill Dupleix, now *The Times Cook* in the United Kingdom, wielded an immense amount of power in Australia's food scene, often creating new trends out of nothing more than personal interest. Several noted chefs publicly complained about Durack, which was picked up outside of the food pages. Yet the irony of the situation wasn't lost on many: Durack had helped create Perry as one of Australia's first 'celebrity chefs', and the shake-up incurred by taking away a hat ensured more publicity for both Perry and Durack, and *Good Living*. This was compounded when in the next year Perry was re-awarded the full serving of 'hats'.

If this smacks of conspiracy theory, it also lays bare the thin veneer of objectivity within the hyped-as-science mode of restaurant reviewing. While strict ethical standards may not be breached by such behaviour, the close if not closed nature of the food scene makes objectivity hard to sustain.

However, for many food journalists ethical worries come in quite a different form. As Cherry Ripe and others attest, restaurant reviewing is hard on the soul. While many hearts wouldn't bleed for Perry – now the head of a considerable empire – much harder are the cases where you know the chef is unknown or just starting, working eighteen hours, trying to do their best, and yet on the night you visit his or her establishment it just doesn't work. Newton gives an analogy of judging cheese in terms of how to deal with the personal effects of reviewing: 'I can say that "that's a so and so cheese which I like usually", and then when I taste it I find it's awful. It's the same with reviewing a restaurant when I can say, "Even though this man is a very nice man, it's a crappy restaurant".'[17]

The human dimension of restaurant reviewing recently came to a head when a French chef killed himself following a bad review. Bernard Loiseau's restaurant in the Burgundy region of France was awarded three stars by the *Guide Michelin* in 1991. In 2003 La Côte d'Or went from nineteen to seventeen points in the *Gault-Millau Guide*, which, in fact, wasn't enough to lose him his three-star rating. Nonetheless, his suicide set off an avalanche of fury against food critics. Paul Bocuse, an established celebrity chef, is reported as saying: 'These critics are like eunuchs: they know what to do but can't do it'. He added that 'the profession is going to react'.[18]

SUBJECTIVITY, PASSION AND ETHICS

The possibility of causing someone to commit suicide adds gravity to any consideration of the power of food critics. It does seem in Loiseau's case that it may have been more of a reaction to the financial problems he was experiencing from having expanded quite rapidly. Nonetheless, the examples above demonstrate some of the problems facing food critics trying to grapple with the outcome of making and breaking stars, as well as the standard ethical principles of objectivity. Are their views biased? Are they completely personal? The spectre of subjectivity is never far away.

How subjectivity is understood is a really crucial question for all journalists, but it is most tellingly evidenced in the case of food journalism. Alan Saunders, the host of Radio National's *The Comfort Zone* and a columnist on food matters in the *Sydney Morning Herald's Good Weekend* section, makes no bones about the personal nature of what he writes. By personal he seems to mean that the subject matter involves himself: 'The article I'm

writing at the moment is about something I found at the very back of my
·fridge'. The personal nature of the subject matter makes for a closeness to his
audience:

> *I think it's inevitably closer than if I were Laurie Oakes, for example,*
> *because I imagine that readers don't feel that they can tell Laurie Oakes*
> *anything other than that they like him or don't like him, unless they're*
> *politicians. Whereas people do give me information ... I think it's the*
> *nature of the subject.*

Saunders is clear that 'our notions of what constitutes news and what we
expect from newspapers and indeed other media outlets have changed
hugely. Newspapers are far more like magazines.' In Saunders' opinion this is
both good and bad:

> *Bad in terms of a loss of an old-fashioned notion of public, political*
> *events ... good in that there are parts of our lives which we ought to*
> *take seriously and perhaps more seriously than we used to.*[19]

In this example, and in others, one hears an articulation of subjectivity,
proximity and situated perspective that privileges interest over disinterest,
passion over detachment. This combination begins to raise radically different
ideas about media ethics. Instead of an ethics based in detached objectivity,
ethics here becomes a way of thinking and doing that touches upon everything. The perspective of the food journalist is very located, interested and, to
an extent, partial and particular. How could it be otherwise when food and
eating are immediately about our bodily, sensual and very particular experiences? Listen, for instance, to Lyndey Milan – the Food Editor of the *Australian
Women's Weekly* – as she describes a food experience:

> *I had gone to Melbourne for [a cooking] Master class and there was*
> *this cheese dinner on the night before and I had been shopping, and I*
> *couldn't find any clothes to fit me and I thought I just have to change*
> *careers because putting on 5 kilos a year is no good. Oh well, I have*
> *changed careers twice before. Then I went into this cheese dinner and*
> *there was this waiter with a silver salver and the beautiful crisp white*

linen napkin and these little jolt balls of something. I popped one in my
mouth, it was an explosion of duck liver mousse and sherry, and it was
just like I'd come down from my second orgasm.[20]

In Newton's terms,

it's impossible to be objective because of the simple fact that food and
wine are topics you write about and subsume. These are the only topics
that become, literally, a part of the writer. Add to that the very private and
personal nature of taste and flavour – history, experience, mood – and
I just don't see how you can be objective when writing about food.[21]

Cherry Ripe concurs:

Food is subjective. Because food boils down to a matter of taste or
issues of whether it's healthy food or not. And you can't, I don't think,
sit on the fence. Well you can obviously in that things must be factual,
but food is a much more subjective area.[22]

These voices attest to the impossibility of applying a conventional ethical framework of detachment and disinterest to food journalism. If for some this merely reinforces the dubious nature of food journalism, it also hints at a broader sense of media ethics based on an acknowledgement of the media as part of social and personal life, and not merely a reflection of it. As a subject that spills into every facet of life, however soft it may appear, food is intimately connected to hard issues. From the effects of genetically modified crops and foods, to the inequities of food distribution and the local conditions in which it is produced and consumed, it's clear that increasingly food cannot be separated off into a comfort zone, or treated as gossip. As I mentioned earlier, many food journalists are frustrated by such treatment of food. They are also highly critical of the way that so-called hard news handles food-related items. With little background knowledge of food, dubiously funded research gets trotted out as fact. Hard news journalists simply have neither the time nor the experience and knowledge of the field to be able to properly contextualise news-breaking stories. Meanwhile over in the life-style food pages, those who have the necessary background are constrained to writing gossip columns about what's hip and hot in the food scene, or how to make the newest trendy cocktails for your friends. In Cherry Ripe's words,

> *One could wish that editors would take a broader view and be more adventurous and believe their readers to be more intelligent, that they would actually like to read more about this. Not just have it glossed over as a very nice life-style thing.*[23]

While the life-style treatment of food is problematic, food and life-style journalism doesn't have to be seen as the Bermuda Triangle of journalism. There's no law stipulating that serious journalism necessarily has to equate with news reporting. And indeed political opinion writers are taken immensely seriously. Conversely, the perception that life-style is of necessity frivolous greatly hampers those who are trying to convey important stories and issues. Whether it is about new research on the health properties of food, or about the relation between food production and consumption, these are issues that arouse the passion of some food journalists – and they should be of central concern to us, the eating public.

As I've argued, food journalism departs from traditional journalistic notions of objectivity. Detachment and distance are at odds with the passionate, subjective and close relationship of food journalists to their topics and ultimately to their readers. Detachment also goes against the intimate nature of food journalism – in Newton's words, 'an intimate and convivial form of journalism'. 'Convivial', living together, life-style, commensality, eating together – all of these terms refer us to something more than a purely passive transmission of facts from journalist to reader. Like it or not, eating is a life-style issue, if we understand life-style in the deepest sense of the term. What and how we decide to eat affects us – in obvious physical ways – just as it always connects to families, relationships, health, as well as local and global environmental concerns. Part evangelism, part education, food journalism allows consumers to become more actively reflective on a wide range of issues.

This begins to sound very close to what many thinkers are exploring in terms of an everyday ethics, and the role of ethics in our everyday living. Paul Rabinow, a noted American academic and the author of many books concerned with ethics, argues that ethics should be seen as being at odds with morality. Morality provides a set of codes which we are to follow, like sheep.

On the other hand, ethics is seen as an active and constant reflection on one's actions. As Rabinow puts it, an attitude 'rooted in an ethics and not a morality, [is] a practice rather than a vantage point, an active experience rather than a passive waiting'. [24]

It would be silly to simply apply a complex philosophical argument to quite different circumstances and practices. Nonetheless, the interviews I have conducted with both food journalists and their readers provide ample evidence that food and eating prompt different levels of reflection. As John Newton comments, 'Food enters culture, it enters politics, it enters history; it is a way of looking at the world. You can look at the world through food and see everything.' It is, he says, 'hard to know where it stops'.[25] As we've seen, this makes food journalism hard to fit within strict codes of media ethics. Of course, the dodgy practices of 'comps', the collusion with restaurants or any perception of nepotism needs to be closely regulated. In fact, perhaps more than any other genre, food journalism need to be strictly scrutinised. Over the long term, the costs of a free lunch and the culinary gravy train have resulted in the loss of respect for food journalism within the wider reaches of the media, and may have promoted a public lack of interest and respect for food writing.

That food journalism has not been taken seriously has devastating effects on how the general public understands the wider issues that are, or should be, at the centre of food journalism. Rather than being the poor cousin to real journalism, food writing can offer a paradigm for the newer genres of media. As it challenges the conventional and no longer useful distinctions between soft and hard, objective and subjective, reporting and opinion, food journalism raises intense issues for the media, and for us, its consumers. As it deals with scientific research and technological innovations, questions the sustainability of certain food production practices, and broadens our appreciation of the tastes of other cultures, food journalism relates crucial spheres directly to readers. It brings these issues, and the information neces-sary for making choices about life-styles, directly into our lives.

And what of the judgement that I cited at the outset – that life-style food journalism is but a shameless promotion for the Good Life? Well, of course one can complain that food journalism is mainly directed to an affluent elite, and that it is shameful to read and write about new varieties of mangoes when people are starving. While it's beyond the scope of this chapter, it could also be argued that food journalists have been central to the 'trickledown' effect of information about better food products and healthier ways of eating. As I mentioned, through some of their efforts it is now common to see organic items in major supermarkets. And as they become ever more widespread, the price of better produce also begins to fall. This is not to say that there are not serious issues about how class and economic position severely restrict what and how you eat. Nor is it to ignore the fact that we don't pay enough for our raw produce – although we may pay too much for processed foods and restaurant meals. And as several of the food journalists I interviewed attest, these are precisely the type of stories that food editors are loath to promote in the life-style pages, or indeed elsewhere.

In sum, the state of food journalism in this country could be better. To make it so requires the efforts of journalists, editors and, perhaps most important of all, us – the eating public. And as I've argued, this requires that food journalism be taken seriously. On this, I'll give the last word to John Newton who argues passionately that the state of the food media could, or should, be seen as a reflection of the state of society:

*You don't have food critics in the Congo. In direct opposition to some
who think that every time you have an expensive meal you kill a baby,
I think we should be striving towards a society where there is enough
affluence for everyone to choose to be able to eat well. To eat well, and
to choose what you eat is a basic human right. I think that the presence
of Elizabeth David or Terry Durack or Cherry Ripe or Matthew Evans or
Alan Saunders is evidence of a stable society, or you could call it
civilisation. This is a roundabout way of saying that it may be soft,
but food writing is as essential as hard news.*[26]

NOTES

1 Nigel Slater, *Real Food* (London: Jonathan Lovekin, 1998). All the TV chefs as a matter of course produced books and tapes to accompany their series, and some even have CDs to accompany the cooking of their recipes.
2 http://www.prospect.org/V11/18/hoffman-a.htm accessed 10 February 2003.
3 The material referenced in this chapter was enabled by funding by a three-year ARC Large Grant, 'Alimentary Identities', of which I am the chief investigator. The project charts the influence of the food media in Australia and Canada in terms of

propagating ideas about national belonging. The interviews with John Newton, Cherry Ripe, Jürgen Goth, Don Genova, Alan Saunders, Lyndey Milan, and with 'ordinary', non-industry individual readers, were conducted over the last three years by myself, Robyn Clough, Amira Ibram and Wendy Gibbons. My thanks to those interviewed, and to my research assistants on the project. I especially want to thank John Newton for his friendship, generosity and sharing of knowledge about the food scene in general, and Sydney in particular. My material is overly weighted towards Sydney because the research project primarily focuses on Sydney and Vancouver, as the two major Pacific-Rim gateway cities in Australia and Canada.

4   Elspeth Probyn, *Carnal Appetites: FoodSexIdentity* (London and New York: Routledge, 2000).

5   'Foodies' refers to amateur and professional lovers of food with an investment in knowing about all aspects of food.

6   Taken from Press Wise – a British-based organisation dealing with aspects of journalism. http://www.presswise.org.uk/Objectivity.htm accessed 10 February 2003. For other sites concerned with journalistic codes of ethics see the Society of Professional Journalists (http://www.spj.org/ethics_code.asp; the Radio-Television News Directors Association (http://www.rtnda.org/ethics/code.shtml).

7   The International Food, Wine and Travel Writers Association was founded in Paris in 1954, and is now located in Los Angeles – which may or may not say something about where food writing is going. As an ex-waitress, I especially like the fact that the ethics code sets out the duty of a food journalist to tip the waiter for any free meal. http://www.ifwtwa.org/code_of_conduct.htm accessed 10 February 2003. See also the British-based The Guild of Food Writers' Ethical Guidelines (http://www.gfw.co.uk/edthics.html) which follows similar lines.

8   John Newton interviewed by Elspeth Probyn, 4 February 2003. Newton is a free-lance food writer whose work regularly appears in the *Sydney Morning Herald* in the Tuesday *Good Living* section and now more often in the Saturday 'Metro-politan' section. He edits the annual *Cheap Eats* guide (www.cheapeats.com.au), and has written several food books and novels.

9   Joe Crea, 'Food for thought: You are what you eat ... and do.' *FineLine: The Newsletter On Journalism Ethics*, 2: 3 (June 1990), 5.

10   ibid.

11   Mark Jurkowitz, 'Controversy simmers over well-connected food editor' *Daily Globe* 5 February 2003. http://www.boston.com/dailyglobe2/036/living accessed 10 February 2003.

12   Interview conducted by Wendy Gibbons for the 'Alimentary Identities' project, Vancouver, 28 November 2001. Goth has a national CBC (Canadian Broadcasting Corporation) radio show, and has worked for the major Canadian broadsheets and food magazines, and Food TV Network.

13 Interview conducted by Wendy Gibbons for the 'Alimentary Identities' project, Vancouver, 10 August 2001. Genova has worked for CBC Radio, and written for *The Globe & Mail*, a national newspaper, as well as for food magazines.

14 Ruth Reichl, *Comfort Me With Apples: More adventures at the table* (Sydney: Allen & Unwin, 2001), 251.

15 'Adrian', interviewed by Robyn Clough for the 'Alimentary Identities' project, 3 May 2002.

16 John Newton interviewed by Elspeth Probyn, 4 February 2003.

17 ibid.

18 Per-Henrik Mannson, 'Three-Star French chef Bernard Losieau Dies; suicide believed', *Wine Spectator Online*: http://www.winespectator.com/Wine/Daily/News accessed 1 March 2003.

19 Alan Saunders interviewed by Amira Ibram for the 'Alimentary Identities' project, 2 May 2001.

20 Lyndey Milan interviewed by Elspeth Probyn 20 September 2001. Milan occupies one of the most high-profile food jobs in Australia. (Over the past decades, the *Australian Women's Weekly* can be credited with introducing new culinary ideas to an Australian mainstream population.) Milan is also the President of the Australia Food Media Club (http://www.foodmediaclub.com.au) and has extensive experience as a food writer and editor.

21 John Newton interviewed by Elspeth Probyn, 4 February 2003.

22 Cherry Ripe interviewed by Elspeth Probyn, 6 February 2003; see her interview in this book.

23 ibid.

24 Paul Rabinow, 'Introduction: The history of systems of thought', in Paul Rabinow (ed.) *Michel Foucault. Ethics, Subjectivity and Truth. Essential Works of Foucault 1954–1984. Vol One.* (New York: The New Press, 1997), xix.

25 John Newton interviewed by Amira Ibram for the 'Alimentary Identities' project, 23 April 2001.

26 John Newton interviewed by Amira Ibram for the 'Alimentary Identities' project, 23 April 2001.

INTERVIEW WITH CHERRY RIPE
BEYOND **FOOD PORN**
(FOOD WRITER AT THE *AUSTRALIAN*)

Given your experience over a number of years and across different media genres, what do you think is the most important ethical point for you as a journalist?

Due to the comparatively low circulation figures of our newspapers and magazines by international standards, because our population is so small, it's rare for journalists or people working in the media to be forbidden from taking freebies, whether it's international travel or just being bombarded with inducements, or new products, or being invited to free meals, new restaurants or product launches by PR companies. It has become widespread practice in this country. Newspapers don't have the budgets to be able to insist that journalists pay for – or claim expenses for – many of the things, which in other countries at the quality end of journalism are forbidden.

I always try, if I've ever received a freebie, to declare it in a 'go last', so you know that 'Cherry Ripe was a guest of ...'. But twelve years ago it was very rare to see such declarations of interest at the bottom of an article, and it is still not universal practice.

For instance, the ABC food magazine recently ran a ten-page spread on Spain without mentioning that the author had visited Spain as a guest of the Spanish government. But it is actually one of the tenets of the journalists' code of ethics: 'Do not allow any payment or gift or other advantage to undermine accuracy, fairness and independence. Where relevant, disclose.'

#124

It is true that the more respected the publication, such as the *Australian*, the *Age* or the *Sydney Morning Herald*, the less likely it is to allow their journalists to accept, for instance, free meals to review restaurants. You only have to look at restaurant reviews in suburban newspapers to realise that the reviewer has had a free meal.

I dislike reviewing restaurants because one must give an honest opinion. If you're a powerful restaurant critic, you are then in the position of being able to put a small business – a restaurant – out of business. It's a tricky ethical question that has to be weighed up. The suicide of the French three-starred Michelin chef, Bernard Loiseau, shows how seriously restaurateurs do take reviews – or, in his case being downgraded by the restaurant guide, *Gault-Millau* – and their potential impact on business.

I am disturbed about the increasing tendency in the food media for creeping product placement, and what they call 'advertorial', where across the top of a page in a glossy magazine it might be called 'A such and such promotion', where somebody has actually bought the space but it's laid out in the style of the magazine so it looks like editorial. A recent non-food example was the half-dozen pages paid for, and devoted to the NSW Premier and his wife in the *Australian Women's Weekly*.

You've talked to me before about the amount of unsolicited free products sent to you.

There's a whole industry that has developed out there in public relations which is devoted to promoting food products. Multinational PR companies, like the one which spin-doctored the first Iraq war for George Bush Senior, also now promote foodstuffs. In the last decade there's been an exponential increase in the number of media releases, phone calls, and sample products that one gets sent as a journalist.

Does it ever work?

Well it doesn't for me.

So in no way do you get interested in something that is sent?

[*Pause*] Yes, I do. For instance, there was recently a new variety of mango launched. I was sent a basket of them, and that was intriguing because it's a product that tastes good; it creates employment for a farmer, it's good for you because it's this really bright orange mango with lots of antioxidants. So yes, I suppose there are different levels of products. At the other end of the spectrum you get sent fat-, sugar- and salt-laden, very commercial products that you'd find in the supermarket. Usually I pass them on.

However, there are certain newspapers which are dependent on such products and releases. They actually have almost a whole tabloid page each week devoted to these new products, some of which are of questionable nutritional value, and some of which are basically junk. Or sometimes manufacturers are trying to invent a new category. For instance, now that we're all supposed to be drinking more water, and there are people out there who don't like the flavour of tap water, manufacturers have invented this whole new category of flavoured waters. There are about six new waters on the market and some of them are what they call pharma-foods, nutri-ceuticals. They're enhanced with all sorts of minerals and herbs such as ginseng and ginko biloba, which supposedly have health-giving properties.

Sometimes being sent such products backfires, though. Reading the contents label of one such drink I'd been sent, I discovered it contained St John's Wort. Unfortunately St John's Wort is a prohibited food ingredient by our food authority FSANZ [Food Standards Australia New Zealand], which I pointed out in print, and was consequently threatened with legal action by the manufacturers. But, had they not sent me the product in the first place, I doubt I would have discovered it.

Talking about the general reader, we've been trying to explore the idea of what types of connection there are or could be between a journalist and their readers. And one of the interesting things about food media is that, in a fairly basic way, people may take up your ideas, go to the restaurant or whatever. What are your thoughts about your relation to your readers?

I write from the point of view of providing readers with information that they can apply to their daily lives, whether it's about the environmental problems of in-sinkerators, which pulverise vegetable matter and transfer the pollution problem from landfill to sewage disposal, or biodegradable take-away containers or cutlery. Or it might be restaurant trends to look out for – menus that offer small dishes that can be ordered tapas-style to make a meal.

Or, if I'm going to recommend a restaurant I will set out the reasons. Obviously every restaurant experience is entirely subjective, but I hope readers will enjoy it too. In that case, it's basically just reporting on my experience and letting them judge for themselves whether they want to go and have a similar experience.

Have you ever been bothered by the recurring idea that the journalist does not offer his or her opinions but only offers facts, which seems to me to be pretty hard in this context?

You can't do that with food. Food is subjective. It boils down to a matter of taste. Reporting must be factual, but food is such a subjective area. A dish I might find over-salted, another person might find to their liking. I might detest mango sauce or kiwi fruit with fish, but it may appeal to others.

Which is what makes it so interesting. However, for a long time food journalism was also seen as kind of soft compared to 'hard news', and as a frivolous extra. How have you dealt with that type of perception, either from other journalists or from the general public?

In the last decade and a half since I've been writing about food, it certainly has been recognised that there are critical issues surrounding food, whether it's the bio-diversity of the food supply with organisations like Slow Food, which have sprung up in defence of old varieties of fruit and vegetables and breeds of domestic animals, or the land degradation due to certain agricultural practices. Those issues have actually come into food journalism, which fifteen years ago was either 'this is a restaurant worth eating in' or at that time, with post-nouvelle cuisine, the 'cult of the chef' had begun, and food suddenly became fashionable. The chef-as-celebrity phenomenon is still with us, all through the magazines and newspapers. Food pages have created food sections, which in turn have created celebrity chefs who then contribute to the magazines. Neil Perry writes in the *Qantas* magazine. Luke Mangan writes in the Fairfax press.

> **Your job as a food writer seems to be a combination of science in terms of nutrition and agriculture, and knowledge about how restaurants and the food industry actually work, as well as a bit of a gossip columnist. How does one possibly train to be a food journalist?**

I think you train to be a journalist – I came from rock journalism – but you must have an interest in food, because if you don't have that passion for food it's not going to come out in your writing. It helps to have a knowledge of agriculture, of how food is produced, but I think you do need a basic journalistic grounding, which I don't think a lot of people in the food media have. But then there's been such an explosion in a more visual type of recipe-driven food journalism that serious print journalism has taken a back seat. The popularity and proliferation of food magazines and the explosion of food on television has meant a diminution in serious content. It has also been replaced by food as spectator sport, or food as entertainment, with the cult of personality on television. You only have to say 'Jamie' in a food context and everyone knows who you're talking about, or 'Nigella'.

> **So in terms of particular issues that you care about, are there any that couldn't be written about, either because of the structure of the food media or for other reasons?**

More for other reasons. I've noticed the shift away from issues-based food journalism. In newspapers, and I guess this fits in with the tabloidisation theme, editors aren't so interested in serious food issues any more, such as urbanisation and subdivision. It has meant that we are covering fertile, productive land – such as the Sydney Basin – with the built environment, pushing agriculture out onto more marginal land.

There's also an acceptance by journalists of taking things at face value without necessarily querying them. For instance, you see research findings reported in the papers every day, increasingly funded by companies looking for a particular outcome. For instance, a large American chocolate company might pay for research to prove that there are antioxidants or polyphenols in chocolate, and then publish the findings that chocolate is good for you. If that research had found that chocolate was bad for you it would have never seen the light of day.

In which section of the newspaper would that story see the light of day?

News! But it's usually reported uncritically, in the sense that who paid for the research – and that it might have been outcome-driven – is not mentioned.

What other issues might you find hard to get across?

Well, this is subjective. For instance, I personally find it appalling that companies whose products aren't widely accepted to be the healthiest, such as multinational fast food hamburger chains, have actually managed to wheedle their way into sponsorship of school sports! There's been hardly any critical comment or ongoing debate about that – even under a Labor government in New South Wales.

And again, that would presumably be a story considered outside your mandate?

I have written about that, but increasingly food is being compartmentalised as 'feel good' life-style area. It's not being dealt with as critically as it deserves to be.

What about obesity as a news story?

In the last three months there has been a huge amount written about obesity by journalists who aren't food journalists – enormous features and a rash of stories. There were major articles of 2000 or 3000 words on front pages of newspapers' features sections.

But not in food pages.

No, but I think those articles were generated as a result of McDonald's being taken to court in America. Obesity is an issue that is receiving more widespread coverage. Even the investment bank UBS Warburg is now advising its food clients that they need to watch out for this type of litigation because, just like the tobacco companies, increasingly food companies whose products are less than supremely healthy are going to be targeted and sued by people similar to those who sued McDonald's in America. And that's going to affect the company's share price, so it's actually going to become an issue for the financial pages.

Does that again put it further away from your mandate to talk about food?

Well I'm just one journalist, and I think it's good that there is greater interest in it. Ten years ago you almost never saw a food story in the news pages. Now there's one just about every day, whether on the health benefits of eating fish or McDonald's in the United Kingdom starting to sell fresh fruit.

Another issue which has become general news is genetically modified (GM) food, although I believe it is still under-reported. For instance, there was a major government report in Britain released on Christmas Eve which was highly critical saying that 'Yes, genes from GM crops could cross into weed populations, and that the safety belts around GM crops needed to be extended'. I heard a report on BBC Radio but I haven't read anything about it in print, no doubt because it was released on Christmas Eve – and guess which is the only day of the year when there are no newspapers? Christmas Day. So it didn't get newspaper coverage.

In terms of an overall view of what's happening to writing about food, on the one hand we have an explosion of interest in it, but as you said it has now become sort of celebrity, lifestyle, gossip…

Glamour, 'gastro-porn', salivating over photographs, but amidst all of that, there are serious issues getting buried such as food miles – which I have written about. It's a major concern of the Food Commission in the United Kingdom. It's the distance food travels from paddock to plate, and the energy it consumes in between, from harvesting to processing, transport to super-market warehouses, from there to supermarket shelves, and then to the place of consumption by the consumer.

And this is despite years and years of food writers telling us to eat what's local, and what's seasonal.

Yes. Seasonality is disappearing. People now expect strawberries and asparagus all year round. Then they go to supermarkets and look for the cheapest available. Yet we're not prepared to pay for quality.

Another huge issue which is not factored into what we're paying for at the supermarket is the long-term cost to the farmers and to the land, such as the environmental degradation of intensive farming. It is not reflected in the price of the food we're eating. But it's going to become evident down the track because the soil is getting so depleted, and river systems more polluted.

How does this affect your ethical engagement as a journalist?

It illustrates that I do take a subjective position. I am concerned about these issues, but they're never mentioned when you look at a glossy picture of a meringue cake with strawberries – whether it's run-off from cane fields affect-ing the Barrier Reef, to the development of genetically modified strawberries. At the Food and Agriculture Organisation of the United Nations in Rome, I've seen photographs of strawberries which have a deep sea fish gene in them to resist frost. The leaves had icicles dripping off them, but the strawberries were still plump and rosy because they had a flounder gene in them.

So do you think that the general public has any idea, and any hope of learning, about some of these issues?

I think they've got a hope of learning about them, but I think they've got Buckley's of changing them. The food industry is enormous, and controlled by giant multinational interests. Potato farmers in Tasmania are being screwed by some US company. The prices to farmers are being screwed downwards. Look at the poor milk producers. Deregulation was supposed to help them, but they're being driven off the land. Milk is cheaper now than it was five years ago in comparative terms. The people making the money are the super-markets. I did a survey of apple prices recently. Apple farmers are getting about the same price as they were ten years ago but all their costs have risen. Organic chicken producers are getting less for their poultry now in actual dollars terms than they were ten years ago.

If you could re-envision your job and your role, what would it look like?

I'd like to see more of the serious issues back on the table. We can't go on expecting food to become ever cheaper. We should be looking more closely at the real costs of industrial agriculture, processed food, and the control and ownership of the food supply, as well as the advertising of food and the labelling of food. The deceptions committed in the labelling of food are myriad. A 'lite' icecream or yoghurt might be 97 per cent fat-free, but frequently the kilojoules from fat have been replaced by just as many – if not more – from sugar.

And the writing about food?

One could wish that editors would take a broader view, and be more adventurous and believe their readers to be more intelligent, knowing that they like to read more about such issues, not just have food glossed up as a very nice life-style thing.

Ethics impossible?
Advertising and
the Infomercial

ANNE DUNN

INTRODUCTION

IS THIS COOL OR WHAT? THE HIP HOP E-MAIL LIST YOU SUBSCRIBE TO invites you on a free ride to a mystery destination where one of your favourite bands will do a concert especially for you and your like-minded peers. It's a great day out, although you notice that the refreshment tent is sponsored by a company that makes alcoholic fruit drinks. Hip young people wander amongst the crowd, offering free bottles of a new brand you haven't seen before. Of course, you don't have to take them.

Here's another one. Your workplace is smoke-free but you haven't kicked the habit yet. There you are with the other office smokers, freezing on the foot-path for your hit, and a pretty girl with a lovely smile comes and offers you a cup of hot coffee. Good one! As you gratefully accept it, she tells you it is 'courtesy of' – and names a brand of cigarettes.[1]

Welcome to the world of guerilla marketing.

Most thinking about ethics in advertising tends to focus on regulating and curbing advertisements that are seen as problematic. Advertisements that are perceived by audiences to be sexist (or too sexy), that use discriminatory stereotypes, may encourage behaviour our society defines as deviant, or that unfairly target children – these are seen as examples of unethical behaviour by the advertising industry. Such advertisements are regularly the focus of concern in the media and of complaints by the public.[2]

Given the kinds of scenario I began with, consumer complaints are the least of the industry's worries when it comes to ethical considerations. The more pressing ethical debate about advertising today is about changes that

#133

erase altogether the admittedly sometimes faint line that has existed between advertising messages and the more disinterested entertainment and information functions of the media.

Complaints about individual advertisements are rarely couched as any challenge to advertising on a meta-level, questioning its place and role in the world. Naomi Klein has recently both documented and stimulated grassroots challenges to the relentless invasion by advertising of public and private spaces, in her best-selling critique of global, multinational corporate manufacturing and brand marketing, *NO LOGO*, but even Klein does not really question the assumption that we, the audience, must consume.[3] Her argument is emphatically not with free-market capitalism. It is rather that we must be able to buy things that have not been made in ways that economically exploit the makers, and that we must protest against the advertising of unhealthy products, such as tobacco, and against such threats to civic life as the commodification of education through corporate sponsorship.

Advertisers tend to respond to complaints by considering the potential impact on the *marketing* relationship between advertisers and consumers, but seldom in terms of the *ethical* nature of that relationship. But perhaps it is time we thought about the nature of that ethical relationship and how it is being damaged by the explosion of 'under the radar' marketing that technological and cultural change are driving.

Advertising has had to be nimble in its response to these kinds of changes, and success for the industry is mixed. The advertising industry's battle – to catch the consumer's attention, to differentiate the product, to aid consumer recall, to overcome consumer resistance and always and everywhere to increase sales – goes on. As an example of one tactic amongst many that raise ethical questions, I look at the infomercial, a television advertisement that is presented as something else, as information or entertainment programming.

ADVERTISING AND THE CONSUMER

Beginning in the mid-1960s, advertisements have moved from the modern into the postmodern era, using intertextual references and, particularly in film and television, co-opting other genres and forms to create forms of art and entertainment that disguise or even subvert the fundamental goal of selling a product.

For example, the Steven Spielberg film *Minority Report* (2002), set in the future, is on one level a critique of a culture of shopping, yet simultaneously demonstrates that that culture is here now. In one sequence, an urgent narrative strand of kidnap and escape, our hero, played by Tom Cruise, stops his customised Lexus car at a Gap store, to buy clothes for his hostage.

Audiences will only accept so much product placement, however. *Minority Report* did not make the box office returns it was expected to. Another example, the James Bond film, *Die Another Day* (2002), released around the same time, featured so many brand name products that it attracted media derision.

In his book *The Conquest of Cool*, Thomas Frank traces a turning point in the advertising industry to the 'counterculture', the changes in personal and social attitudes that define the 1960s.[4] His argument is that a new consumerism arose at this time, which Frank calls 'hip consumerism', and its culture was that of youth:

> *And when business leaders cast their gaze onto the youth culture*
> *bubbling around them, they saw both a reflection of their own struggle*
> *against the stifling bureaucracy of the past and an affirmation of a*
> *dynamic new consuming order that would replace the old.*[5]

The key to this new order was image. It began when legendary Madison Avenue ad man David Ogilvy created the ESP, the emotional selling proposition, which replaced the concept that had dominated advertising for so long, the unique selling proposition (USP). The USP told you, the consumer, the 'reason why' you should buy this product; what it offered that no competitor could match. It was about the product, whereas the ESP is about the target, the consumer.

Market research techniques that are used to create market segments, in order to identify and monitor consumer preferences, tastes and uses for products, enabled image branding. And segmentation in turn created life-style advertising, an approach that makes the product secondary. Ads of this type show people in the kind of environment, and doing the kinds of things, that the advertisers believe the target market either does or aspires to do. The successive campaigns for Coca-Cola are classics of the type. In every era, the people who are shown enjoying and wanting to drink Coke are young, beautiful and have lots of friends and exist at leisure in what seems to be an endless holiday. The idea is that consumers relate to the life-style invoked by the cultural meanings and values associated with particular products, not the utility of the goods or services.

Both the USP and ESP approaches date from an era in which advertising was treated as a science; even the creation and marketing of a brand image could be achieved following predictable 'laws'. According to Frank, this modernist approach was turned on its head in the 1960s, with the rise of a movement articulated by young, mainly middle-class Americans and quickly taken up around the world. This was the 'counterculture', and it was brilliantly recognised and exploited by Bill Bernbach, one of the founders of the Doyle Dane Bernbach (DDB) agency.

Bernbach is credited with leading the 'creative revolution' in advertising and did so by reflecting back to consumers their 'distrust of advertising and dislike of admen',[6] with wit and a visual style that differed dramatically from the received wisdom of graphic design of the 1950s. Such now-classic campaigns of DDB as those for the Volkswagen 'Beetle', Avis or Alka-Seltzer gleefully sent up the textual features and discourse of advertising, in a way that is recognisably postmodern. The advertisements called attention to themselves as advertisements. The Alka-Seltzer campaign, for instance, included a 1970 television commercial showing the making of a television commercial for a fictional product, ludicrously portrayed, of spicy Italian meatballs in a jar. The hapless actor is shown having to do take after take, in each of which he eats some spaghetti and meatballs, ending up with the kind of indigestion that, of course, only Alka-Seltzer can relieve.

The joy of the ad, still present if it's watched today, is that it acknowledges the audience's knowledge of the artifice of advertisements, and provides this as entertainment while still being an extremely successful advertisement itself in terms of consumer recall and sales. Frank argues that the work of Bernbach and the DDB agency was truly revolutionary because it ensured no less than the immortality of the consumer society. This 'new aesthetic of consuming ... would become ... a cultural perpetual motion machine transforming disgust with consumerism into fuel for the ever-accelerating consumer society'.[7] The co-opting of the 'counterculture' was complete.

Suspicion and dislike of consumerism and its advertising lackey have not gone away as a result of the so-called 'creative' style of DDB and those who followed. In the decades since, advertising has continued to make use of the textual features and discourse, not only of advertising itself but also of other media forms, such as the television soap opera (for example, the long-running Nescafé Gold Blend series of advertisements) or, particularly, in information campaigns for such things as road safety, television news or documentary.

In the 1990s television advertising managed a double bite at the same cherry by using scenes from movies in which the product placement was purchased in advance, or popular songs written in order that they should be used later in the soundtrack for advertisements.[8] In so doing, advertising has contributed at least since the 1960s to what French postmodern philosopher Jean Baudrillard was to call 'hyperreality'.[9] Hyperreality is the creation of models or simulations of reality (for example, the Alka-Seltzer television advertisement depicting the making of a television advertisement), in order not just to represent reality but also to engender another reality (so, in the narrative of the Alka-Seltzer ad, only Alka-Seltzer is not fake). Television critic and sociologist Ellis Cashmore suggests that, 'In the hyperreal age, we have become preoccupied with authenticity: We value the original, the genuine article, the real thing.'[10] In fact, as Frank points out, this is a preoccupation that goes back to the end of the 1950s and 'it [always] was and remains difficult to distinguish precisely between authentic counterculture and fake'.[11] There is no point in attempting the distinction: the brand image or the 'product person-ality' is as real as the thing it simulates; it is self-referential, it is 'hyperreal'. But hyperreality is defined as much by what it omits as by what it includes; in the case of advertising, it serves to disguise the fact that our choices are limited to the point where 'consumer sovereignty' is itself an illusion.

Technological change of a kind by now familiar, change that can be sub-sumed under the title of 'digital convergence', has fragmented advertising's traditional markets, right down to the single consumer. Advertisers cannot assume people will be assembled in the same place, in front of one of four or five TV channels from around six o'clock each evening, positioned to receive a mass advertising message.

Not only have television channels proliferated via cable and satellite, there are also many other ways of spending an evening at home, including in front of a computer, or using the television monitor and a plug-in device to play an interactive game. More than this, since the advent of the home videotape recorder and the remote control, technology has steadily increased the consumer's opportunity to avoid television advertising, which is the last thing advertisers want. Machines with large digital hard-drive storage capacity and computer chip intelligence, such as Ti-Vo or DVD recorders, can be programmed to avoid advertisements (or, of course, to be selective of which are viewed, and this too should not be forgotten).

Against this must be set the sheer availability of a range of digital devices, which means that as consumers we make ourselves known; we literally signal our availability to advertisers. Mobile phones, in combination with information generated by credit card databases, enable advertising to locate and reach individual consumers with marketing messages tailored, if not yet to that individual, then to specific demographics. The *only* promotion done for a new action movie recently was via SMS (Short Message System) messages to mobile phones; young men were the target audience for the film. The campaign (and perhaps the media publicity it then attracted) produced respectable returns for the film. We are being swept towards the vision of advertising's future offered in Spielberg's *Minority Report* faster than we may imagine.

Within the next few years it is predicted that software using artificial intelligence to identify people by age, race and sex may be placed behind cameras in shopping malls.[12] Marketing messages tailored to the demographic identity of the passers-by will be instantly selected and pitched by a speaker in the wall. Such a scenario presupposes not an unprecedented level of public surveillance, since shopping malls are already full of security cameras, but a level of *targeted* surveillance that troubles many people, in order to sell more things. Klein referred to 'the colonization of public space';[13] futurist Creed C. O'Hanlon describes us as surrounded by 'the incessant buzz of the media-saturated life'.[14] These phrases aptly express the fears many people have that the ubiquitousness, the unavoidability of advertising, has reached unacceptable levels. What needs to be acknowledged is that fear may not be the only response; for many people equally, contemporary advertising is an often pleasurable, playful and unthreatening part of their lives.

Less than a generation ago, in the 1980s, media researcher Hugh McKay could describe the effectiveness of advertising as limited, strongly modified by the direct, personal experience of individuals, because it had to reach people by the indirect, impersonal media. McKay describes ways in which 'people protect themselves from mass media effects',[15] a phrase which makes the assumptions, first, that there are mass media effects and, secondly, that they are to some degree noxious, since we act to 'protect' ourselves from them.

It is true that we may choose what newspapers or magazines we'll read, and read others seldom or not at all. We may watch only some television programs – our favourites – with any attention or regularity, and most people only listen regularly to one or two radio stations. But the spaces in which we can escape from advertising altogether are getting harder to find, and advertising is more embedded in the media than ever before. Placement deals for brands and products in Hollywood movies provide one example, infomercials in television another.

INFOMERCIALS AND ETHICS

Infomercials began to appear in the 1970s on cable television channels in the United States. In 1999, US$105.8 billion worth of product was sold in the United States via infomercials.[16] The infomercial is a hybrid form of television that attracts strong criticism for being 'disguised' advertising; that is, advertising in the guise of television programming or, in the print medium, where it is called 'advertorial', as editorial content.

Perhaps the best known recent form of hybrid television is 'reality TV'. Programs such as *Big Brother*, which are not only hybrids of documentary and soap opera but also cross-media platforms, offer commercial sponsors with product placement integrated with direct marketing. When viewers in Australia rang up to vote on whom to evict from the house and put on hold, they were offered the chance to order the pizza that the house residents had conspicuously been eating. An estimated 20 per cent did so. Pizza sales also went up for the principal competitor to the sponsors, suggesting that young consumers discriminate between brands, even if the embedded advertising put the idea of eating pizza into their minds.

As Jane Roscoe has pointed out, much of the pleasure of watching what most viewers know to be a highly manufactured 'reality' comes from 'glimpsing the authentic moment'.[17] If the authentic is what we trust, and what we trust we are more likely to buy, then of course the authentic is precisely what advertisers will seek to simulate. This is one reason for the growth in popularity of the infomercial as a marketing tool: the integration of advertising and information in television formats that do not present themselves as ads, but as some other kind of program.

The director of one company that devises and makes infomercials was recently reported as saying that 'infomercials work for advertisers as they deliver information in a way that television viewers trust'. While traditional advertising 'builds an emotional bond to a brand', the 'rationalisation approach (of infomercials) builds credibility'.[18]

Direct marketing is growing in Australia at the rate of 17 per cent a year, and across all media, advertisers spent A\$16.2 million on direct marketing in 2000.[19] In one two-hour weekday morning program, *Good Morning Australia*, an average of thirty-two minutes was taken up by infomercials. Integrated marketing, content integration – these are the terms that advertisers use to describe, for instance, the use of a limited range of painting and decorating products on a home renovation show. The infomercial deliberately creates ambiguity by mirroring a format that is different from a TV commercial. It may be the magazine format of the life-style program, or the style of a 'chat show' interview, hosted by a celebrity, giving the appearance of independence from the product being discussed, while having advertising – paid promotion – as its primary purpose.

In programs such as the home renovation or cooking show, there is no indication that the products used and recommended are all from one or two manufacturers, or that there are many other brands from which to choose. The deliberate ambiguity of the infomercial reflects the nature of direct marketing techniques. Such techniques have grown in popularity with advertisers worldwide, not only in response to the fragmentation of mass media but also to get around legislation that prevents mainstream advertising, on public broadcasters, for instance, or for products such as tobacco.[20]

If we look at this practice from an ethical point of view, the intention to create ambiguity could also be called deception. Certainly this is what Plato meant when, in the *Republic*, he argued in his famous allegory of the shadow in the cave that to create the reflection of a reality and treat that image as real is a dangerous and immoral illusion.

In most media advertising markets, outright deception or misinformation is not only unethical but also illegal. However, for many people there would appear to be no simple line between advertising that turns out to be a con and program content that turns out to be an advertisement: both are perceived as deceptive. The suspicion that there is something 'sneaky' about advertising is a long-held one in the history of advertising, and assumptions about noxious media effects have been argued since the advent of comic books.[21]

Not surprisingly, regulatory authorities reflect such beliefs in the way they act. In the 1950s, concern about so-called 'subliminal advertising' in the United States, prompted by Vance Packard's *The Hidden Persuaders*,[22] ultimately led to legislation banning its use.

In 2001 in the Australian state of New South Wales, the Minister for Fair Trading appointed the independent Fair Trading Advisory Council (FTAC) to investigate 'advertising dressed up as editorial content'.[23] The minister did so in response to complaints by consumers: nearly 3000 of them in a two-year period. The great majority (more than 90 per cent) of these complaints were from people who, as the result of seeing an infomercial, had ordered and paid for goods, which were then never delivered. This is a form of dishonesty unrelated to the form of advertising and so does not concern us here. The remaining complaints fell into two broad groups: that products were misrepresented, and that the advertising *method* was deceptive. This is not the same as saying that people watching infomercials actually were deceived; rather, that they perceived them as having the potential to deceive.

The disappearing line that infomercials represent, and that the FTAC inquiry was set up to investigate, is between 'editorial content' and advertising. It is one of the most problematic areas of ethical consideration, and historically one of the most jealously watched over, not by advertisers but by journalists. One of Australia's most respected journalists, Michelle Grattan, has written of the breaking down of the 'wall' between marketers and editors in the newspaper industry.[24] The degree to which advertising and marketing have come to dominate newspapers in the 1990s has not been much discussed in Australia, but has been extensively analysed and commented on in the United States. Grattan, writing in 1998, describes how the *Los Angeles Times* was reorganised in 1997, so that 'each editor would have a business partner – a brand manager – working alongside, responsible for galvanising the entire business side of the team'.[25]

Although debate in Australia has been limited, opinion here, as in the United States, is divided between those who believe there is a threat to journalistic integrity and those who believe it is possible to achieve 'a natural marriage of editorial integrity with the commercial imperatives we must address to ensure not only survival, but a successful future'.[26] If media are financed to an increasingly greater extent by advertising, which is the case in most countries of the world, the potential exists for advertising to exert pressure on editorial content. An ethical question may also arise when editors or journalists decide what they will or will not cover on the basis of the potential effect on advertisers; in other words, if journalists anticipate advertiser pressure and practise self-censorship. This suggests that it has to be journalists who are the watchdogs, which is one way of describing their traditional role after all, but there are good reasons of self-interest for business to act ethically too. Unethical behaviour can be disastrous for business, as the collapse of HIH insurance in Australia, or those of the US corporations Worldcom and Enron, demonstrate.

The dilemmas discussed so far are familiar to those who work in newspapers or commercial radio and television; but what of the new media? Journalists and editors working on Internet publications are in a medium that makes a far less obvious distinction between editorial and advertising than the 'old' media of print and broadcast. Moreover, most news web sites are in a precarious financial situation, putting them under direct pressure to generate revenue. Since most Internet users are still resistant to paying for content, advertising is even more important as a source of profit. While banners and pop-up windows make advertising obvious, hyperlinks can take site users to advertising without warning or without it being explicit that the linked content is advertising. It is also possible for news sites to 'incorporate links to retailers of products mentioned in editorial copy', enabling a transaction between advertiser and publisher, whereby 'each item sold generates a commission for the news company' and of course provides 'a direct economic incentive to say nice things about' the product.[27] The Internet, as well as mobile phone SMS messaging, data casting and interactive TV potentially take the 'infomercial' to a new level.

The 2001 FTAC inquiry defined an infomercial in its background paper as:

[A]n advertisement that is styled as a presentation of information for interest or entertainment. It may be unclear whether it is an advertisement or part of normal programming content ... [Anyone watching] may be led to believe that products are featured on their merits rather than recognising these promotions as paid advertising.[28]

It was not surprising, given this definition, that the final report on the inquiry, released in 2002, should have concluded that 'Infomercials are paid advertisements *disguised* as program content, usually screened during lifestyle and current affairs programs'[29] (italics added). The final report of the inquiry identified the form of infomercial in which a product's 'inventor' or 'developer' is interviewed in a chat-show format, as 'potentially deceptive'. The 'interview' in this form of infomercial may conclude with the suggestion that viewers phone the freecall number appearing on their screen. This marketing technique is called direct response television (DRTV), and the Infomercial Inquiry's report criticised it for encouraging impulse buying. The Infomercial Inquiry considered that consumers are more likely to buy on impulse when the sales message is delivered with a 'contrived sense of urgency', produced by exhortations to the effect that this is a 'limited time only special offer'; and this was often the case in relation to infomercials.

Another form of infomercial is a whole program that purports to bring 'new' products to segments of the television audience; the inquiry's final report uses home renovators as its example. In this case the key deception is by omission, in that viewers are not told that an advertiser has paid to have their products featured on the show. To all intents and purposes, the program appears 'to be exercising independent judgment ... when it is actually a vehicle for product placement and promotion'.[30] The Infomercial Inquiry found 'significant problems' with some infomercials, sufficient to warrant their recommendation that a Working Party be formed, comprising 'industry and Government representatives', to set up and manage a self-regulation scheme, with a specific code of practice for infomercials. In many if not most countries, infomercials do not have even the usually rather cursory guidelines and regulations limiting the claims of traditional advertising. The FTAC inquiry recommendations to set up a self-regulatory body and a code of practice thus put New South Wales 'at the forefront of international policy initiatives to promote regulatory reform and effective self-regulation'.[31]

ETHICS AND CODES

Codes, whether called codes of practice, codes of ethics or codes of conduct, have become the universal panacea for ethical problems; every industry has to have one, it seems.[32] Codes tend to be seen as the avenue of first resort by industries that feel threatened with external regulation. They have become associated with a self-regulatory approach to industry, one that successive Federal governments in Australia and elsewhere have favoured since the 1980s. Originally, codes of conduct were established as a way of claiming professional status for activities such as journalism, public relations or advertising. To speak of 'professional conduct' suggests commitment to ethical principles and standards. But how effective are codes of practice or codes of ethics in promoting ethical behaviour?

Codes may have a number of uses, not only or not necessarily including oversight of ethical behaviour. Sanders has identified four functions of professional codes: protection, education, public relations and damage limitation.[33] While Sanders is talking about ethics and journalism, these functions can be seen as well in the codes that pertain in the advertising industry, such as the code of ethics of the Australian Association of National Advertisers (AANA), which represents providers of goods and services; of the Advertising Federation of Australia (AFA), which represents advertising agencies; or the code of practice of the Association of Direct Marketers of Australia (ADMA).[34]

The *protection* function of these codes refers to consumers and to advertisers themselves. For example, both the AANA and the ADMA codes contain standards setting out that advertisements 'shall not be misleading or deceptive'[35] or that '[a] member organisation shall not make misleading or deceptive claims about an offer delivered through direct marketing'.[36] These clearly are intended to protect the consumer. But both codes also refer to minimising risk to advertisers or direct marketing member organisations. Specifically, the codes insist on compliance with relevant legislation and statutory controls. The AFA code advises 'Don't bend the law' and 'Look after your colleagues'.[37] These paragraphs also act as *damage limitation*. The *education* function is explicit in the objectives of the ADMA code, which includes the objective to 'promote a culture among member organisations of conducting their businesses fairly, honestly, ethically and in accordance with best practices'.[38]

Sanders discerns a *public relations* function in codes in two things: 'articulating occupational ideals' and 'atoning for past sins by forbidding practices which have come to be publicly unacceptable'.[39] The 'SMS Issues Industry Code', developed in August 2002 by the Australian Communications Industry Forum, provides a very clear example of the PR function. It is expressly designed to forestall public rejection of the potentially intrusive and prolific use of location-based marketing via SMS text messages using mobile telephony.

Under the SMS code, individuals targeted by unsolicited marketing offers are supposed to be told they have a choice before they can be targeted with other offers, including the choice to opt out altogether of marketing within individual text messages. The Federal Privacy Commissioner described the new code as 'a step in the right direction' but insisted that unsolicited SMS offers would be viewed as a 'gross invasion of privacy'.[40]

Less than a year later, an article in Sydney's *Sun-Herald* cited advertising industry magazine *B & T Marketing and Media* as reporting that Australian advertisers were making 'good progress with the new medium' (of SMS marketing). Companies targeting young people in particular, such as Channel V, Virgin Mobile, Coca-Cola and *Girlfriend* magazine, were 'spearheading creative use of SMS as an advertising medium in Australia'.[41] The main import of this article, as with most others on the subject, was that text message marketing is intrusive and unwelcome because it is usually unsolicited.

It is rare to see an article reporting that the young targets of SMS marketing (who use SMS so much themselves) may enjoy and value the entertainment, information and offers that such advertising usually contains. Yet, in Britain SMS has boomed for advertising, often in the form of competitions, suggesting a degree of consumer co-operation. The *Sun-Herald* article made no mention of the new SMS Issues Industry Code.

The Infomercial Inquiry recommendation, that an industry body be established to regulate infomercials and develop a code of practice, is couched in terms of the 'long term health and future development of the industry'; that is, with the function of protecting the industry. The code of practice would clearly be established in the first instance also for reasons of damage limitation and public relations. However, the FTAC report sees an education function for such a code, referring to the 'greater understanding of issues' and 'the opportunity to develop best practice guidelines for the industry generally'.[42]

Discussion of media ethics often contains the argument that the main problem with codes of ethics is also a problem of self-regulation, and it can be summed up as one of accountability. Even where an industry is obliged to develop a code of practice (as is the case for the broadcasting industry in Australia, for example), if the penalties for breaching the code are weak, their effective contribution to ethical practice is marginal. This viewpoint can only lead to skepticism ('nothing changes') or insistence on a level of response that would serve to undermine the philosophy of self-regulation ('there ought to be a law against it …'). Media reporting of codes often criticises them for being 'toothless', even while urging that codes be established in preference to legal sanctions. And, as the example of SMS marketing described earlier suggests, this attitude can completely overlook the agency of consumers.

Tough sanctions or not, codes alone will never provide answers to the hard questions because ethical thinking and behaviour do not reside in codes. There is more to being ethical than following rules. There is a growing recognition of this in business ethics generally. The preamble to the Advertising Federation of Australia's Code of Ethics states in part:

> *This Code is not a set of rules encased within a legalistic framework. Rather, it is a combination of broad principles and specific issues which set standards of behaviour for people working in the advertising industry. Equally we have an obligation to understand and adhere to our clients' industry codes of conduct. The AFA does not seek to act as police, judge or jury on the issue of ethics. We see our role more as a guide to agencies as they navigate their way through advertising's grey areas.*[43]

The preamble concludes with an undertaking to settle written complaints 'with the advice and assistance of the St James Ethics Centre', a not-for-profit centre set up to promote ethics and which does a lot of work with Australian business organisations.

One of the ways in which the Ethics Centre does this is to give people the tools to be able to interpret and apply codes, since this requires what Belsey and Chadwick call 'a reasoned basis in ethical theory'.[44] The emphasis in theories of ethics can be either on the behaviour itself, the act and whether it is wrong or right, or on the person acting and whether that person is of good moral character. Theories that emphasise behaviour have been divided into those that emphasise acts of duty (such as Immanuel Kant's categorical imperative) and those that emphasise the consequences of acts (such as John Stuart Mill's Utilitarianism). Theories that emphasise the actor, associated in the first instance with Aristotle and St Thomas Aquinas, put the focus on character. The contemporary version is known as 'virtue ethics'.[45] Virtue in this approach has nothing to do with self-righteousness or priggishness. It is about realising our true selves as human beings and thereby achieving our human purpose, which might be called happiness, defined somewhat differently by Aristotle and by the Christian Aquinas. But for both, virtues are 'excellences of character', goods in themselves, and 'tendencies to act in certain ways'.[46]

Most codes of ethics place an emphasis on the act rather than the actor, in that they tend to be lists of what those bound by the code should and should not *do*. The Advertising Federation of Australia (AFA) code of ethics for its advertising agency members is full of such statements as: 'Strive for excellence in everything you do' and 'Give clients your best efforts and advice, without fear or favour'. This is not to say that the advertising and marketing industries ignore questions of character altogether. The AFA tells its members to 'Be honest'. Similarly, the AANA describes the object of its code of ethics as being:

> *to ensure that advertisements are legal, decent, honest and truthful and that they have been prepared with a sense of obligation to the consumer and society and fair sense of responsibility to competitors.*

Again, the virtues of honesty and truthfulness are invoked. In this code we also have the concepts of *obligation* and *responsibility*. Both of these involve the notions of duty and accountability; and both are often present in professional codes. But overall, both the ADMA and the AANA codes, as with most, rely on dutiful compliance, regardless of the moral inclinations of the individuals concerned. Stick with the code of ethics/practice and you'll be OK, goes the argument. The trouble is that, when the going gets tough, the code can be interpreted in ways that are self-serving.

When the Infomercial Inquiry was launched in 2001, the direct marketers, represented by ADMA, were affronted. In its submission to the inquiry, ADMA expressed concern that the inquiry could unfairly affect the reputation of 'many responsible business organisations'. It argued that deceptive advertising was not the main problem; the majority of complaints were that goods paid for were never delivered.[47] This is disingenuous or perhaps really misses the point that complaints are not likely to result if deceptive marketing is successful. ADMA's submission failed to see that consent cannot be given if a project is deceitful. To disguise a marketing message as an information program, or to present it in the guise of news, is to commit two sorts of moral failure. First of all, it is to treat other human beings as means to an end, and not as ends in themselves. Secondly, it fails to respect others' capacity to act (their moral agency), by putting them in a situation where they cannot make an informed, rational decision because of the deception involved.

The Department of Fair Trading made a recommendation, which the Infomercial Inquiry adopted, that a disclosure statement along the lines of 'This is a paid advertisement for [product or service]' should be superimposed at the beginning and end of every infomercial, and again whenever a direct response is called for from viewers, in the form of details of how to order the product or service. This was in effect a best practice recommendation, since some infomercials, such as the three-minute *Infobreak*, were already using this kind of superimposed text or announcement at the beginning and end of the program.

CONCLUSION

Network television stands to lose in the long run if infomercials that look like entertainment-based programming continue to proliferate. Just as advertisers fear that a few traders making false claims or failing to deliver can damage the credibility of the direct marketing industry as a whole, so too television networks need to consider whether the presence of infomercials could damage the credibility of regular programs. Even before the Infomercial Inquiry finished, the Nine Network announced it was discontinuing morning infomercial shopping programs and replacing them with classic movies. Nine denied this was in response to the inquiry. Channel Ten changed the way in which the infomercials in its program *Good Morning Australia* were presented, to make it much more obvious they were paid promotions. The final report of the inquiry suggested these two changes alone indicated 'a move away from this type of material and its attractiveness to the broadcasting industry'.

Grattan concludes her analysis of the 'the commercialised culture' of newspapers with the argument that it is one cause of the poor regard in which most people hold journalists, because it is a culture that treats both institutions (newspapers in this case) and people, the readers, as a means to an end. The result is that 'readers – the customers – have mostly lost the feeling of special identification with the papers they buy.'[48] Readers who feel this way – dispensable – will be more prepared to stop buying newspapers. And if they do, then advertisers will also stop buying space. The same goes for infomercials and television.

The arguments being made by Grattan and the FTAC Infomercial Inquiry are business appeals: lose the readers or viewers and you'll lose the advertisers. But it is also an ethical one: it is not right to treat people as tools or things. The many changes to the ways in which advertising messages now seek us out and permeate our lives, which Naomi Klein has summed up as a change from 'commercial interruption' to 'seamless integration',[49] can make consumers feel as if they are being taken for suckers. And people don't like the feeling. The Advertising Federation of Australia's guide to its code of ethics asks the question 'Why do advertising agencies need a Code of Ethics?' The answer given is that:

> *We are fortunate to occupy a role in society where business, creativity and the media overlap. This role brings with it both opportunities and responsibilities. Our industry relies on* **trust***. We need to act with integrity to gain trust – from our clients, colleagues, suppliers, consumers and our critics. (Bold in the original)*[50]

Advertising techniques that abuse trust will in the long term no doubt damage the market – the product may not sell, people will become still more resistant to commercial messages, and new, tighter regulations may result. But more than this, unethical behaviour always has the potential to increase social cynicism and lessen the faith people have in their society to treat them with respect. In the end, ethics – in advertising as in any aspect of our lives – is about the quality of human relationships, the way we treat each other.

NOTES

1   Both stories are true although neither took place in Australia. See S. Brook, 'Lavender grows in sweet new climate', *Australian*, *Media* section, 6–12 February 2003, 4.
2   Consumer complaints are handled by the relevant watchdog body, usually set up by the advertising industry itself, as part of a self-regulatory regime.
3   Naomi Klein, *NO LOGO* (London: Flamingo, 2000).
4   Thomas Frank, *The Conquest of Cool* (Chicago and London: The University of Chicago Press, 1997).
5   ibid., 28.
6   ibid., 54.
7   ibid., 68.
8   For example, see R. Guilliatt, 'Look what they've done to my song', *Sydney Morning Herald, Good Weekend*, 8 February 2003, 27.
9   Jean Baudrillard, *Simulations* (New York: Semiotext(e), 1983).

10   E. Cashmore, … *And There was Television* (London and New York: Routledge, 1994), 186.

11   Frank, *The Conquest of Cool*, 8.

12   S. Lowe, 'Ads about to see you coming', *Sydney Morning Herald*, 15–16 February 2003, 5.

13   Klein, *NO LOGO*, 492.

14   C. O'Hanlon, 'Back from the future', *Bulletin*, 18 February 2001, 55.

15   H. McKay, in K. Fowles, and N. Mills, *Understanding Advertising: An Australian Guide*, TAFE Educational Books (Sydney: UNSW Press, 1981), 159.

16   FTAC, *Infomercial Inquiry: Final Report* (Parramatta, New South Wales: Department of Fair Trading, 2002), 18.

17   J. Roscoe, 'Real entertainment: New factual hybrid television', *Media International Australia*, No. 100, August 2001, 9–20.

18   Tim Buchanan, director The Buchanan Group, quoted in J. Schulze, 'The infomercial world expands', *Australian, Media* section, 4–10 July 2002, 3.

19   FTAC, *Infomercial Inquiry: Final Report*, 17.

20   S. Brook, 'Lavender grows in sweet new climate', *Australian, Media* section, 6–12 February 2003, 4.

21   D. McQuail, *Audience Analysis* (Thousand Oaks, California: Sage, 1997).

22   V. Packard, *The Hidden Persuaders* (New York: D. McKay Co., 1957).

23   Department of Fair Trading media release, 21 June 2001.

24   Michelle Grattan, 'Editorial independence: An outdated concept?' *Australian Journalism Monographs* 1 (May 1998).

25   ibid., 5–6.

26   Steve Harris, formerly editor and publisher of the *Age*, quoted in Grattan, 'Editorial independence', 8.

27   K. Bowd, 'Left in technology's wake? Codes of ethics and online news', *Australian Journalism Review* 24: 2 (December 2002), 48.

28   FTAC, *Infomercial Inquiry: Background Paper* (Parramatta, New South Wales, Department of Fair Trading, 2001), 4.

29   Department of Fair Trading media release, 2 August 2002.

30   FTAC, *Infomercial Inquiry: Final Report*, 17.

31   ibid., 12.

32   Bowd, 'Left in technology's wake?', pages 43–4 argues that codes of practice or conduct are different 'in composition and aim from codes of ethics'. However, her definition of organisational codes as focusing 'on acceptable or unacceptable conduct' seems to me to have ethical implications, so I do not make such a distinction, using instead Sanders' different functions for codes. See K. Sanders, *Ethics and Journalism* (New Delhi, Thousand Oaks, and London: Sage, 2003).

33   Sanders, ibid., 142.

34   The ADMA Code of Practice is online at http://www.adma.com.au/consumer/codeOfPractice.htm. The AANA Advertiser Code of Ethics can be found at http://www.aana.com.au/1_about_aana/1_02_code.html.

35 AANA code, 1.1
36 ADMA code, 2001, Section B, Paragraph 1, p.4.
37 Advertising Federation of Australia (AFA), *A Guide to the AFA Agency Code of Ethics*. The code of ethics can also be seen online via http://www.afa.org.au. Paragraph 5.4, p. 3, accessed 23 February 2003.
38 ADMA code Section A, Paragraph 5.4, p.3.
39 Sanders, *Ethics and Journalism*, 142.
40 P. McIntyre, 'Self-regulation saves consumers from SMS spam', *Australian, Media* section, 29 August–September 2002, 10.
41 *Sun-Herald*, 'Mobile junk turns SMS into SOS', 23 February 2003, 15.
42 FTAC, *Infomercial Inquiry: Final Report*, 33.
43 AFA, http://www.afa.org.au/index2.asp?pid=ethics 2001, accessed 23 February 2003.
44 A. Belsey and R. Chadwick (eds), *Ethical Issues in Journalism and the Media* (London and New York: Routledge, 1992).
45 Sanders, *Ethics and Journalism*, 32.
46 ibid.
47 FTAC, *Infomercial Inquiry: Final Report*, 22.
48 Grattan, 'Editorial independence: An outdated concept?', 21.
49 Klein, *NO LOGO*, 3.
50 AFA, http://www.afa.org.au/index2.asp?pid=285 2001, accessed 23 February 2003.

INTERVIEW WITH JIM MOSER
PITCHING TO THE 'TRIBES': NEW AD TECHNIQUES
(MANAGING DIRECTOR FOR CLEMENGER BBDO, SYDNEY)

Can you comment, first of all, on the suggestion that mass media advertising is less successful and popular now with advertisers than it has been in the past?

When television was introduced fifty or sixty years ago, that was going to be the death of radio and it wasn't. When the video recorder was developed, that was going to be the death of cinema, and all cinemas have done is grown since that's happened. When the Internet came out it was going to completely change everything in terms of consumption habits and mass-market advertising, and that didn't happen. What I do see is our industry, particularly mass-market advertising, continuing to grow year on year.

What about the argument that there are some segments of the consumer market that are more resistant to the commercial message than others, especially young people?

I would completely agree with that. To reach teenagers today we probably wouldn't employ television. They're a really difficult group to capture and influence with a commercial message, or what's seen as a commercial message.

#152

There's a lot of different ways that advertisers are trying to reach and influence this group, and I think probably one of the best would be Frucor [a New Zealand-based company, makers of energy drinks 'V' and 'G Force']. [Their] energy drink is so clearly targeted towards teenagers and young adults. When they initially launched that beverage they did not use conventional mass media. They went to niche media, or underground media, targeting small publications that were just about what was happening in Sydney; and distributing postcards in shops. They sponsored programs and events that young people would go to, but it wasn't an overt commercial sponsorship.

They also had a very clear strategy about who they were talking to; and they separated their target groups into four 'tribes' as they called it. One was the tribe Boarders, both snow and ski, or both snow and surf. Another was the gay and lesbian crowd. Another was music people, who are passionate about music; and the fourth was students. They designed on-the-street marketing programs to talk to each of those groups differently. Only after they were able to infiltrate those segments did they go to mass-market advertising, and they did go to television. But their television was very quirky and it was totally unexpected in terms of anything ever done in that category.

When you were talking about that particular approach, you used the word 'infiltrate'. One of the things that concerns some critics is the suggestion that the whole object of these approaches is to disguise the fact that the consumer is receiving an advertising message. Do you think that's the case and, if so, do you think it matters?

I have absolutely no issue with it. If you go into a car dealership and you talk to a car salesperson, that car salesperson is going to employ a number of different tactics in order to get you to purchase a car, and it's no different from any sort of sales operation. It's finding a way to present whatever it is that you're trying to sell in its most positive light. So I don't think we're doing anything in terms of misrepresenting the brand. We're not giving out any misinformation, we're not putting out any overt lies. There's no trying to mislead anybody. It's just equating that particular brand with something that is quite positive and something that's important to that group. To me there's nothing immoral in that sort of synergy.

You don't see it as a covert activity?

I think people are smarter than that. I mean, just because the energy drink is going to be at a music festival or a surfing competition down at Bondi, I don't think it's any sort of subterfuge. They're smart enough to know that there's a commercial imperative behind why they're there, but that doesn't necessarily inhibit whether they choose or don't choose to consume that product.

What about, for example, planting messages on e-mail lists, fake messages, which are in fact advertising?

I'm not that familiar enough with any of that to really comment on it. I would have a bit of an issue in that sense.

Why would you have an issue with that?

Well, because they're inserting an advertising message in something which is not designed to be a commercial environment. However, I think there have been a couple of companies that have been successful at using some sort of viral e-mail. They're usually a visual image, which is just meant to entertain and to make people laugh; and the only reason why somebody passes it on from one person to the next is because it's made them laugh. There's an entertainment value or there's a point to it that they want to make to whomever they're sending it to. If there's an advertising message that's part of that communication I don't have any issue with it because we're just putting it out in the market, and if somebody wants to take that and send it off to somebody, that's their prerogative.

One of the arguments against the infomercial is that people who are watching it are unable to distinguish between information and entertainment and advertising. Would you mind commenting on that?

Certainly, I think every infomercial that I've ever watched is a blatant commercial message. They're demonstrating products, they use basic sales techniques, there's lots of excitement generated, and they try to make it somewhat entertaining. I've never really had an issue with any of those because to me they've always been so clearly for commercial reasons.

But how do you distinguish, and maybe this is a stretch, how do you distinguish something like that from somebody else selling on another program, for example, their new movie release or their new CD? Now to me that is a more hidden sales effort than an infomercial because that is blatant commercialism in terms of trying to promote a product and the product just happens to be a movie. And it's no different from when a new band releases a CD. They go on a talk show circuit or they play on different programs and try to sell more of their CDs. It's no different when they go on tour to promote sales of that CD – and it works. It's just a different method in terms of trying to sell your product.

Is it impossible to escape advertising now?

I think sales, not advertising, but a sales message, or a compellingly persuasive message.

So you'd agree it is impossible?

Virtually. But it's also impossible in any shop you go into, because you go to a sales assistant and they help you in terms of clothes that you might be buying and they're also selling. I mean, everybody's always selling something. It's what makes the world go round. As long as I see at the top in clear letters that it says advertisement or commercial message, then I don't have an issue with it.

The producers of the major soap operas and the producers of the major daytime programming going back thirty, forty, fifty years, were always the huge detergent manufacturers and they actually produced the programming. Clemenger itself, as a company, started out as a radio production company back in 1946, and they produced radio programs and then within those programs were sponsor messages, and if you look back in history that's been quite common.

I think advertisers are going to start to produce more and more programming. We already see it for example on Channel Ten, you have *Pepsi Chart*, and it's a program designed for teenagers which is produced by Pepsi but airs on Channel Ten, and it's all about bands and music. And there's loads of other programming that I think advertisers will start engaging in, and selling to networks or syndicating, that will have their message embedded in that program; and I don't really have any issue with that either.

What about product placement in film and television?

Well, product placement is something that's been around for quite a bit. I mean, you pay a lot for movies. If you look at the most recent James Bond movie, my God, it's getting so commercial. And you know as long as people are willing to go to the movies and pay money [they will go to] see that. If they go too far it becomes too commercial and that turns people off, so they'll stop going. Movie producers will then come back a bit to something that is more acceptable to a wider audience.

And they've turned some of that content back into the TV commercials, haven't they?

Exactly, and we've done that with VISA. They are one of the sponsors of the most recent James Bond film and we've produced a very extensive VISA commercial that's used throughout Asia, Australia and New Zealand that uses Pierce Brosnan and plays on his character as Commander Bond.

So your feeling is that that will go up to and no further than the point at which consumers resist it?

Exactly. It's an open market place, so if they take the commercialism too far, and it's something that people aren't willing to accept, then they won't spend their money on it.

What do you think about research that says people don't watch TV ads?

There isn't a single person that I've ever met who will ever admit they are influenced by advertising. Nobody wants to say that, 'Yep, that influences me' or 'Yep, that has some way of determining my behaviour'. None of us want to feel as though we're susceptible to those sort of influences. It's no different from a salesperson who's trying to sell us something, we'll say, 'No, no, no, it has nothing to do with the salesperson. I made up my own mind and made the decision myself.' We all like to believe that, but I don't think that's necessarily how things work, and the reason why I laugh at [research] like that is, if that is true, then how is it that when we do research, people can so easily recall the advertising? Recall of numbers for something that is highly entertaining can be extraordinarily high. There are even lines such as 'Just do it' that [have entered] the vernacular.

The reality of today is that there's virtually product parity. Whereas before, it took Colgate two years to copy Proctor and Gamble in terms of their new innovation, they can now copy it within a matter of weeks or months, so there isn't one specific product innovation to use as leverage. Now your competitors catch up overnight; so that's why, from an advertising standpoint, it's about the emotional relationship that a brand has with consumers; and why it's so important to match the values that are expressed as part of that brand with the values of the user.

It's not necessarily the rational benefit side but the emotional benefit side of brands – and the best way to communicate that is in very entertaining, very absorbing communication.

For instance, the Clemenger BBDO (Sydney) campaign for Hahn Premium Light beer won the 2002 Advertising Federation of Australia Effectiveness Award Gold Pinnacle.

That particular advertising does not talk about any rational benefit – we never talk about the fact that it's a light beer, which is the rational benefit of Hahn Premium Light. We don't talk about anything in terms of that particular beer.

What we found is that there are two barriers to the consumption of light beer. One is that if you're drinking light beer it looks like you're not able to handle alcohol, so it's a 'wussy beer'. The second is that every light beer produced up until Hahn Premium Light compromised on taste; so not only were you feeling a little silly holding a light beer, it didn't even taste very good.

Lion Nathan did an extraordinary job in terms of making that particular light beer taste good, and to make the taste profile consistent with what you'd have in a full strength beer – so that was first and foremost a big deal.

Secondly, the advertising had to be able to make you feel proud to hold a Hahn Premium Light in your hand. We did that very cleverly by bringing

Michael Caton in and making it very sort of pleasant, funny, very warm, take-the-piss-out-of-yourself, which is a strong Australian trait, and very humble. The ad portrayed people who are absolutely passionate about what they do yet they have bad taste in virtually everything they do. But the one thing that matters the most to them is brewing great beer, so that's where they've put all their taste.

Finally, it wasn't just the advertising that was successful. Lion Nathan has an extraordinary distribution system so we could get Hahn Premium Light out in virtually all premises as well as every liquor distribution point across Australia. And the bottle they chose suggested purity, clarity and crispness, and gave you some clue in terms of what it was you were drinking. It all sort of worked together.

9 Diary of a Webdiarist: Ethics Goes Online
MARGO KINGSTON

IT WAS MEANT TO BE A WEEKLY ONLINE COLUMN ON FEDERAL POLITICS, a mere change in the forum for my work. It was my price for agreeing to do another stint as the *Sydney Morning Herald*'s chief of staff at our Canberra bureau in 2000, so I didn't lose my public voice while doing a behind-the-scenes organisational job. A year later it was my full-time job, yet until I agreed to do this chapter I hadn't systematically considered the ethics of it all, or how my ethical duties as a journalist were adapting to the Internet experience.

After *Sydney Morning Herald* editor Paul McGeough gave me the column, online editor Tom Burton pointed me to a couple of journalists' weblogs in the United States, where specialist reporters jotted down developments in their area, inside stories, and comment. The advantage for me was that I had no deadlines, so could write something now and then when I had time.

I had a quick look, got scared, and decided to start with a blank page and see what happened. When the technical people sent their design for the Webdiary page, I was horrified that they'd included my e-mail address. I had organised a silent home number after receiving hate snail mail and abusive phone calls while covering the Wik legislation and Pauline Hanson's 1998 federal election campaign, and the last thing I wanted was to invite an onslaught. 'Get used to it', Tom said. 'Interactivity is the future.'

The first entry began: 'Welcome to my Canberra diary. I'm allowed to say what I think, whenever I like, and lucky you can interact if you like. The down-side for this indulgence is that all the words stay forever so I can be judged for my sins.'[1]

It's ironic, thinking back, that I was so loath to encourage reader feed-back. My experience covering Pauline Hanson had convinced me there was

#159

something very wrong with the relationship between journalists and the public they supposedly served.[2] When would the media address our endemic disconnection with the people? And how could we do it?

Webdiary was my answer. Far from an onslaught of hate mail, interesting e-mails – on the topic I'd written about, other topics, and the idea of inter-action between journalist and reader – started rolling in. Most were so good I made the decision that would transform the page: to publish them as a matter of course.

A big plus for readers was that they could talk one-on-one with a journalist. Being able to drop the formality of letters to the editor style and say, 'I think you're wrong, and here are some questions for YOU', proved deliciously tempting. For me, admitting in writing that, Yes, I hadn't thought of that, or, You're right, or Here's where you're wrong, began an exciting, unpredictable public conversation with readers.

Pretty soon I had more e-mails than I could publish, and it dawned on me that I had absolute power over the space. What appeared did not depend on a decision of the editor/deputy editors/assistant editors, based on the mix of news, the space available, and the competition on the day. It depended on what I decided. I had no excuses if something went wrong. I set the tone.

The decision to publish readers' contributions also transformed my ethical considerations. Writing an online column entails the same obligations, but a different delivery mechanism. When you let readers join the show and help direct it, accountability is no longer a sham but a reality. Online ethical codes drafted for hardcopy journalism must adapt and stretch to fit a medium less planned, more open, faster, and much more in-the-moment.

At first I had a full-time, demanding job, and Webdiary got tossed off in spare moments. My response to the trust my bosses had put in me was instinc-tive – not based on reading the Media Alliance's code of ethics, to which I am bound. It's funny, but often you don't know what you've got until someone else describes it. Two years after Webdiary began, *Lateline* program presenter Tony Jones said of Webdiary: 'Kingston's net site is irreverent, straight-shooting and interactive. The readers get to answer back, often at length and apparently uncensored. You could describe it as participatory journalism with an attitude.'[3]

While writing this chapter, I asked long-time Webdiary contributor John Wojdylo for his thoughts on Webdiary and its ethics:

The running conversation that arises between readers is richer in form than at any of the Internet forums I have seen, with the exception of a handful of Usenet newsgroups. The exciting thing about the format is that Webdiary has the potential to be part of the pulse of contemporary life, influencing and being influenced by it. The moderator controls what is published in Webdiary, and it comes out under her name; therefore, 'Webdiary ethics' means 'the moderator's professional ethics'. The moderator selects the contributions to appear and often makes minor alterations to them.

Whichever decision the Webdiary moderator makes, the result is aggressive: it isn't possible to satisfy everybody, because some demands are contradictory ... Knowing how to use power responsibly is the essence of ethics – in Webdiary, or anywhere else.[4]

Doesn't the word 'power' leap from that description! My first bout of introspection about my responsibilities was in 2001:

I spoke to a Rotary lunch on Wednesday on the topic 'Playing politics in post-egalitarian Australia', which made me think about what this page has turned out to be, and what's the philosophy that's come to underpin it.

1. *After following Pauline Hanson around in 1998, I realised that I didn't know much at all, had been lazy in accepting the truths of the experts without thinking about it, and was generally out of touch. I was also convinced that conversation across viewpoints was vital to national coherence and the search for a new consensus.*

2. *I had three main assets:*

   (i) *I have access to information and an opportunity to scrutinise people of power because of my job and the paper I work for.*

   (ii) *I am independent. The only constraint I have is in speaking completely openly about the company I work for, although over the years I've come pretty close. That means I can be trusted – not to be objective, but to be honest.*

   (iii) *After going through the agony of using the 'I' word in my Pauline Hanson book, I have thrown off the shackles of the myth of objectivity, which is really an excuse to hide the truth*

*from readers, not expose it. It also falsely sets the journalist up
as observer/judge, not participant.*

*(iv) Once you get over that one, you stop being defensive about
criticism and realise that publication of criticism is a sign of
confidence, and its censorship proof of insecurity. It also means
that since everyone's sitting at the same table, genuine
engagement is natural.*

*As it's turned out, the page has become an open-ended conversation
with me as facilitator, as well as general rave merchant. What's the
point of that? A big thing in its favour is that no-one believes anyone
HAS the answers/the complete picture, any more. We are in a transition
of thinking, ideologically and philosophically, about our society and its
values. To scream at and deride those who have different starting points
castrates the debate, not enlivens it. It's also depressing.*

*What I love about this page is that intelligent people from many
starting points are interested in other thoughts. It's exhilarating. It cleans
out cobwebs and lifts feelings of disempowerment or hopelessness.
It's also a pretty big challenge to the mainstream, in that it's privileging
ideas over who has them, and intellectual debate over rhetoric and
conflict-thrill.*[5]

The first thing I decided was that the space would be safe for readers –
that they would trust it, and that I would trust them. It quickly became clear
that most readers were inclined to my worldview; so the space would quickly
become predictable, boring, and of no use if people of a different mind felt
there was no place in Webdiary for their voices to be safely heard. So I didn't
ridicule or deride contributions, and published most e-mails critical of me,
my style, and my substance.

Invariably, when people of one view begin to dominate, other readers
balance them. The Tampa issue triggered a torrent of e-mails from readers
appalled at what was happening and desperate to get their response on
record. After a few days supporters of government policy and people unsure
of what to think began to e-mail me, both balancing the page and beginning
weeks of detailed, passionate engagement. This year, e-mails antagonistic to
the American position on war with Iraq dominated published e-mails in the
lead-up to George Bush's address to the nation. Almost at the precise moment
I began to feel uncomfortable that anti-Americanism was overwhelming the

page, several readers wrote pieces 'in defence of America' and the American people.

This has not stopped several readers bitterly complaining that Webdiary lacks balance. I publish complaints, and make the point that Webdiary's content is self-selecting by writer/readers. Webdiary reflects the contributions of readers, and it's not my job, unlike in opinion editorial pages, to impose a top-down balance. Publishing and responding to criticism invariably triggers contrarian pieces from readers, re-balancing debate as if by magic!

Being so open to criticism means I've been forced to get a much thicker skin. Journalists are under constant pressure to write what the powerful want written, and not delve into what they don't. Threats are commonplace. We are unpopular. I've found, however, that developing an honest, open, transparent relationship with readers eventually built my confidence. I began to trust them! Giving virtually automatic rights of reply to readers who disagree with me, and to publish readers' contributions, not only enriches my thinking but gives real meaning and muscle to the code of ethics.

When I asked long-time Webdiarist Polly Bush for a comment on what Webdiary's ethics were, she wrote:

> *The problem is when you dip your toe into the water on the complex*
> *topic of ethics (and Webdiary for that matter), you end up with more*
> *questions than answers. I was thinking about this relationship between*
> *reader/contributor, yourself and the only word that kept coming up was*
> *'trust'– but is trust ethics?*

Yep. That's what it is. And yet, ethics codes have done little or nothing to improve the relationship between journalist and reader. Many readers have given up on journalism, and journalists, because they feel powerless. Many don't even know there's a code of ethics, or if they do, they feel powerless to enforce it. How many papers publish their ethical codes, or that of the Media Alliance? How many television and radio proprietors let their listeners and viewers know about it?

Most media groups are extremely loath to print corrections. They're by nature defensive, partly because they don't want to undermine confidence in them, partly because there's effectively no accountability for their breach, and partly because they fear getting bogged down with complaints from relentlessly partisan players. Who do you complain to? What's the process for resolution? Suggest setting up and publicising a process for accountability, and everyone runs a mile. Apart from defamation law, we're not used to accountability, and we don't like it.

As ethical questions have been raised and debated on Webdiary, I've realised that ethics – when laid on the table for open discussion between writer and reader – can be a tool of empowerment. What I hadn't done before writing this chapter was to make my ethical obligations clear. So I've decided to publish the Media Alliance code and the *Sydney Morning Herald*'s code in a prominent permanent position of Webdiary's home page, along with the procedure to complain to the Alliance. If readers want to complain to my paper, I've asked that they e-mail me and my online editor. I will publish complaints on the Webdiary with my initial response, and ask for reader comment, which I will publish and reply to on Webdiary, as could my editor. I hope this will cement confidence in my good faith, and the sense that ethical matters need not be matters for confrontation, but for conversation and resolution.

This procedure will add depth to the occasional navel-gazing debate in Webdiary, invariably triggered by a provocative e-mail that makes me think about where Webdiary's going. In 2001 I wrote the Webdiary Charter, published on the right-hand column of Webdiary as a permanent reference point for readers, in response to this e-mail from Paul McLaren:

> *Please excuse my ignorance, but I am perplexed by the object of your section of the* Sydney Morning Herald. *Could you please tell me why I should contribute? It seems very interesting but a little pointless unless, like I suspect, I am missing something.*[6]

The ethics of Webdiary evolve in consultation with readers as issues arise, and ethics discussions are not confined to interpreting the principles set out in the code. Readers have insisted that it's much wider – they're interested in how the media and journalists work, and are prepared to challenge the basis of our right to be critical of public figures, insisting that journalists too are public figures needing scrutiny. Trust breeds demands for greater accountability.

At the end of 2001, I wrote a series of columns berating Peter Reith over the Telecard scandal. Reader Jack Robertson wrote a passionate piece calling me, and my profession, to account for our double standards. He demanded to know what WE were paid, details of relationships between journalists and political players and details of when our owners had heavied us.[7] (To my regret I disclosed my pay, a disclosure now used by rightwing webloggers as a weapon of attack.) The process of answering Jack's questions, or explaining why I wouldn't, opened the floodgates to a torrent of e-mails critical of the media, and extended Webdiary's focus from politics to the media.

My editors over the years had always pooh-poohed my suggestion for a media section or page as boring for readers, who'd see it as navel gazing. They were wrong. I made Jack into Webdiary's 'Meeja Watch' commentator, and he and others now regularly critique media coverage of issues and prominent media figures. Jack took the debate further with '52 ideas for a healthier Australian news media', encouraging readers to think constructively about change.[8]

Through Webdiary, readers have forced me to think harder about and justify my ethical stances, and those of the profession. The controversy over the Laurie Oakes disclosure of the affair between Cheryl Kernot and Gareth Evans inspired debate of the highest quality on the appropriate line between public and private lives, when I was overrun with reader e-mails disputing my support for Oakes in a *Lateline* debate.[9] At the end of it, I wrote a piece clarifying and adjusting my position. Webdiarists had influenced my view and forced from me a detailed statement of my position.[10]

This is ethics in action. Ethics are ideals, not black letter law. They rely on the judgement of journalists trying to apply the principles in good faith, readers trusting them to do so, and regular dialogue between the two when real-life examples crop up.[11]

NOM DE PLUMES

The issue of anonymity raises the most difficult issue for online journalism. The Media Alliance code of ethics states:

> 3   Aim to attribute information to its source. Where a source seeks
> anonymity, do not agree without first considering the source's motives
> and any alternative attributable source. Where confidences are
> accepted, respect them in all circumstances.

In newspapers, writers must identify themselves. Anonymous contributions are not considered appropriate. Yet journalists quote anonymous sources all the time, too often becoming tools for their sources to influence debate behind the scenes. We make judgements all the time about which source to trust, when and how, and know that we're usually being used. This is a closed world to the reader.

Online, you can't usually check whether writers are real or writing under false names. And anonymous comment is commonplace. The issue flared up when contributor Tim Dunlop challenged my decision to allow readers to write reports on marginal seats under *nom de plumes*. After 'Stephen Henderson', a member of the Democrats, wrote a report on the seat of Parramatta, Tim saw red:

> *I think the practice of people writing under false names on your web site is appalling. From what I've read, they say nothing that is particularly 'radical' or anything that would threaten their jobs and yet they feel the need to hide behind a phoney identity. It sucks, and I don't think you should encourage it. It shows contempt for your readers. And surely such sanctioned dishonesty is not good for journalism in general.*[12]

The resulting debate was fast and furious, but I stood my ground.

> *I want real people to have a voice. Many can't because of the stupid censorship that suffocates them, where people can't be themselves by speaking as a private citizen because of the crappy constraints of their public or private sector jobs. I know it's hard, and I could be caught out, but this marginal seats idea is about perspective and opinion. I want interesting readers to be able to say interesting things to interested readers. No-one who's offered to write for me on marginal seats has offered to write under their real name yet. How about it?*

I didn't change my mind, but I came up with a policy. I asked readers to tell me if they were writing under a *nom de plume*, and to give reasons why, which I publish at the beginning of each *nom de plume* piece. I can't enforce the rule, but many contributors comply.

There is a critical exception. I would never publish personal slurs under a *nom de plume*, as a matter of basic fairness. I strongly disagree with the *modus operandi* of www.crikey.com.au in this regard, and believe that whatever its considerable merits, it cannot lay claim to being a site that complies with the code of ethics.

Of course, Webdiary does not seek to break news. If I get a story, I write it for the paper, and I give readers' news tips to the *Sydney Morning Herald* news desk. Crikey, which has as a central aim breaking news, is different. But in my view a journalist's web site cannot ethically publish serious allegations or personal attacks under cover of anonymity. A policy of fulsome corrections is not good enough. The code also bars publication under the rule that allegations should be verified before publication. In a *Lateline* debate on media ethics, Tony Jones asked: 'Isn't this, though, one of the things the Internet is famous for – no censorship, no boundaries?' I replied: 'Yeah, but it doesn't mean that I don't disapprove of some of the things on Crikey as a journalist'.[13]

OFFENSIVE MATERIAL

The Media Alliance code of ethics states:

> 2   *Do not place unnecessary emphasis on personal characteristics,*
> *including race, ethnicity, nationality, gender, age, sexual orientation,*
> *family relationships, religious belief, or physical or intellectual disability.*

I'm more relaxed about this requirement on the Net, as are my readers, partly because it is a deliberate choice to log on. Racism is the red-button issue in contemporary Australia. Australians tend to live in enclaves of the like-minded these days, creating a terrible barrier to understanding and national unity. I once agonised over whether to publish a contribution from a racist One Nation supporter, and did so, without complaint from readers, some of whom responded respectfully to the contributor. My use of 'Yanks' recently triggered a barrage of criticism from readers who suggested the word was a term of abuse. When I dropped it to avoid causing offence, other readers protested that the term was neutral. I took up 'Yanks' again after an American general used it while praising Australians for pre-deploying troops to Iraq. That settled it, I said, and no one disagreed.

In 2002, *Media Watch* asked me whether I'd known that a link to a page of Henry Lawson poems directed readers to a racist site, and if so, would I still have published the link? I wrote in Webdiary:

> *The implication, I assume, is that if I had done so I would have been*
> *knowingly promoting a racist site, something which right-minded*

*people would not do. I thought hard about the question, and finally
decided I would have done the same thing.*

*He's the first great poet of Australian identity, Lawson, and he was also
deeply racist, antagonistic in the cruellest sense to both the Aboriginal
peoples and Chinese migrants. This was a mainstream view then, and
since Tampa you'd have to say it hasn't left the mainstream yet.
But does that take away from Lawson's importance, or artistry,
or capacity to move us?*[14]

So I told *Media Watch* I would still have provided the link, and raised
the fors and againsts of a nationalistic response to the bombing of Iraq, with
the poetry and political views of Lawson as a case in point. I pointed out to
Media Watch that during the terrorism laws debate I'd published a press
statement from the far-right National Civic Council, which worked hard to stop
the laws, claiming they paralleled Hitler's actions in the prelude to World War
II. Is that promoting racism? No. It's acknowledging that groups of opposing
persuasions can come together on certain issues. And it's inviting readers to
consider what those groups have in common, and why.

CONFLICTS OF INTEREST

In 2001, Don Arthur, a regular contributor on welfare policy, raised the matter
of reader conflicts of interest.

I was thinking over what you were saying on Late Night Live *about*
Inside Out *attracting people who are not part of peak groups. Here's
something people ought to know about me. I can afford to study full
time because I've got a scholarship – it's called an Australian
Postgraduate Award (Industry). My industry partner is Anglicare (WA).
I'm not exactly sure how the money thing works but Anglicare puts
up some of the funds and is involved in setting the research topic.
I have three supervisors, two from Edith Cowan and one from
the industry partner. Sorry I didn't say this earlier.*

I replied:

I can't see anything remiss in not disclosing this, unless you mentioned Anglicare in a piece, or were writing on religious charity or the like. But Don's disclosure does raise the question of independence on this page ... Don, I can't check out every contributor and investigate hidden agendas. Basically this page is a trust exercise. I run most of what's sent in, with my judgment being pretty simple – is it interesting, is it repeating previous contributions, is it accessible? So it doesn't matter who's name is on it, in that sense, which is – apart from trying to free people from the constraints their work places put on their freedom of speech – why nom de plumes are cool with me. But I do ask that if it would be reasonable to perceive a bias, or conflict of interest, in what you write, that you disclose this. Like the marginal seats reports – if you're a party member, just say so. Also, if you've got expertise in an area you're writing on, I'm sure readers would appreciate that information too.[15]

Since then, many readers have disclosed their affiliations.

PLAGIARISM AND CORRECTIONS

There's been one instance of plagiarism that I know of, notified by a reader. I published his e-mail and gave readers the low-down on the issue. Many readers have pointed out inaccuracies in my work, and others', and I correct them as soon as possible. Since the explosion of weblogging in early 2002, there are many more critical eyes on Webdiary, and many webloggers take delight in pointing out errors. This adds another layer of accountability to the site. With all control in my hands, I have no excuse for failure to correct; and any fear of correcting is far outweighed by the fear of losing credibility with the reader who points out the error.

So has all this openness and honesty got me anywhere? Last year New South Wales Premier Bob Carr accused me at a press conference of blaming the Bali dead for their for own deaths in a column in Webdiary. I was horrified, fearing my reputation had been destroyed by a powerful man's lies. Rather than rush into print defending myself, I published the relevant extracts from the press conference, a transcript of Carr's subsequent radio interview on the matter, and the column I thought he could have based his false allegation on.[16]

The next day, we ran a 'Your Say' forum on the front page of the *Sydney Morning Herald* online on Carr's anti-terrorism laws, the subject of the press conference. Several readers demanded a forum on the Carr–Kingston dust-up, got it, and hopped right into it after reading the material. The verdict on Your Say and in Webdiary e-mails was overwhelmingly in my favour – with some admitting to surprising themselves by defending a journalist! That's got to be progress.

NOTES

1 'Welcome to my diary ... and now for the GST', http://old.smh.com.au/news/ webdiary/2000/07/04/FFXX7LRU6QC.html
2 See Margo Kingston, *Off the Rails: The Pauline Hanson trip* (Sydney: Allen & Unwin, 1999).
3 http://www.abc.net.au/lateline/s606072.htm
4 John's column, 'On Webdiary ethics', http://www.smh.com.au/articles/2003/ 01/30/1043804455034.html
5 'Disclosure and you', http://old.smh.com.au/news/webdiary/2001/04/05/ FFXGPMRU6QC.html
6 'What's the point?', http://old.smh.com.au/news/webdiary/2001/04/26/ FFXMPMRU6QC.html
7 'Questions to you journos', http://www.smh.com.au/articles/2003/01/16/ 1042520716364.html
8 '52 Ideas for a healthier Australian news media', http://www.smh.com.au/articles/ 2003/01/20/1042911317531.html
9 'Your say on the Cheryl Affair', http://www.smh.com.au/articles/2002/07/04/ 1025667034744.html
10 'An affair to remember', http://www.smh.com.au/articles/2002/07/09/ 1026185040530.html
11 DRAFT CODE OF WEBDIARY ETHICS

I want you to trust Webdiary. That's the ideal at the core of all professional ethics codes, which are guidelines for conduct which aim to achieve that ideal. I'm a journalist bound by two codes of ethics drafted to apply to traditional journalism. I've adapted the code to meet the responsibilities of running Webdiary, and set out guidelines for your contributions. These guidelines are always open for discussion and debate on Webdiary and can be clarified and added to as issues arise.

My obligations

1 I will strive to comply with the Media Alliance and *Sydney Morning Herald* codes of ethics, which will be in a prominent position on this site at all times.
2 In particular, I will correct errors of fact on Webdiary as soon as possible after they are brought to my attention and will disclose and explain any

inadvertent breach of my ethical duties on Webdiary at the first available opportunity.

3 I will respond on Webdiary to all non-frivolous queries or complaints about my compliance with the codes and give a copy of queries or complaints to the online editor.

4 I will not belittle or show disrespect for any reader's contributions I publish, or to any person who emails me.

5 I will do my utmost to ensure that Webdiary is a space to which all readers, whatever their views or style, feel safe to contribute. If you are offended by something in Webdiary, feel free to respond. I won't publish any material which incites hatred.

6 I will let you know when archives have been changed except when changes do not alter their substance, for example, corrections to spelling or grammar. I will amend archived Webdiary entries to include corrections of fact and advise you accordingly.

7 I won't publish all publishable emails, but I will read every one unless there's too many to reasonably do so in the time available. If I haven't been able to read all emails, I'll let you know on Webdiary.

8 My decisions on publication will be made in good faith, without bias towards those I agree with or am sympathetic towards.

9 I reserve the right to edit contributions.

10 I will publish most contributions made in good faith which are critical of Webdiary's content or direction, or of me.

My expectations of you

As a journalist I'm bound by ethical codes; as a contributor you're not. Still, there's a few guidelines I'd like you to follow. David Davis, who's read and contributed to Webdiary from its beginning and helped draft these guidelines, explains why. 'Webdiary encourages free and open debate. The guidelines for contributors are not designed to curtail this, but to remind you that just as you live in a community in the real world, the same is true in the online world. Being part of a community carries many rights, but there are responsibilities. Rather than eroding the rights, these responsibilities actually protect them.'

Ethics of contributors

1 If you don't want to use your real name, make up a *nom de plume* and briefly explain, for publication, why you don't want to use your real name. _anonymity_

2 Disclose affiliations which you think could reasonably be perceived to affect what you write. For example, if you are writing about politics, disclose your membership of a political party.

3 Don't plagiarise, that is, don't use the ideas of others without telling us where they came from, and don't copy the writings of others and pass them off as

your own. There's no need. Put quotes around the words of other people, and tell us who they are and where you got them from. If you've used online sources for your contributions, include the links so others can follow them up.

4 Be truthful. Don't invent 'facts'. If you're caught out, expect to be corrected in Webdiary.

5 Robust debate is great, but don't indulge in personal attacks on other contributors.

6 Write in the first person. Remember, we're having a conversation here.

12 'Last dispatch from Canberra', http://old.smh.com.au/news/webdiary/2001/02/ 09/FFX8RJRU6QC.html

13 See footnote 3.

14 'Webdiary watch', http://www.smh.com.au/articles/2002/10/25/1035504881026.html

15 See footnote 4.

16 'Bob Carr and me', http://www.smh.com.au/articles/2002/11/19/1037682014953.html

10

Control-SHIFT: Censorship and the Internet

KATE CRAWFORD

JOSEPH GUTNICK IS A WEALTHY, MELBOURNE-BASED BUSINESSMAN. HE IS an orthodox rabbi who made millions as a mining mogul while also developing a reputation in philanthropic circles. But what may earn his place in the history books goes beyond his business acumen or his charitable reputation, while being intimately related to both.

It began when Gutnick was given a starring role in an investigative article in *Barron's Digest*. *Barron's* is a weekly financial magazine published in the United States by Dow Jones, the corporate parent of the *Wall Street Journal*. The now infamous 7000-word piece – *Unholy Gains* by William Alpert – ran with the sub-heading: 'When stock promoters cross paths with religious charities, investors had better be on guard'. From Gutnick's point of view, it all went downhill from there. This appeared in print and on the *Barron's Online* web site, hosted on a server that distributes web pages from a corporate office in New Jersey. Meanwhile, in Melbourne, Gutnick read the article on the web site and discovered that his generosity to charities had been impugned as a cover for suspect dealings. He was not amused.

I'm not really concerned with the claims about Gutnick's affairs or whether they are defamatory. What's of keen interest to me, and, for different reasons, thousands of media publishers around the world, is how cases such as these could be used as instruments to limit what you can publish on the Internet.

Gutnick's lawsuit is just one of many in recent years that raise questions about what constitutes acceptable speech on the Internet, how broadly those rules apply, and who they apply to. These cases do not always hinge on

#173

defamation; they are more likely to be instigated under new, wide-ranging copyright laws, such as those seen in the United States. But the result is the same – web sites are being removed, material is being banned, and concern is growing that we are witnessing a new kind of Internet censorship.

It seems to me that this is not so much a new means of control as an old means being applied in a new medium. But there are important differences – the Internet does not operate in the same way as television, radio or print. What effects do we see when defamation law and copyright law are used to restrict speech on the Internet? And how do these differ from state-sponsored Internet censorship regimes such as the one we have in Australia? Isn't the Internet supposed to be the great medium of 'free speech' anyhow?[1]

Before we can answer these questions, we need a framework to understand how speech is controlled on the Internet – an analytic of censorship, if you will. This is not intended as a comprehensive summary of approaches to online censorship, but just as a consideration of two modes of control over online content.

Until recently, the established take on the Internet was that it was an inherently free medium – that its distributed global architecture somehow gave it an inbuilt immunity from censorship and control. John Perry Barlow, co-founder of the Electronic Frontier Foundation civil rights group, proclaimed the freedom of the medium to the US government in his widely dispersed Declaration of the Independence of Cyberspace:

> *I declare the social space we are building to be naturally independent of the tyrannies you seek to impose on us. You have no moral right to rule us, nor do you possess any methods of enforcement we have true reason to fear.*[2]

Barlow's manifesto is very much a document of its time, and it reveals the twin rationales for the belief that the Internet is beyond externally imposed controls – no one had moral jurisdiction and no one had the technical capacity. The Internet was built as a decentralised and diffuse network: spread across millions of servers, it was supposed to be impervious to national borders and independent of any central authority. In this utopian conception of the network, any attempt to block forms of content would fail: in the oft-quoted words of Net-libertarian John Gilmore, '[T]he net interprets censorship as damage, and routes around it'.[3]

This is no longer the case, if it ever really was. The Internet has metastasised and become mainstream. States are convinced of their moral authority over the Internet, and the technical capabilities to censor have advanced: we can point to Internet censorship regimes in China, Saudi Arabia, Singapore and Burma.[4] Western democracies are not exempt, although in some cases the means of control may be less direct or centrally governed. While the Internet can still be a powerful means for expression, it is also maturing as an instrument of control.

TWO MODES OF CONTROL

In analysing acts of censorship, we can distinguish between two levels of operation. On the one hand, censorship acts on particular works to remove them from view, to make them unavailable to the public. In this sense, censorship operates on the level of the specific site, as a targeted response to a particular situation. On the other hand, censorship can be seen to function in accordance with abstract, generalised moral principles, such as upholding community standards or protecting minors. In this second sense, censorship operates as a framework, a 'regime'.

To varying degrees, acts of censorship operate simultaneously on both of these levels. Defamation cases such as *Gutnick v. Dow Jones* have a specific and finite outcome, yet they produce generalised effects as they make their way into common law. Institutions with a generalised censorship charter enact their broad principles in specific cases by ordering the removal of particular works from public view. All acts of censorship involve a mixture of specific and general objectives, and produce a mixture of specific and general effects.

The Internet's massively distributed architecture has brought this distinction between the 'specific' and the 'general' into sharp relief. The sheer size of the global Internet – reaching across hundreds of separate jurisdictions – has made it relatively simple for content producers to avoid censorship restrictions or to go entirely unnoticed by their would-be censors, rendering the 'general' dimension of censorship largely ineffective. While generalised censorship is very difficult to achieve on the Internet, specific acts of censorship can (and do) take place in the networked world and the tools to do so are evolving to become more stringent and effective.

So let's return to Gutnick – his case can furnish us with some clues as to how the lines of control are being re-drawn on the Internet, and whose interests that might serve.

GUTNICK VERSUS BIG MEDIA

Gutnick's argument ran like this: Internet material is 'published' in the territory where it is downloaded and read. Thus, when Gutnick woke up in the morning to read a potentially defamatory article about his business investments on a US web site, it was effectively being published in Australia, and as such was actionable under Australian laws. Dow Jones countered, via its celebrity barrister Geoffrey Robertson QC, that the article was not published in Australia – only in a US print magazine and on the web server in New Jersey. Therefore any defamation case could only be brought in the United States. To decide otherwise, Dow Jones argued, would be catastrophic for free speech and Internet publishing worldwide – suddenly publishers could be held liable according to the laws of any and every country that had access to the Internet. A story published in the United States, for instance, could simultaneously be subject to the wildly varying laws of Malaysia, Finland and Cuba, as well as those in the United States. Chaos and confusion would reign.

The reasons behind these arguments are a little more self-interested. Gutnick wants to prosecute in his home state of Victoria as he is more likely to win. Simply put, under US law the plaintiff has the burden of proof to show that the allegedly defamatory statements are false, whereas in Australia the defendant must prove that a statement is true. Dow Jones, while it has a point that the media industry could be editorially hamstrung if it were subject to all possible international jurisdictions, is also coming to the defence of free speech on the Internet because of the threat to its bottom line. The cost of legal double-checks on all potentially defamatory articles, cross-referenced with different legal systems, would be astronomical. enormous.

By the time Gutnick's case reached the Australian High Court, Dow Jones was joined by the *Washington Post*, the *New York Times*, CNN, Reuters, Yahoo and Amazon. The big media players, across the traditional and new media sectors, decided it was time to throw in their weight. The decision had the potential to affect them all.

But despite all that corporate media muscle, the High Court made the decision no one expected: it agreed with Gutnick. In short, defamation law is based on damage to a person's reputation. Gutnick's reputation could be damaged wherever the libellous material was received – in this case, Victoria – so the court decided he should be allowed to pursue action in that state. In the words of Justice Callinan, to do otherwise would be to allow US law to dictate how defamation is considered in other territories:

What the appellant [Dow Jones] seeks to do, is to impose upon Australian residents for the purposes of this and many other cases, an American legal hegemony in relation to Internet publications.[5]

Whether or not Gutnick will succeed in that defamation action remains to be seen. All the High Court did was allow the possibility for him to sue in Australia for material posted on the Internet in the United States.

It may sound like a trifling, Australia-specific decision; nitpicking over the definition of 'publication' for the purposes of determining if a local business-man can sue a foreign publication. Dr Matthew Collins, barrister and author of *The Law of Defamation and The Internet*, wryly commented that it is the 'first time an ultimate appellate court has to decide where material is published'.[6] And in many ways the decision is simply a straight application of the existing case law for defamation in print, radio and television, without making any special exemptions for the fact that the material was online. But while it is an Australian ruling, it is likely to be treated with authority in other countries with a similar system of common law, such as Canada, the United Kingdom and Singapore.

The world's major media producers saw an immediate danger and responded with routine hyperbole about the opening of floodgates. Headlines included: 'A dark day for the Internet'; 'Libel without frontiers shakes the net'; 'How Diamond Joe's libel case could change the future of the Internet'; and my personal favourite from the *Wall Street Journal*, 'We wuz robbed'.[7]

Gutnick's case has yet to be decided, but it could provide a new legal mechanism by which to control information on the Internet: namely, to have news stories or entire web sites removed, even if they are hosted in foreign nations with different laws. This is a targeted, specific form of control, and in Gutnick's case it may seem justified – a libellous article will be removed, damages awarded. But this tool can now be applied by different parties and with broader ramifications. We are already seeing jurisdictional decisions made along the same lines in the United States.

In January 2003, just a few months after the Gutnick decision in Australia, a Los Angeles federal judge ruled that movie studios and record companies can proceed to sue the parent company of Kazaa, currently the world's most popular file-swapping service. Kazaa is an heir to Napster; it allows Internet users to connect to each other and share and swap music and video files. Despite the fact that Kazaa was created by Sharman Networks – a company based in Australia and incorporated in Vanuatu – it can now be actionable for breach of copyright in California. As such, it is now more likely to face the same future – or lack thereof – as Napster.[8]

The Kazaa case raises a further point. The dominant media and entertainment companies may be arguing for free expression in defamation cases, but in copyright cases such as the one brewing over Kazaa, we can witness a very different response. Here the aim is to shut down peer-to-peer clients, to remove forms of exchange from the Internet that are not seen as profitable to the movie-making and recording arms of the media industry.

While the general objective to prevent downloading of copyright works from the Internet is near impossible, broader copyright provisions are providing corporate interests with the means to censor and remove specific online services with considerable efficacy.

about copyright.

WELCOME TO THE DIGITAL MILLENNIUM

Intellectual property, and its distribution over the Internet, is the central issue in an emerging, complex battle. In the opening sorties, the industries that make profits by investing in copyright works are winning. Media and entertainment companies are now finding ways to control the flow of information using copyright protections that have been expanded for the digital realm.

Consider this: how do you regulate the use of someone's intellectual property in a medium where everything already exists as a copy? To access a web page, your computer is basically creating a copy of a version hosted elsewhere – it reads the Hypertext Mark-up Language and translates it into words and images on your screen. Then you can easily copy and paste that text into any document you choose. If you access a music file on the Internet and download it, you have made a perfect digital copy. The same goes for video. Communications theorist Cees Hamelink calls the Internet 'one enormous photocopying machine'.[9] So how can this kind of activity be monitored or regulated, let alone prosecuted, on a network as vast and decentralised as the Internet?

This is the concern articulated by the major players in Hollywood and the recording industry. These are companies that make profits by publishing and distributing other people's intellectual copyright – books, articles, films and songs. Suddenly they were faced with a global network that could publish and distribute these items without the middle-men. In short, media and entertainment companies had not yet figured out a way to protect their profits in the digital realm, so they began to lobby furiously – chequebooks in hand – for extra government protection via copyright laws.

The results of this cash-heavy lobbying are only now being evidenced – currently in the United States, and in the foreseeable future in Australia. In short, the balance has shifted from favouring consumers – who could simply download what they liked – to companies, who have now secured powers in the digital realm that exceed those in the offline world.

It began with entertainment industry bodies such as Hollywood Motion Picture Association of America (MPAA) and the Recording Industry Artist Association pushing for every possible way to develop stricter copyright laws, from mandatory copy-protection technology in all digital devices, to giving companies the authority to hack into the computers of people who had downloaded copies of films and music.

Arguments for greater industry protection haven't always worked – back in the 1980s, when Jack Valenti, President of the MPAA, argued the videotape recorder was the 'Boston strangler' of the American film industry,[10] the US Congress was rightly skeptical and decided against enacting videotape recorder protection bills.

But something changed by the 1990s – according to law professor and author of *Digital Copyright,* Jessica Litman, it was 'thanks in large part to the massive increase in lobbying money spent by entertainment industries', so that, all of a sudden, 'most members of Congress would agree that more copyright protection is always better than less'.[11]

One of the results of this newfound concern to increase copyright protection is the controversial *Digital Millennium Copyright Act of 1998* (DMCA). Amongst other things, this Act was designed to make it easier for copyright holders to fight piracy. Under the Act, if a party believes their copyright has been infringed, they can send a demand to an Internet Service Provider (ISP) to remove the offending material. If the ISP complies immediately, it cannot be held liable for contributing to copyright infringement. The site owner can file a counter-complaint if they feel their site has been unjustly removed and a court can then decide whether or not to reinstate it.

The DMCA has been widely criticised for its 'guilty until proved innocent' model. Sites are simply removed when a complaint is received, and will only be restored if they are proved legitimate. It gives a great deal of power to complainants – all they have to do is protest to an ISP about a site, and the ISP will take it down immediately for fear of further legal action.

It's not just ISPs that are affected by this law. Google, the world's most popular search engine, was recently found to be within the long reach of the DMCA. Google was issued with a complaint by the Church of Scientology that its search results included links to a site that was using copyright material by L. Ron Hubbard. The disputed site was, unsurprisingly, a damning critique of Scientology and was using the works of L. Ron Hubbard as part of its evidence against the church. Google was required under the DMCA to remove links to that site or be liable for infringement, despite the fact that Google was not responsible for the content and the site itself was based in Norway.

To date, the DMCA has been used in dozens of cases to restrict publication and expression. For instance, it was used to put a Russian computer programmer in jail, to deter a Princeton professor from publishing research, and to remove articles from magazine web sites.[12] It has even been invoked in an attempt to force ISPs to hand over the names of customers who are suspected of swapping music files on the Internet.[13]

But if we use the Watergate investigative method, and follow the money, we see who is benefiting from such legislation: the major players in the media and entertainment industries. The considerable investment spent on preserving their offline monopolies in the online world is paying off.

Marc Rotenberg, director of the Electronic Privacy Information Centre and co-editor of *Technology and Privacy: The New Landscape*, sums up the new mood in the United States. In an article in *Salon*, he argues that copyright law:

> *has become the silly putty of media attorneys and Washington*
> *lobbyists, stretched in space and time to protect all manner of activity,*
> *including business techniques and technological protocols that were*
> *probably not the kinds of things initially envisioned by the framers*
> *of copyright law.*[14]

Rotenberg reflects one of the key points being made by the widely published critic of copyright law, Stanford law professor Lawrence Lessig. In Lessig's latest book, *The Future of Ideas*, he demonstrates how dominant media players are manipulating copyright laws – originally designed to promote publication – as a way to dampen innovation, restrict free expression and protect their monopolies. 'This is the reality that the current law has produced. In the name of protecting copyright holders ... we have established a regime where the future will be as the copyright industry permits.' These large media companies 'are in effect getting more control over copyright in cyberspace than they had in real space, even though the need for more control is less clear'.[15] He concludes his book by arguing that we are witnessing a counter-revolution on the Internet where control is overturning freedom. 'We move through this moment of an architecture of innovation to, once again, embrace an architecture of control.'[16]

The specific applications of copyright law to the online realm that we've considered demonstrate a clearly defined goal to target individuals and services, rather than aiming for general or moral principles. Instead of attempting to stop all individuals from swapping music files or from criticising L. Ron Hubbard, the approach in these cases is to attack specific hubs of activity – the Recording Industry Artist Association closes down Napster, or the Scientologists block sites from Google. These actions have a finite conclusion, and an achievable set of objectives – they operate on a micro-level rather than a macro-level.

However, there can also be generalised principles in play behind these applications of copyright law. The arguments mounted by Hollywood lobbyists and recording industry executives alike are often framed in terms of theft of intellectual property: every individual who downloads music from the Internet is a thief. Edgar Bronfman Jr, chairman of Seagram (parent company of Universal Studios), argued that file-sharing technologies turn all their users into criminals and, in a dubious analogy, likened Napster to the former Soviet Union, in that it takes 'advantage of each person's least admirable qualities'.[17]

Without going into the flaws of the 'downloading is stealing' rhetoric, a generalised charter to block all file-sharing from the Internet to 'protect artists from theft' is almost impossible to achieve. As we know, the Internet as it exists today is too dispersed and distributed for these generalised approaches to censorship to be consistently successful.[18] Without substantial changes to the technological foundations of how the Internet operates, file-sharing will continue even when big services such as Napster are shut down. In contrast, using copyright law with precise objectives to target individual services or sites on the network can succeed. Established interests can use these means to great effect, and individuals and online services can be isolated and silenced.

AUSTRALIA AND THE SPECTRE OF THE DMCA

Australia may be compelled to develop its own system of wide-reaching copyright controls in the digital realm – an antipodean version of the US DMCA. The Australia–US Free Trade Agreement, currently still under negotiation, aims to remove certain trading inconsistencies between the two countries. One of the issues flagged for discussion is developing greater uniformity on copyright legislation. Recent reports indicate that the United States is recommending that Australia enact its own version of the DMCA, as a necessary part of 'the two nations "harmonising" key legislation on commerce'.[19]

If Australia does institute a similar copyright regime to that of the United States, ISPs would be held individually liable for content infringements unless they agree to remove web sites as soon as they receive a complaint. Just as in the United States, we would have a system that favours the copyright holders, and forces Internet publishers to prove that they have not infringed copyright before their web sites could be reinstated.[20]

Australia's online civil liberties group, Electronic Frontiers Australia, expressed its concern at the reports. The executive director of the EFA, Irene Graham, laid out the potential threat posed by widening copyright provisions in Australia:

> If we get a similar system to the US we will certainly see more attempts
> to remove material from the Internet. The DMCA has been used by big
> corporations in the US as a tool of censorship on the Internet. Australia
> already has the government's Internet censorship regime to deal with –
> this would add another threat to speech on the Internet.[21]

CENSORSHIP AND THE VILLAGE IDIOT

The Australian Internet censorship legislation provides a very useful case study – mainly due to the fact that there are few other examples of online censorship regimes in the West. So few, in fact, that when the *Broadcasting Services Act (Online Services)* (BSA) was passed, we earned the moniker of 'the global village idiot' by the president of the American Civil Liberties Union, Professor Nadine Strossen. Strossen made the observation that the legislation was unworkable because of the ease with which it could be circumvented; and troubling, as it gave an 'an open-ended license for who-ever's enforcing the law to inject their values into it'.[22]

The Federal government passed the BSA back in 1999 when moral panic about Internet porn was running high. The Act gave the Australian Broadcasting Authority the power to receive complaints about web sites, and issue take-down notices to ISPs to have unsuitable material removed from the Web.

Naturally, the regulations only apply to Australian ISPs and only affect the Australian content they host. Web sites originating overseas are beyond the government's reach. So what constitutes unsuitable material? The government applied a method similar to that used in film and video classification. According to the Act, anything classified R (material requiring an adult perspective, or simply unsuitable to minors), X (sexually explicit material) or RC (refused classification, such as child pornography) is prohibited content and must be removed. There is one exception – online R-rated material is permitted if the site requires adults to supply their credit card, driver's licence or birth certificate before they can access the content.

While these are similar classification criteria to film and video content, the media could not be more different in their means of distribution. Films, for example, are distributed in Australia via a small number of film distribution companies. Material on the Internet is distributed by thousands of content producers, and received by millions. Banning a film is a question of issuing an edict to a single distributor – banning a type of classified content on the Internet affects a large number of people and is extraordinarily difficult to patrol.

The Internet classification guidelines are intended to be tougher in application than offline media. Cinemas are not compelled to check the identity and age of all adults wanting to see an R-rated movie; and, in the offline world, X-rated movies can be mail-ordered without ID or credit cards. But something about the Internet warranted stronger controls – namely, what the minister identified as 'the widespread availability of the Internet to minors', particularly in the home.[23]

This is the underlying moral framework of the legislation – to protect children from unsuitable content on the Internet. However, given such a generalised objective, it is impracticable for the legislation to succeed. There is no evidence to suggest that children are any more protected from online pornography today than they were before the legislation came into effect in 2000.

In fact, there is considerable evidence to the contrary. The story is told in the statistics: the ABA's reports on the scheme reveal how few sites are actually taken down. For example, in 2000, the ABA received 491 complaints, of which 139 were determined to be prohibited content, but only 22 were found to be hosted in Australia. Therefore only 22 sites could be issued with take-down orders. Even this figure may have been exaggerated upward by the government, according to research by the Electronic Frontiers Australia group. To put the official number of removed pages in context, recent estimates suggest there are over eight billion pages of data on the Web.[24] There is no way to check if the sites, once removed from a hosting service, did not simply spring up elsewhere on the Internet using a different ISP.

The Internet censorship scheme is both inefficient and extraordinarily expensive – costing around $2.7 million per year, on government estimates. But according to a spokesperson for Communications Minister Senator Alston, the BSA is achieving its objectives, as 'the removal of these illegal and highly offensive sites means families feel comfortable about their children accessing the Internet'.[25]

This kind of oratory attempts to disguise the minimal impact of the scheme, while highlighting the ultimate futility of the government's putative goal. There are multitudes of readily accessible porn sites on the Web, and the numbers are growing. If a porn site is shut down, the owner can move it to a different ISP, host it overseas, or just set up a new one. Families that feel secure in the knowledge that the Australian government has somehow made the Internet 'safe' are being misled. The onus remains on them to educate their children about using the Internet, or to regulate their usage. The government's generalised objective to 'protect the children' is another example of symbolic politics, along with 'defending the Australian way of life', 'the war on drugs' and 'the war on terror'. While these have a rhetorical impact, from a practical perspective they are empty claims.

This generalised mode of Internet censorship, premised on general moral principles, is comparatively inefficient. As long as there is unsuitable content available to minors on the Web, the legislation has failed to meet its articulated goal. Even when a few targeted sites are removed, the overriding objective is not achieved. Given the heterogeneous and polycentric structure of the Internet, specific sites can be silenced, but shutting down entire genres of expression is exceedingly difficult.[26]

the difficulties of Internet censorship.

AFTER THE SWITCH IS THROWN

The idea that the Internet is inherently a medium of free expression and democracy is unsustainable. The Internet can be controlled, monitored and censored. But as Internet theorist Manuel Castells points out, it has not yet become a total architecture of control:

> The Internet is no longer a free realm, but neither has it fulfilled the
> Orwellian prophecy. It is a contested terrain, where the new,
> fundamental battle for freedom in the Information Age is being fought.[27]

By attempting to map the modes in which speech is now being controlled online in the West, we can identify two levels of operation: the use of a generalised (and necessarily moral) objective, more typically driven by the state, and the use of specific objectives to silence key sites or services.

However, it is important to recognise that these approaches are not opposed to one another, where one is purely state-focused and the other is solely in the hands of the market. The libertarian state-versus-market dialectic does not hold up to much scrutiny in this context. General and specific censorship objectives are used in varying degrees by both state and corporate interests. Furthermore, government policies on the Internet and market interests are mutually implicated, evidenced by the multi-million-dollar corporate lobbying for digital copyright protections. The two do not have clearly separated aims or methods. But the role of moral guardianship is one traditionally adopted by state bodies, and as we've observed in Australia, generalised moral censorship objectives are proving to be less effective in a medium as decentralised as the Internet.

It's too soon to gauge how much impact defamation law will have on the Internet, but we are already witnessing the growth of copyright as an instrument of control online. As demonstrated in the work of Lawrence Lessig and Jessica Litman, widened copyright laws have been used effectively for silencing critics, restricting research and closing down file-sharing activities.

If the tools to control content on the Internet are multiplying, and their use increasing, what does this mean for the development of the Internet as a medium? According to Marc Andreessen, the co-author of the first web browser and founder of Netscape, the period of innovation and freedom on the Internet is over.[28] In this view of the future, the dominant players are left to fight it out over the Internet's development – it's over to Microsoft, AOL Time Warner and News Corporation. The last two lines in Lessig's *Future of Ideas* are bleak: 'The switch is now being thrown. We are doing nothing about it.'[29]

Dutch Internet critic Geert Lovink disagrees.

It's fairly easy to draw up a gloomy picture, but that's not how I see it …
I always see crisis as an opportunity. It creates space to regroup and
rethink strategies. So what needs to be done is setting up independent
Internet infrastructures, software, communities and content. Another
virtual world is possible![30]

The critical difference between the pessimism of Lessig's vision of an architecture of control and Lovink's model of independent resistance is one of knowledge. If the majority of Internet users, and the members of the broader public, are barely aware that the Internet is facing increased censorship and control, then they cannot begin to resist it. To adapt a line from Kathryn Bigelow's film *Strange Days* (1995), the Internet is not 'like TV only better' – it is a medium that allows for direct participation. And as we become informed about the options before us, we have the ability to make active choices about the kind of Internet we wish to participate in, and the means of expression that will be permitted to flourish there. If we as media consumers and producers know the rules of the game, we can create our own virtual spaces in the gaps between the specific and the general operations of control.

NOTES

1   For my part, I will note that I am as leery of the term 'free speech' as I am of 'free market', but that's a topic best kept to a different chapter. I will use it in a loose shorthand for the time being, with invisible inverted commas.

2   John Perry Barlow, 'A Declaration of the Independence of Cyberspace (1996)', in Peter Ludlow (ed.), *Crytpo Anarchy, Cyberstates, and Pirate Utopias* (Massachusetts: MIT Press, 2001), 28. There have been so many critics and commentators over the years who followed this line that it's a little unfair to pin it on any single individual. The belief that the Internet is inherently free is less commonly found these days, and generally only by those still under the sway of the Californian ideology espoused by Nicholas Negroponte, Louis Rossetto, and others from the *Wired* orthodox church.

3   Cited in Howard Rheingold, *The Virtual Community: Homesteading on the electronic frontier* (Cambridge: MIT Press, 1993), 7.

4   For example, all Internet traffic in China must go through the Chinese government's own filtering system – or firewall – which regularly blocks particular Internet addresses. It has now earned the name of The Great Firewall of China. According to a study by researchers at the Harvard Law School in 2002, at least 18 931 sites were found to be blocked to Chinese Internet users out of a sample of 204 012 sites. A similar but less extensive system of government filtering is used in Saudi Arabia, and Harvard researchers are also tracking its development. See The Berkman Center for Internet and Society, at http://cyber.law.harvard.edu/.

5   The transcript of the High Court judgement, in *Dow Jones & Company Inc. v Gutnick* of 10 December 2002, can be found in the Australasian Legal Information Institute database: http://www.austlii.edu.au

6   As quoted in Darrin Farrant, 'The world logs on to Gutnick's Internet case', *Age*, 28 May 2002.

7   'Editorial', *Australian*, 11 December 2002. David McCullagh and Evan Hansen, *CNET News.com*, 11 December 2002; David Fickling and Stuart Millar, *Guardian*, 11 December 2002; *Wall Street Journal*, as cited in Mark Glaser, 'Aussie libel ruling: Bad or horrible?', *Online Journalism Review*, 12 December 2002.

8   In February 2001, Napster was found by the 9th Circuit Court of Appeals in California to be illegally copying and distributing music and was effectively shut down. For a timeline, see 'Napster: Life and death of a P2P innovator' at the Berkeley Intellectual Property Weblog at http://journalism.berkeley.edu/projects/biplog/

9   Cees J. Hamelink, *The Ethics of Cyberspace* (London: Sage Publications, 2000), 157.

10 Cited in Sam Costello, 'How VCRs may help Napster's legal fight', *The Industry Standard*, 25 July 2000. http://www.thestandard.com/article/0,1902,17095,00.html accessed 22 November 2002.

11 Cited in Damien Cave, 'Chained melodies', *Salon*, 13 March 2002. http://www.salon.com/tech/feature/2002/03/13/copy_protection/ accessed 20 November 2002.

12 The full list of cases where the DMCA has been used can be found at the Chilling Effects Clearinghouse: http://www.chillingeffects.org.

13 In late 2002, the Recording Industry Artist Association (RIAA) tried to use the DMCA to compel an ISP, Verizon Communications, to hand over the name of a customer accused of illegally trading music files. Verizon refused, and at the date of publication was appealing the case in court. This is the first time the RIAA targeted an individual for swapping songs on the Internet, rather than suing companies such as Napster. See Declan McCullagh, 'Verizon appeals RIAA subpoena win', *CNET News.com*, 30 January 2003. http://news.com.com/2100-1023-982809.-html accessed 30 January 2003.

14 Marc Rotenberg, 'Internet liberation theology', *Salon*, 7 November 2001. http://archive.salon.com/tech/review/2001/11/07/lessig/ accessed 17 November 2002.

15 Lawrence Lessig, *The Future of Ideas* (Random House: New York, 2001), 201–2.

16 ibid., 268.

17 Quoted in Costello, 'How VCRs may help Napster's legal fight'.

18 Here I am specifically referring to the Internet as it is used in the West, not under authoritarian or totalitarian regimes. In political systems that already operate with rigid media controls and constant Internet filtering, a more generalised approach to censorship can be effective – as noted above.

19 Simon Hayes, 'US tightens Net copyright', *Australian*, 28 January 2003.

20 We are already seeing the attention of major music corporations beginning to focus on possible copyright breaches in Australia. In February 2003, Sony, EMI and Universal launched legal action against Melbourne, Sydney and Tasmanian universities over students allegedly downloading music illegally on their networks. See Sue Cant, 'Why the record giants are putting our unis in a spin', *Sydney Morning Herald*, 25 February 2003.

21 Irene Graham, personal interview, 3 February 2003.

22 Quoted in Kirsty Needham, 'Alston defends content law after "idiot" charge', *Sydney Morning Herald*, 25 August 1999.

23 Department of Communications, Information Technology and the Arts, press release 19 March 1999. http://www.dcita.gov.au/Article/0,,0_1-2_1-4_13648,00.html

24 Statistics on the number of pages on the Web vary wildly and increase dramatically every few months. This estimate comes from research conducted by the Google search engine company, announced on 6 April 2002.

25 Quoted in Christine Jackman, 'Net surfers dob in porn sites', *Courier-Mail*, 17 April 2001.

26 There may come a time when the technical infrastructure underlying the Internet allows for far more widespread applications of control. There are several ways this could be achieved, but this is beyond the scope of this chapter. For more on this topic, see Lawrence Lessig, *Code and Other Laws of Cyberspace* (New York: Basic, 1999).

27 Manuel Castells, *The Internet Galaxy: Reflections on the Internet, business and society* (Oxford: Oxford University Press, 2001), 171.

28 Quoted in Lessig, *The Future of Ideas*, 266.

29 ibid., 268.

30 Lovink, personal interview, 1 February 2003.

INTERVIEW WITH LINDA JAIVIN

REPRESENTING THE
ASYLUM SEEKERS
(NOVELIST AND SINOLOGIST)

**How did you initially become interested in the issues
surrounding asylum seekers?**

After *The Monkey and the Dragon* came out, I had a couple of ideas for novels
in mind; but I was so angry about the whole 'children overboard' business, the
Tampa, and our treatment of asylum seekers, I wanted to do something which
addressed that issue first. I had been interested in writing for theatre for a long
time, and it occurred to me that what I wanted to do was to write a comedy
with a very punchy message about asylum seekers. I came up with the idea
for *Seeking Djira*, which is about a bunch of self-obsessed Australian writers at
a writers' centre who are unexpectedly confronted with an asylum seeker who
has escaped from Villawood [a detention centre in Sydney]. Everyone's very
confused about who the other people are: he thinks he's stumbled into some
weird, dysfunctional family, and they think that he's the famous Middle
Eastern poet who they're expecting. So it's a comedy of errors, written in the
style of a classic bedroom farce. Anyway, I was starting to write this play when
I realised I'd never met an asylum seeker, and had no idea how to do the
character. I went to Villawood with the intention of going only a few times,
to do some research. But I became very involved with the people I met and
so, since November 2001, my whole life has revolved around asylum seekers.

#189

How have the mainstream media been covering the issue of asylum seekers?

While there are some journalists doing a valiant job of trying to cover the situation fairly and fully, and there have been excellent books on the subject by journalists including Peter Mares and David Marr, media coverage in general has been marred by ignorance on the one hand and wilful distortion on the other. Sometimes you can't tell which is which. We have some newspaper editors who have adopted an extreme anti-asylum seeker stance, and everything they publish has a slant on it. They always seek to make both asylum seekers and the people who help them look bad; a classic example is the *Daily Telegraph*, which publishes articles with headlines like 'Five Star Asylum' about Villawood and Woomera. Even some of the coverage which attempts to be more fair suffers from an inability to get at the facts because the media are officially banned from access to asylum seekers in detention. Of course, a number of journalists have effectively defeated the ban, visiting the centres as ordinary visitors, conducting phone interviews with detainees and so on. The [Australian] government's press releases and pronouncements, meanwhile, tend to demonise asylum seekers, encourage use of completely inappropriate terms like 'queue jumpers' and 'illegal immigrants', and present a one-sided and often misleading picture of the truth.

What has been the effect of the severe restrictions on filming inside refugee detention centres? How has this influenced public opinion?

The effect of restrictions on filming inside the centres is that most Australians don't have a clear picture of life behind the razor wire and, more importantly, find it hard to put a face to asylum seekers; it is just that bit more difficult for the public to recognise asylum seekers as people like themselves. By keeping asylum seekers faceless and nameless, it's easier to foment resentment, distrust and even hatred against them. All this breaks down when, thanks to smuggled-in cameras and so on, asylum seekers have been able to present themselves and their stories on such programs as the *Sunday* program, *A Current Affair* and *Four Corners*. They become real people then, harder to ignore, and deserving of our compassion and care. The print media can do this as well with images that go with stories. For example, there was a profile in the *Sydney Morning Herald* on Mohsen Soltanyzand, an Iranian asylum seeker.[1] He wrote poetry, and some visitors decided to put his poetry to music and make a CD. The album was dedicated to children in detention, and all proceeds were given to the ChilOut (Children Out of Detention) organisation. Because he had his name out there, it gave the newspapers a chance to do a profile on him. It turned out he was a legitimate refugee, deserving of our protection, as the Refugee Review Tribunal finally affirmed in a second hearing, after he'd been in detention for almost four years. I know many of the cases in Villawood pretty well, and Mohsen is not the only genuine refugee whom the process had failed.

When you read the details of Mohsen's life, and look at his photo, it makes you think, 'Where was I in my late twenties and what were the subsequent four years like for me? How many things did I do? How many places did I go?' You try to imagine what it would have been like to flee your country under terrible circumstances. Individual stories have the power to move people. The effect of the ban is to make it as difficult as possible for people to access these stories.

How important is it that these stories about life inside detention centres get out?

I think it's terribly important. When people realise that an asylum seeker is not just a blurry image of a man seen from a distance with dark features, on a boat, or tearing at a fence, that he or she is a human being, they realise that there is something terribly wrong going on. They might even be moved to try to change things.

What other methods are refugee rights activists using to get these stories out there, and what other avenues are being explored?

There are so many avenues. There's a billboard campaign, advertisements in the mainstream media, and different groups doing things on the Internet. The Internet has been a powerful tool for the dissemination of information on asylum seekers, whether through dedicated sites, such as those run by ChilOut, Just Refugees and the Refugee Action Collective, or because it's so easy to find and download reports such as that by Human Rights Watch on mandatory detention in Australia. Human Rights Watch and Amnesty International are just two international groups that make readily available information about asylum seekers and the Australian detention system. The Edmund Rice Centre published a well-researched and easy-to-understand article, 'Debunking the Myths on Asylum Seekers', on the Internet. It has been downloaded and reprinted in many different formats and has proved a very useful tool for refugee advocates trying to persuade others that asylum seekers are not 'illegals' or 'queue jumpers', and that Australia is not exactly being swamped by refugees.

Then there are creative approaches, like incorporating concerns about asylum seekers and detention into books, plays, films and artwork. I don't think that plays are going to change the world, but writing is what I do best, so I try to make a contribution this way. A number of artists have responded to the theme of detention in exhibitions such as 'Border Panic', which was put on in Sydney's Performance Space in 2002. Annette Hughes and Geoffrey Datson put Mohsen's poems to music and on a CD. There are a lot of examples of artists and writers doing things like this.

What's important to keep in mind is that we are living in a time when the media have an extraordinary amount of power, and I mean media in the broadest possible sense. If governments and corporations get their message across by clever, if often dishonest, manipulation of the media, we must work out ways to manipulate the media just as cleverly, but with the intent of putting across the truth. It's vital that we reach the people who rely on talkback radio and the *Daily Telegraph* for their information about what's going on.

Personally, I think that demonstrations, particularly those which involve potentially violent confrontations with police or attempts to tear down fences at the centres, are probably the least effective method for change, because they tend to alienate mainstream Australians, when what really needs to happen is to bring them on side.

Is culture jamming, and other unorthodox means of getting messages into the media, an effective tactic for changing public perceptions of a political issue?

I think culture jammers have done some excellent work. Mickie Quick has created a street sign alteration kit so that anyone can turn one of the signs for 'Refuge Island', which have a symbol of an adult leading a child across the street, into a political statement: you add an 'e' to 'Refuge', put a gun in the hand of the adult, and stick a map of Australia under the image.

In this very confrontational time, when so much hatred and bigotry is being whipped up around this issue, culture jamming is a great way to get people's attention – you surprise them, make them laugh and then make them think. You don't approach the public as an enemy but as a potential co-conspirator, sneaking into their consciousness.

What is your analysis of the use of language in the mainstream media coverage of refugee stories?

The government constantly tries to confuse the term 'illegal immigrant' with 'asylum seeker', an obfuscation in which some media are willing participants. In fact, in terms of the international convention on this, if you are seeking asylum, you are not entering a country illegally. The media ought to be more careful about the way they parrot the government's language. I was very disappointed when at one point the *Sydney Morning Herald* ran a little news item that used the words 'illegal immigrant' where it should have used 'asylum seeker'. The word illegal predisposes the reader to think of the person as bad.

Then we can go back to the example of the 'five star asylum' appearing in the *Daily Telegraph*. That was such a joke in Villawood. Many of the claims in that article were absolutely fallacious or taken out of context. It implied that things that had been provided to some detainees as gifts from visitors, such as personal stereos, were standard issue – and taxpayer provided. It claimed that the detainees have access to e-mail and the Internet, which they don't. It was an absolute, bald-faced lie. In another case, on reporting the New Year's Eve attempted mass break-out and fires at Villawood, the headline screamed 'Detainees declare war' – and never bothered to mention that the detainees involved in the trouble didn't include a single asylum seeker. They were all visa over-stayers and criminals awaiting deportation. The one section of Villawood where there was no trouble at all, Stage Two, is where most of the asylum seekers are housed. When things like that go out through a mass media outlet like the *Daily Telegraph*, it generates an overwhelmingly negative response towards asylum seekers. The purpose is achieved instantly.

Have you ever given up on even-handed mainstream news coverage of asylum seekers?

I don't put aside hope that the mainstream media, who are most guilty of vilification of the asylum seekers, will eventually recognise that they've been taken for fools by the government, and that they were used in a profoundly unjust cause, with terrible human consequences. Fish might learn to fly, too. On the other hand, I think it's important to see that not all of the mainstream media are against asylum seekers or buying into the government's line; probably most media would come up with mixed scores on this issue. I'm just about to walk across the street and get the *Australian* because I understand they have a vaguely sympathetic piece in today's issue. I think that dedicated journalists with integrity can always, at some point, break through and get heard.

> **Do you think that alternative media outlets, such as independent news web sites, are free to get around the editorial limitations you've described in the major presses? Or are they simply subject to different forms of control and censorship?**

I think that's the idea of those sites, to get around editorial limitations. I'm not familiar enough with them or the way they're operated to comment on the censorship they exercise over content. It's a good question.

> **You've experienced some censorship on the Internet related to your novel *Eat Me*, haven't you?**

I'd given a reading from *Eat Me* at a bookshop in San Francisco – The Booksmith – a great little bookshop with a good web site. They posted a blurb about *Eat Me* which was completely inoffensive, saying something like 'Four women from Sydney discuss their erotic lives and fantasies'. They pictured on the site the US cover of the book, which actually won a design award: there was a 'boy' cover – a banana with two plums at the base – and a 'girl' cover with a split papaya. Cyberpatrol, a large Internet filtering software company in the United States, a 'Net nanny', which is subscribed to by a huge number of libraries and educational institutions, as well as by individuals, decided to ban the entire Booksmith site because of the description and the cover. Cyberpatrol told Booksmith the only way they would remove the ban would be to remove all information about my book from their web site. Interestingly, Cyberpatrol didn't go after Amazon.com, which also had a picture of my book.

Anyway, Booksmith refused to remove my book and told them to bugger off. This incident generated much discussion on the Net and during Banned Books Week that year, and in the end Cyberpatrol withdrew its ban. That was very revealing because it demonstrated that you can stand up to these bullies and win. Booksmith has my eternal gratitude and admiration for risking a tremendous amount of business on principle. They just told Cyberpatrol that it was wrong.

I remember that your book received considerable coverage as a result of the ban and the subsequent furore.

Yes, sales of *Eat Me* shot up!

So online censorship worked in your favour in the United States.

Absolutely. Funnily enough, in China, there have been instances where both authors and artists have just begged to have their work banned. It means instant success. The people who are behind acts of censorship never seem to understand this, which is probably just as well, in some ways.

But my deep fear is that as we enter this crazy, ridiculous war for oil and follow the United States into the Middle East, that we will end up with some version of the state of emergency which governments so happily impose in wartime. This will be connected to the new anti-terrorism legislation in this country which curtails civil liberties in a number of very significant and frightening ways. If the government uses this to censor its critics, of mandatory detention or anything else, things could get very ugly.

NOTES

1   Tony Stephens, 'Poet's words from behind the wire', *Sydney Morning Herald*, 9 October 2002.

11 The Ethics of Porn on the Net

KATH ALBURY

IN LATE 1995 I BEGAN RESEARCHING MY HONOURS THESIS ON 'Representations of heterosexuality in media and popular culture'. I soon realised that there was a rich vein of heterosexual representation to be explored in popular men's magazines – that is to say, soft-core porn. Researching amateur images in soft-core pornography led me to consider the broader genres of explicit sex media (... which is, of course, a nice way of saying the 'soft' stuff led to the 'hard' stuff).[1]

Initially friends and colleagues were apprehensive when I discussed my work – although I did get plenty of flirtatious offers of 'research assistance'. By 1998–99, however, things changed. Where the topic of my porn research had once been a sure-fire conversation stopper, it began to receive a great deal of informed (and amused) interest in both academic and non-academic circles. It was clear from these conversations that many more people had become familiar with the diversity of pornography as a media form – and that the Internet had played a major role in this familiarisation. Pornography was no longer the scary and/or embarrassing secret they hid under their beds. It was being openly accessed – and discussed – in my friends' nice middle-class homes and offices. Yet this same openness and ease of access represented a growing source of anxiety for many, particularly those who were already dubious about the production and consumption of sexually explicit magazines and videos. Friends and colleagues who had previously avoided any exposure to explicit material (for moral and/or political reasons) felt that the Internet had created an avenue for pornographic 'home invasions'. These conversations and interactions have helped shape my study of pornography as a form of popular 'sex-media', a project which currently involves

#196

interviewing local producers, consumers and distributors of commercial and non-commercial porn.

This chapter reflects on some of the different issues that have been raised by my particular brand of 'feminist porn research'. Specifically, it looks at the ways that the Internet has not simply brought porn into the home, but has in fact facilitated a kind of 'domestication' of pornography, by allowing porn fans to become amateur pornographers in their own bedrooms. Most importantly, it allows those who feel left out of mainstream explicit and non-explicit media representations of sexiness and sexuality to create the kind of porn they want to see. As one of my interviewees, a lesbian porn producer/performer, put it, producing this kind of cottage industry or DIY porn 'is like a freedom to wear sexy clothes, or get naked or be exhibitionist … but do it … where our sexual preferences lie.' I will explore some of the moral oppositions to the production and consumption of pornography, and suggest that the alternative forms of Internet porn might be better understood in relation to a framework of sexual ethics, and 'everyday experimentation'.

It is clear many people believe that pornography on the Internet is signifi-cantly different to other kinds of porn. Indeed, there are some significant differences – but 'different' is not always 'worse'. Before exploring Internet pornography in detail, it is worthwhile revising some of the traditional reasons for opposing pornography in general.

WHAT'S WRONG WITH PORNOGRAPHY?

The production, distribution and consumption of pornography have tradition-ally been understood in terms of morality. The moral issues involved, however, tend to vary according to one's school of thought – or politics. The Judeo-Christian view might be summarised as follows: sex is, ideally, a matter of procreation, and an expression of *private* 'married love'. As such, it should be confined to the bedroom of married heterosexual couples, and never per-formed in public, or for profit. Pornography depicts non-reproductive sex acts, performed for profit between two or more unmarried, and not necessarily heterosexual, partners. Not only do these images depict immoral sex – they incite masturbation, which may in itself be an immoral act.

Leftwing opposition to pornography has tended to emphasise Marxist and/or radical feminist moral perspectives, which overlap somewhat with the religious/conservative position summarised above. From a Marxist perspective, it could be argued that all porn performers are 'alienated' from their own sexuality, since pornographic sex is performed as labour, rather than simply for the purposes of recreation or procreation. Pornography is inherently immoral, then, because it encourages its performers to sell that which should be most sacred to them – their sexual bodies, and/or intimate encounters with sexual partners. The feminist addition to this argument asserts that women as a class are particularly exploited by pornographic industries. Pornography, according to this argument, 'dehumanises' or 'objectifies' women, by depicting them in explicit sexual poses. Pornography not only publicly sells or 'commodifies' something that should be free (and private), it depicts a male fantasy of idealised, ever-available female sexuality.

Many feminists argue that explicit pornography (that is, material that could be classified X-rated) is part of a general social tendency for men to view women as sexualised objects, who are only valued for their ability to service men – physically and emotionally. As such, porn can be viewed as one end of a spectrum of other popular media images of sexuality; from erotic novels to advertising billboards, television and cinema productions, self-help manuals and women's magazines.

Both conservative/religious and Marxist/feminist critics of pornography and other forms of sexual media might argue that the 'commodification' or 'objectification' of women's bodies is inherent to most of Western media and popular culture. However, it is visual imagery, particularly explicit photographs and videos, that is most often presented as literal 'evidence' of sexual exploitation.[2]

In summary, pornography is widely considered to be immoral primarily because it:

- makes something 'public' that should be private;
- encourages people to exchange sex for money;
- exploits women by representing them as being sexually active and available; and
- represents a limited range of body types as sexually appealing.

But if porn is immoral, does that mean it is unethical? Is it free from codes of conduct, internal value systems, or 'best practice' guidelines? My answer to these questions is no.

Although there is plenty of misogynistic porn in circulation, pornography has, until recently, been the only form of media where women have been seen to experience strong sexual desire and sexual pleasure. And, as I will argue, it is still the only form of popular media where women and men who deviate from the agreed norms of physical attractiveness by being too fat, too old, too kinky, or just too 'ordinary', can be acknowledged as unique sexual beings. As much as 'sex sells', there are many, many people who want to share their most intimate sexual moments freely and publicly. Internet pornography demonstrates all this, and in doing so it offers a tremendous challenge to traditional arguments about what porn is and what it does.

PORNO COMMUNITIES

Much of the pornography available online is produced and distributed in ways similar to traditional commercial pornographic magazines and videos. Some web sites take the form of magazines, to which consumers subscribe; and many of the images are taken directly from existing print or video porn. On the Internet, X-rated content comes to us at the click of a mouse, with no need to physically visit sex shops, or other 'restricted premises'. This is one source of anxiety about porn – the idea that explicit media can 'invade' the home, our most private space. Yet the most interesting Internet pornography is produced at home – by amateurs, community chat groups and collectors.

Unlike traditional broadcast media, such as film and television, the Internet allows us to talk back, to become publishers (and pornographers) in our own right. The Internet has allowed a remarkable blurring of the categories of 'publisher', 'distributor', 'performer' and 'consumer'. Provided they have sufficient funds (approximately $1000), the home enthusiast or amateur in any field can start up a web site or join a chat list which allows them to air views on almost any topic. The purchase of scanners, and digital still and/or video cameras allows the home enthusiast to take their fandom one step further by 'borrowing' favourite images from print media, videos and, of course, other web sites to re-post in archives, catalogues or swap forums. Even better, if the amateur harbours a fantasy of actually performing in pornography, they are able to fulfil exhibitionistic fantasies in safety and relative anonymity.

This boom in home publishing technology, combined with the Internet's capacity for opening up national and international distribution networks, means that Internet porn both is, and is not, a very different beast to the porn films, videos and magazines of the 1970s and 1980s. While there have always been underground networks for the collection and trading of both commercial and homemade pornography,[3] the Internet has allowed for a tremendous upsurge in amateur distribution and networking amongst fans and consumers.

The term 'porn collector' may evoke images of creepy, furtive (male) loners with minimal social skills. However, as British sociologist Don Slater found in his ethnographic research into one online collector's site, sex-pic traders feel themselves to be part of a virtual 'community', much like other special interest groups. Rather than experiencing shame or alienation, Slater's interviewees enjoy participating in a pleasurable alternative to everyday life. Especially when:

> the chat [on the IRC (Internet relay chat) site] … can itself become eroticised as representations, flirting, heated and pleasurable sex talk, cybersex, in which the actual encounter between participants becomes, as the typical comment goes, 'like being inside a piece of interactive pornography'.[4]

This desire to voluntarily immerse oneself in 'interactive pornography' is not exclusively the province of male porn fans. In his study, Slater found that female informants particularly appreciated the Internet as a place where they could 'explore desires which are too taboo, embarrassing or dangerous for offline life: mainly bisexuality, exhibitionism, group sex and promiscuity'.[5]

These research findings resonate with the experiences of my Australian interviewees. For example, 'Craig', a Victorian webmaster, publisher and party promoter, believes that the growth of Internet sex sites and phone chat services has allowed heterosexual women in particular to feel safer and more confident in their experimentation with alternative sex practices. This involves more than anonymous chat – both male and female guests at Craig's Melbourne parties have become increasingly comfortable with incorporating a little online exhibitionism into their night's entertainment:

> The very last party we did, we had [a room with] two webcams broadcasting live onto the web, and we put big signs up outside saying to people: 'Don't come near it if you don't want to be filmed'. And it probably got more use than any other room in the place … There's something about having the ability to let your hair down and just for

once in your life, you know, do some amateur porn on a camera, or
jump around and pretend you're a stripper or something like that.

As the British researchers put it, 'These pleasures and transgressions evidently depend on a clear separation of sexuality from "real life"'.[6] Interestingly, though, the separation between sex and real life is not always clear-cut. Slater observed that 'many logged conversations [in his study] move within minutes from tastes in porn to the problems of single-parenthood, money problems, dead-end jobs'.[7]

For Slater's IRC traders, and Craig's partiers, it seems that Internet porn does serve as a pleasurable space where sexual fantasy serves as an escape from the everyday. At the same time, amateur porn and X-rated swap sites seem to demonstrate that sex (even pornographic or taboo sex) is *interconnected* with everyday life. Not only are everyday domestic issues discussed on the pic trading site, the space of the site itself is 'domesticated' in participants' discussions. For example, these may include the formulation of guidelines for online sexual etiquette, and the negotiation of jealousy and competition between online and 'real-life' sex partners. As Slater and his fellow researchers describe it, the study of this particular web community 'shows that the objectification of sexuality on-line appears to be fuelled at least as often by the urge to order sexuality (and IRC relationships and practices themselves) along ethical lines as it is to gratify it transgressively'.[8] I take this to mean that these porn fans do not view their own enjoyment of pornographic representations of sexuality as 'de-humanising' or 'objectifying' to themselves or others. Instead, IRC sex-pic trading is seen as part of everyday sexuality: pleasurable, but not without its problems, and ethical challenges.

Even within the seemingly utopian world of interactive pornography, there are negatives. Online porn fan communities are vocal about their enjoyment, but can be quite critical of what they see as the sausage factory production practices of commercial porn producers, and the generic, poor quality products which can sometimes result. One male porn fan/collector complained, 'I get the feeling that whenever ... I watch an adult movie I'm being sneered at behind my back and treated like a moron [by commercial producers]. I don't appreciate it.'[9] And if heterosexual men, who are, after all, porn's target demographic, are dissatisfied with commercial pornography, those with minority sexual tastes have extra incentive to create their own alternatives. As

Melbourne amateur drag-king/lesbian porn producer Bumpy put it, 'I hate the [mainstream] lesbian porn that I've seen … most of it. It's not sexy. To me it seems very wimpy and straight.' Given this widespread dissatisfaction with the work of porn professionals, it is not surprising that many porn fans decide that they can do better at home.

DOING IT FOR LOVE – AMATEURS ON THE NET

While some fans are content to trade (and chat about) scanned or copied images from commercially produced pornography, many others have seized the opportunity to become porn stars in the privacy of their bedrooms. Although it is impossible to definitively quantify the amount of porn on the Internet, one Australian 'DIY porn' director has suggested that approximately 70 per cent of online porn is produced or modelled by non-professionals.[10] On sites like WatchersWeb.com (motto: '600 000 Visitors every day can't be wrong'), amateur images take many forms. Some involve simple, modest cheesecake or beefcake style pin-up poses, some depict daring outdoor 'flashes' of public nudity; while others involve graphic 'private' performances of explicit sex, complete with full erections, open-leg shots and close-up images of vaginal, oral and anal penetration. Like the IRC trading site community, these men and women are part of 'interactive pornography' – but they have literally put their own bodies (if not always their faces) into the picture.

There is, of course, a great deal of blurring between the categories of amateur and professional pornography. Some sites are entirely amateur in the most classic sense – homemade pictures are posted by enthusiast exhibitionist/voyeurs for the pleasure of their peers, with no money exchanged at any time. Other sites can only be accessed by those who are willing to pay (or at least offer a credit card number for registration purposes), but the models and performers on the sites could be best described as 'hobbyists'. These models receive a fee, but pornography is clearly a cottage industry sideline, not a means of employment. For example, 'Prue' and her partner 'Greg' received A$100 and A$50 an hour respectively for an explicit four-hour sex session for an underground Queensland 'amateurs' site. Even factoring in 'free parking in the city and free champagne', they received a fraction of the fee a pair of professionals might get for producing similar 'hard-core' images.[11]

With an attitude that seems typical of Internet exhibitionists and wanna-be porn stars, Prue was 'thrilled' by the experience, treating the performance fee as a bonus, rather than her primary motivating factor. As she told journalist Rachel Langford:

> We walked out of there, smiling happy customers, only they paid us! ...
> It's interesting to see yourself in that role, and it's really good. I think
> it's really healthy to do that.[12]

While 'Prue' and 'Greg' may well have been tempted to their Internet sex debut by the cash incentive, other amateurs have entered the field entirely at their own expense, only to be 'discovered' online by professional producers, and then crossing over into commercial porn production. As Sydney fetish magazine and web site editor 'Caroline' describes the process:

> The Piss Girl [videos] are from the UK and we had a marketing
> agreement with the people that make them. Basically we saw these
> photographs on the web from this woman with her and her husband
> and they were really sexy and we sent her an email and we said:
> 'Hey, would you like to make a video?' She said: 'Oh no, we just do it
> for free, it's our fetish'. We went: 'Hey, you can make a lot of money.'
> They went 'Oh, ok.'
>
> So, they gave us their first video, we give them 40 per cent, [and]
> we take 60 per cent on every copy sold. We ship it, we duplicate it,
> we advertise it – she doesn't have to do anything except make the
> tape for her 40 per cent. She's now up to [video] number 10 and
> she's raking it in.

THE BEAUTIES OF INTERNET PORN

Traditional feminist critiques of porn have tended to focus on the role of 'women in pornography'. Porn's opponents have argued that pornographic producers, performers and consumers perpetuate an oppressive male fantasy of female sexuality. While some, such as Andrea Dworkin, are concerned that the depiction of women participating in sexual practices implies that all women are 'whores by nature',[13] others are more concerned that pornography depicts an extremely limited and restrictive image of female sexual beauty and attractiveness. Pornographic beauty, it is claimed, is 'unrealistic', since it favours silicone implants, taut aerobicised loins, fake tan, false nails, big hair and Brazilian waxes, over the 'natural' attributes of everyday women. The concern here is that heterosexual men (who, by and large, are porn's greatest consumers) will be so influenced by the idealised (and labour-intensive) images they see in pornography that they are no longer able to appreciate the charms of their 'average' female companions.

Certainly the bulk of professionally produced pornography contains images of fairly conventional pornographic beauty – even allowing for the fact that the typical mainstream porn model is quite a few kilos heavier than the typical model in a fashion magazine. However, the relative accessibility of the technologies that allow 'publication' on the Internet has allowed a wide range of *atypical* pornographic beauties to present themselves to an extremely appreciative audience. As Victorian webmaster and publisher 'Craig' explains, it is the very ordinariness of web amateurs that makes homemade porn so appealing:

> *A lot of Internet webcam sites have become very popular, because people like the factor of seeing someone who is not a paid porn star getting their gear off or having sex with somebody … I think it's kind of like the next-door neighbour factor – they don't really know who it is, but they like the fact that it could be someone they walk past in the supermarket or someone who lives down the street … The biggest growth in porn in the last ten years has been in the amateur area; the other areas are pretty much maxed out.*

Feminists have rightly observed that the 'consensus' view of sexual attractiveness means the vast majority of women and men can never see themselves represented in the media as desirable and sexy. Media producers (for instance, fashion magazine editors) have defended themselves against accusations of bias and discrimination by appealing to 'market forces' – that is to say, the public gets what they're willing to pay for. Given that the majority of media consumers are unwilling to purchase images of, say, very voluptuous or very hairy women, the majority of media images could easily lead us to imagine that all sexually desirable women are in their late teens or early twenties, thin and devoid of body hair.

Internet pornography, particularly the stories and images produced by amateurs, hobbyists and 'cottage industry' pornographers, tells a different story. One of my favourites is Pam Winters' web site Hair To Stay, which caters to 'natural hairy women' (including bearded women), and the men and women who love them. Hair To Stay demonstrates many characteristics that are common in many cottage industry Internet 'fetish' sites, in that it combines erotic content with FAQs (frequently asked questions), personal history, informative articles and peer support links for women with medical conditions (such as poly-cystic ovaries) that might trigger hirsutism. There is, of course, no guarantee that every visitor will take advantage of all the options available on the site. Yet the combination of practical information and pragmatic detail available on this site (and others) seems to undercut the stereotypical assertion that pornography is universally 'dehumanising' and 'degrading'.

On one level the site defies the 'beauty myth' by encouraging not just tolerance, but celebration and eroticisation of women's 'normal, natural' body hair. At the same time, it acknowledges the everyday difficulties faced by women who do not conform to cultural norms. Publisher and webmistress Winters certainly presents a variety of eroticised images of 'the PURSUIT of the HIRSUTE', including an 'Underarm home page' and a 'talk to sexy hairy women' chat line. However, she does not conform to stereotypical images of the simpering, passive woman-in-pornography. Rude or abusive correspondence from visitors to the site is responded to publicly – and bluntly. For example, when men complain that Hair To Stay will not ship videos to their home state, Winters tells them straight: 'YOUR HARD-ON IS NOT WORTH MY GOING TO JAIL'. So much for the presumption that all porn is designed to support phallic supremacy, no matter the cost.

Of course, magazines and videos catering to fetishists (or those whose sexual tastes are not supported by mainstream popular culture) have been around for a long time. In fact, many pornographic web sites, such as Hair To Stay, and Caroline's site, Wet Set, are part of publication networks that include hardcopy magazine and video production and distribution. However, physically accessing the sex shops in which these niche products are sold is not always easy (or legal). The further one is from a major urban centre, the less likely the local shopkeeper is to stock alternative publications. Not to mention the embarrassment factor involved in approaching the counter to request 'unusual' pornography. Depressing as it may be, sexual attraction to very hairy women, amputees, very fat women or men, or even women over 40 is widely condemned as 'kinky'. However, the anonymity of the Internet has allowed national and international networks to open up for people who previously believed they were the 'only ones' who had a particular sexual taste. This proliferation of sexual imagery is a perfect example of Internet porn's ethical sensibility.

WHAT'S ETHICAL ABOUT PORNOGRAPHY?

Talking to [Internet amateurs] I'm struck by the lack of any conventional moral dimension. That's not to say there is no sense of right and wrong. Indeed, the cardinal sin in the world of online erotica is stealing images, but the prevailing view is that if people want to take pictures of themselves and someone else wants to see them, then where's the problem?[14]

Pornographic sex is clearly immoral. But if amateur and cottage industry Internet porn is demonstrably different to the bulk of commercial pornography, does this mean it can be considered ethical? The answer depends on what definition of 'ethics' one chooses. For some, the terms 'ethics' and 'morals' are interchangeable. For others, they represent quite different concepts. According to the controversial French philosopher, Michel Foucault, morality consists of black and white rule systems, the familiar 'thou shalts' and 'thou shalt nots'. One either obeys the rules, or is damned to hell (or perhaps expelled from the sisterhood). As I have noted, while most secular Westerners tend to agree that women have the capacity to experience sexual desire and exercise sexual agency, many discussions of pornography are still framed in terms of a moral struggle of an inherent female sexual 'good' against an objectifying male sexual 'evil'. If good and evil are strong words to be using in the context of secular liberal and/or feminist discussions of sexual behaviour, it is worthwhile considering Foucault's example of some of the more modern terms that can be comfortably substituted for 'old-fashioned' moralising – to the same effect:

[W]hen a judgement cannot be framed in terms of good and evil, it is stated in terms of normal and abnormal. And when it is necessary to justify this last distinction, it is done in terms of what is good or bad for the individual.[15]

The problem with these moralising judgements is that they are generally imposed from the outside, without regard for context, circumstance or timing. This kind of morality is an all or nothing proposal, which leaves no room for the individuals involved to reflect on their circumstances, and decide whether or not they wish to change them. For example, if it is simply a blanket wrong to enjoy or appear in pornography, then it doesn't matter whether an amateur feels in control of his or her situation or not. The amateur may, as in Don Slater's IRC research, think long and hard about his or her own value systems in regard to pornography and Internet chat. Likewise, a cottage-industry producer like Bumpy may have a clearly articulated philosophical framework for her choice of pornographic sexual expression; but this counts for nothing when s/he has been pre-judged by others according inflexible understandings of 'normal' and 'abnormal' sexual behaviour.

In contrast to this kind of morality, Foucault proposes we understand ethics as the way our various beliefs and value systems are put into practice in response to everyday situations and circumstances. For Foucault '… ethics is the considered form that freedom takes when it is informed by reflection'.[16] While moralising judgement is imposed externally, ethical judgement evolves through a personal and community-based process, which may involve precisely the combinations of thought, conversation and action that are evident in amateur Internet porn sites and chat pages. Of course, there are those who will argue that women in particular are not (and should not) consider themselves to be free to choose to enjoy pornography. However, they are arguing this in the face of increasing numbers of women who insist that they can, and do enjoy experimenting with this and other forms of sexuality that have historically been reserved for men.[17]

The 'ethical sensibility', as Foucault terms it, leaves room for reappraisal and adjustment in the face of changing circumstances. This kind of sensibility does not imply a vague 'all bets are off' relativism, but a process of constant experimentation and reappraisal, in which new experiences are integrated, and reflection helps determine future actions. While this may seem very abstract, in the case of Internet pornography it is easy to see this kind of sensibility in action. The Internet may appear to be an unencumbered sexual utopia; however, even the most explicit pornographic web lists and sites have internal guidelines, rules and etiquette. While there are some autocratic (and moralistic) webmasters and mistresses, more often, rules and guidelines are open to discussion and debate, and change markedly according to the consensus of list members and other participants. Unlike offline forums, it is also easy for those who feel that their interests are being excluded, or simply neglected on a particular site, to establish a new list or web site that better serves their interests, or reflects their values. It is important to draw a distinction here between amateur Internet sites and non-consensual or hidden camera sites. Recording and/or posting videos or photographs without the subject's consent or even knowledge cannot be considered ethical, since an ethical sensibility implies consideration of others' feelings and wishes as well as one's own.

CONCLUSIONS

The sheer scope and volume of content on the Internet makes it hard to contain or classify. This may be why Internet porn seems so threatening and all-pervasive. However, it is the Internet's diversity, and capacity for participation and change, which offers to make the most positive difference to the ways that sex and sexuality are represented pornographically.

Internet pornography is often represented as a perverse outsider, forcing its way into suburban homes. However, my exploration of Internet porn sites reveals that a) the suburban bedroom may already be a pretty perverse zone; and b) the 'invasion' may really be a *conversation*, linking bedrooms, lounge rooms, kitchens and garages. While the medium of the Internet offers a new space for sexual chat, experimentation and exhibitionistic play (particularly for women), this space is not necessarily utopian.

The freedom the Internet offers is limited by everyday circumstances of time, budget and other personal pressures. Considering pornography in terms of ethics rather than morals offers an opportunity to see amateur participation in porn as an example of what sociologist Jeffrey Weeks has termed an 'everyday experiment', a form of new sexuality that is both part of, and separate from, mundane domesticity.[18]

While there are plenty of commercial sex sites online, it is as easy to freely exchange sexual gratification on the Internet as it is to buy or sell it. While feminists such as Andrea Dworkin have argued that women who participate in porn are practising 'prostitution', an anonymous woman who exchanges sex chat or dirty pictures with an equally anonymous online mate often does so without any financial gain. This suggests to me that there are other factors to be considered than a simple exchange of sex for cash, or protection.

THE ETHICS OF PORN ON THE NET 209

Amateurs may, of course, choose to move into cottage industry, or mainstream commercial pornographic economies. It is important to acknowledge, however, that whether amateur or commercial, Internet pornography offers a unique opportunity for those with unconventional sexual tastes and appearances to interact in ways that are taken for granted by those with 'normal' interests. It is not simply that Internet porn offers a pathetic consolation to isolated or lonely 'perverts'. Alternative Internet porn sites like 'Amputees are Beautiful', 'Hair To Stay' or 'Zaftig! Sex for the Well Rounded' combine polemic, self-help information, chat pages and resource listings with explicit writing and images. In doing so, they effectively expand definitions of sexual beauty and desire, rather than imposing limitations.

Ultimately, to seek to understand Internet pornography as a simple issue of 'good' representations of sexuality versus 'bad' representations is to back oneself into a moralising cul-de-sac. It is worthwhile, though, to closely examine traditional assumptions about what pornography is and what it does in the light of broader moral judgements about what constitutes 'appropriate' sexual expression – particularly for women. Undoubtedly, the Internet facilitates anonymous sexual experimentation. Whether this is seen as a positive or negative factor will depend on your point of view. By looking at some specific examples of Internet porn, rather than seeing it as a looming, generic threat, some space is opened up where we might relax some of our anxieties about the dangers of cybersex and cyberporn, and see them as part of a spectrum of contemporary sexual tastes and practices. In doing so, we may see some of the everyday ethical sensibilities at work in some (although not all) porn sites and sex-chat lists, and reassess the ethical potential of Internet porn.

INTERVIEWS

'Caroline' – Interview with Matthew Thompson, 31 August 2002.
'Craig' – Interview with Kath Albury, 5 December 2002.
'Bumpy' – Interview with Kath Albury, 11 December 2002.

WEB SITES

'Amputees are Beautiful' http://www.cdprod.com
'Hair To Stay' http://www.hairtostay.com
'Watchers Web' http://www.watchersweb.com
'Wet Set' http://www.wetset.net
'Zaftig! Sex For The Well Rounded' http://www.xensei.com/users/zaftig

NOTES

1 The research for this article forms part of the ARC Discovery Grant funded project 'Understanding Pornography in Australia'. Interviewees' names are pseudonyms. Many thanks are due to research assistants Rebecca Huntley, Anna North and Matthew Thompson for their invaluable contributions. I would also like to thank Gay Hawkins, Alan McKee and the editors of this collection for their ongoing support.

2 Australian state and federal classification laws tightly restrict visual images in magazines and videos, but are relatively relaxed when it comes to books. Although the federal classification body is called the Office of Film and Literature Classification (or OFLC), print literature is seldom subjected to the same degree of regulation as visual images. Although the Internet arguably contains as much written or literary material as it does pictures and video clips, it tends to be classified as a primarily visual medium, according to the same standards as Australian television. No web site with a '.au' suffix is legally permitted to post material which the OFLC considers unsuitable for viewing by a 15-year-old. This legislation certainly reflects popular anxieties about the Internet as a source of particular risk to young people; however, a more detailed discussion of this issue is beyond the scope of my argument here.

3 See Thomas Waugh, *Hard to Imagine* (New York: Columbia University Press, 1996); or Linda Williams, *Hard Core: Pleasure, power and 'The frenzy of the visible'* (Berkeley, Los Angeles: University of California, 1989).

4 Laura Rival, Don Slater, and Daniel Miller, 'Sex and Sociality: Comparative ethnographies of sexual objectification', *Theory, Culture and Society* 15: 3–4 (1998), 300.

5 Rival et al., 'Sex and Sociality', 301.

6 ibid., 304.

7 ibid., 304.

8 ibid., 316.

9 Lawrence O'Toole, *Pornocopia: Porn, sex, technology and desire* (London and New York: Serpent's Tail, 1998), 337.

10 Ruth Barcan, 'In the raw: "Home-made" porn and reality genres', *Journal of Mundane Behaviour* 3:1 (2002).

11 Rachel Langford, 'What women REALLY WANT', *Brisbane Courier-Mail*, 19 October 2002, 36.

12 ibid., 36.

13 See Andrea Dworkin, *Pornography: Men possessing women* (London: Women's Press, 1982).

14 Nick Galvin, 'The porn star next door', *Sydney Morning Herald*, 10 January 2003, 27.

15 William Connolly, 'Beyond good and evil: The ethical sensibility of Michel Foucault', *Political Theory* 21:3 (1993), 367.
16 Michel Foucault, in Paul Rabinow (ed.), *Ethics: Subjectivity and truth* (New York: The New Press, 1997), 284.
17 See Kath Albury, *Yes Means Yes: Getting explicit about heterosex* (St Leonards: Allen & Unwin, 2002).
18 Jeffrey Weeks, *Invented Moralities: Sexual values in an age of uncertainty* (New York: Columbia University Press, 1995).

INTERVIEW WITH FIONA PATTEN
ETHICS **AND SEX**
(SEX INDUSTRY LOBBYIST)

The sex industry and, more specifically, the pornography production and distribution components of it, are often portrayed as if the people involved in them exist in a kind of ethical void. Can you comment on this view?

People sometimes think that only monsters would be involved in commercialising sex – the first thing that gets talked about as soon as the topic of pornography comes up is child pornography. But the vast majority of people in the industry have families and children and have no interest in exploiting children or anybody else for that matter. If you want to look for child pornography, the last place you'd go looking is the sex industry – the industry is not interested in children at all. You're much more likely to find the sexualisation of children in scout halls and churches.

Those of us who work in and with the industry are constantly accused of being immoral; we're under constant moral scrutiny. And that forces us to think very hard about ethical issues. We are forced to do that more than most industries to show that we aren't unethical. Certainly, the industry is very careful about restricting premises and web sites to deter children and teenagers from having access to adult material. We're interested in adult customers, not kids. So much so that a woman sued Sexpo [an annual industry exposition] after being refused entry because she wanted to bring in her child she was breastfeeding.

#212

What about the way younger people are treated in the industry? Isn't the sex industry one which exploits vulnerable young people?

From a commercial point of view if you're talking about prostitution services the best employees are in their late twenties. There's no point in having really young people working in that industry. The problem is that the public face of the industry is often what people see on the street, where you see young people who are having sex to find a bed for the night or to support a habit. They don't see behind the closed doors of a brothel where the average age is 28 and 60 per cent of the workers in Australia have families they go home to. Indeed, drug abuse in the sex industry is about the same as in the general population.

Would you say in that sense that the sex industry is as professionalised as any other large industry?

Absolutely – in many cases, maybe more so. You are extremely unlikely to see people being paid under-award wages, for example. That's because the industry is under such scrutiny. Take adult shops, for instance. X-rated videos are still illegal in all Australian states and owners still run the risk of being sent to jail if they're found to have illicit material. So they are very keen to minimise unwanted scrutiny – you don't take other risks by employing underage staff or by allowing minors anywhere near the premises. I'm sure the same couldn't be said for the liquor industry.

Another area where we have always been well ahead is the issue of privacy. Because our customers do want us to be discreet – some of them don't want to jump up and down and say 'I've been visiting brothels and buying X-rated videos' – that focus on privacy has been instilled. The same is true of Internet porn sites – you'll never find lists of names being sold. It's what customers demand of the sex industry.

Even if many Australians are comfortable with sexually explicit material, surely the real concern is to do with other kinds of material – child pornography and bestiality?

They're talked about in the media because they are the most extreme kinds of pornography and they make the most interesting headlines. Ninety-nine per cent of the pornography industry is centred on the depiction of adults having consenting sex. The kind of material you're talking about is simply not handled by mainstream distributors in the industry – it's the tiniest proportion of material and it's put out there by amateurs or by people who are not involved in the adult industry in any other form. The established companies have online and offline presences and they don't get involved in anything like that – it's not in their interest to do so.

X-rated videos are illegal in all Australian states, anyway. So if you look at it from a purely legal point of view, it really doesn't matter if you sell *Debbie Does Dallas* or *Debbie Does Dogs* [depictions of bestiality would be refused classification] – you're facing the same charge. But you won't find an adult shop selling the latter – it's not the business they're in and it's not what their customers want.

Well, let's turn to the mainstream material now. Can you talk about the ethical issues raised by censoring sexually explicit material? What are your views of the current regime?

I think the censorship regime we have in Australia really infringes on people's individual rights. My view is that, if it's legal to do, it should be legal to watch. Far from loosening up with time, we've watched even greater restrictions put on the X category – and for political rather than ethical or rational reasons. People are often unaware of how restrictive the category is. For instance, dressing up in leather and latex is banned. The notion of what constitutes sexual violence has been taken to the nth degree. For instance, there was a gay film which showed a football game in which a guy gets kicked in the balls in the course of the match – there was no sex going on in this scene, but the film was nonetheless refused classification. You're allowed more violence in a G-rated cartoon than in an X-rated movie and yet they are still banned in all Australian states. I put it this way: I can say, 'Fuck me' in an X-rated film but I can't say, 'Fuck you'.

To make matters worse, the law is full of inconsistencies. In Victoria and New South Wales, for instance, you can show people having sex in a magazine but not in a video. I think it's amazing that the industry has remained as professional as it is under the circumstances, because laws like these are exactly the kind of laws that promote a black market and people selling things out of the backs of trucks. Instead, what we have at the heart of the industry in this country are two very public companies which are listed on the stock exchange.

Surely a key ethical concern for legislators in this area should be whether they are representing the wishes of the bulk of Australians – and surveys consistently show that most people favour making sexually explicit material available to adults. The last large survey put that figure at 85 per cent.

12 Grassroots Ethics: The Case of Souths versus News Corporation

MICHAEL MOLLER

ON 10 OCTOBER 1999, AN ESTIMATED 40 000 PEOPLE RALLIED THROUGH Sydney's CBD in one of the city's largest demonstrations since the Vietnam War. Protesting against the level of corporate influence shaping Australian culture, speakers and marchers demanded that multinational companies listen to community groups. In part a protest against the media's intrusion into ordinary people's lives and passions, the rally was nonetheless sympathetically and widely reported. As the lead item of Sydney's Channel Nine news bulletin, for example, it was portrayed as a mass demonstration against the destruction of a much-loved community institution by a global media organisation. The thousands at the rally opposed the idea that important economic and cultural issues should be determined by, as one speaker put it, a group of 'faceless, gutless bludgers' who had failed to explain to the public why unpopular decisions were being made. As the rally-goers made clear, however, the fight was only just beginning. A year later, faced with the likely disappearance of a popular Sydney icon, nearly 100 000 marched in support of the same cause.

The National Rugby League's (NRL) 1999 decision to exclude South Sydney (known as Souths, or the Rabbitohs) from future competitions sparked a level of community activism rarely seen in Australia. The *Sydney Morning Herald* called this activism 'Passion Play'. Paul Kent suggested that the feeling shown by Souths fans illustrated the emotional poverty of News Limited's ownership of Australia's premier rugby league competition: 'Rupert Murdoch may be the power behind rugby league's revolution, but thousands of passionate fans turned out yesterday to show him they still own the game'.[1]

#216

Opposed to the way the NRL had sought to reduce the number of teams in the competition, supporters insisted that they followed particular clubs rather than the game of rugby league itself. For supporters, following a club demands a certain kind of commitment. Being a fan entails a sense of duty and a responsibility to protect the community of which they are part. This passion is crucial to understanding Souths' struggle, because the ethical practices and demands of supporters make little sense without their emotional commitment. It is through their commitment that fans could lay claim to owning the game. While similar in some ways, the struggle I am referring to does not quite fit the stereotypical image of anti-corporate, anti-globalisation street protests. The two-year battle waged by supporters of the South Sydney District Rugby League Football Club against the NRL and its owners News Limited was a good deal more specific than many anti-globalisation protests; and its opposition to economic rationalism and corporate control of a popular sporting culture was certainly more palatable to the Australian political mainstream.

Souths fans' resistance to the NRL and News Limited was also far better organised, more sophisticated and more successful than most recent protests against global corporate power. Their struggle was keenly followed by television, radio and the print media, particularly in Sydney, helping the club to raise more than $2 million in public donations. Finally, in July 2001 Souths were welcomed back to the competition from which they had been excluded, supporters jubilantly proclaiming a new era for the most successful club in Australian rugby league history.

THINKING AUDIENCES

It is a truism that the media exert a powerful influence on what we see, hear and read about sport. Information about athletes and sports events is extremely popular. But audiences do not always appreciate the role the media have created for themselves, many complaining about the intervention of commercial media in grassroots sporting events. Occasionally, this discontent has led to organised displays of 'people power' such as the campaigns to keep the South Melbourne and Fitzroy football clubs in Melbourne (in 1981–82 and 1996 respectively), and the widespread distaste shown by rugby league supporters during the 1995–97 feud between Super League and the Australian Rugby League (ARL).

Central to supporters' complaints about the media and corporate sponsors is a belief that these organisations are not doing the right thing by ordinary fans who have stuck with the game. For example, in the aftermath of the 1983 'Big League' documentary, the accounting and management techniques of the commercial media were touted as a potential saviour for rugby league. Financial probity, transparency and responsibility are supposed to be mainstays of corporate behaviour, and it was thought these qualities would restore supporters' faith in the game. And for a while, perhaps it did; the late 1980s were very successful years for rugby league, the game's appeal boosted immeasurably by the commitment of Channel Ten. The fans' trust, however, was repeatedly broken in the Super League war as the media and big business laid bare the base self-interest of players, clubs and administrators, as well as themselves.

The 1983 *Four Corners* documentary, 'Big League' is famous for its exposure of corrupt behaviour by some within rugby league and the New South Wales legal profession. In 1977 the president of the New South Wales Rugby League (NSWRL), Kevin Humphreys, had charges of fraud against him dropped.[2] The ensuing controversy resulted in a massive loss of public confidence in those managing professional rugby league. Crowds, which had already been waning due to perceptions of player and crowd violence, plummeted dramatically on hearing the news that the game's administrators were lining their own pockets. The NSWRL had had some success in using video evidence to support a campaign against illegal play, but 'Big League' showed a tough, macho and secretive world in which administrators wielded considerable power without having to account for their actions.

This lack of accountability and professionalism was heavily criticised in the press at the time and opened the door to more extensive media scrutiny. Part of the solution to the scourge of corruption, then, was seen to lie in making transactions between clubs, sponsors and the league more transparent. The media had dissected and analysed the inner-workings of professional sport, forcing the arcane, boozy world of rugby league administration to modernise or perish. Rugby league's new regime elected to modernise, seeing in the media – especially television – a key partner in rebuilding the game's popularity and financial base.

In the years that followed, rugby league courted new media and business partners who would promote the game and help build a new audience. As the relationship between rugby league and the television industry strengthened, the game's administrators sought to expand the competition to include teams from around Australia. Television companies would pay more for broadcast (and later for pay TV) rights if rugby league could deliver audiences in a number of markets.

It was not until the Super League dispute of 1995–97, however, that supporters were made fully aware that expansion of the competition left the traditional Sydney-based clubs vulnerable. Compared with the new franchises operating from Brisbane, Newcastle and Auckland, clubs like Souths were in danger of being cast out as dinosaurs, relics from the past in terms of their management, marketing and supporter base, as well as their ability to compete on the football field.

In the context of a more general process of globalisation, anxiety about the relevance of community clearly affects how supporters think of themselves and their relationship with the commercial media, sponsors and other clubs. Souths fans saw their primary duty as being to the club and to fellow supporters, perceiving business organisations and other clubs as potentially useful allies, but also as possible threats to their community. Fans viewed the media and sponsors as partners who could help assure the club's future, and many were willing to make sacrifices to keep commercial partners on side. For example, there was some anxiety that the cost of fundraising black-tie dinners betrayed Souths' working-class heritage, but was tempered by the realisation that such events raised a lot of money for the club, as well as providing the club with important business contacts. There was constant debate amongst supporters about how best to attract sponsors and media attention, and on whether Souths was selling itself short in its eagerness to court financial partners. The strategies and ethical importance of Souths fans' struggle, then, can only be fully appreciated when they are considered as a response to the rapidly changing political economy of professional sport.

Faced with an increased media interest in sport, especially from television, fans and administrators have had to find ways of making the unique culture of their club relevant to as wide an audience as possible. Grassroots supporters are changing how they support their club, moulding their behaviour in response to modern patterns of media production, distribution and ownership. Barracking for the local team is not the straightforward activity it may once have been. Going to matches is only one form of support, albeit a symbolically important one, but in today's media economy other kinds of support and fan behaviour are at least as significant in the expression of a club's identity. The identity of sports clubs and their supporters is strained by the way the media can isolate audience members from each other, as well as from other athletes. Encouragingly, however, we are also beginning to see the media used in ways that bring supporters together in symbolic and ethical terms rather than geographical ones.

Souths supporters used the media in very active and positive ways, calling upon other fans to show their emotional and financial support for the club. Referring to the sense of obligation they felt to the club which had given so much to so many, fans fought publicly for the values symbolised by the club's history: mateship and respect, caring for one's community, and the need to provide disadvantaged young men with an opportunity in life.

Much of the commentary about the relationship between the media and sport has been unconcerned with what people actually do with the things they see, hear and read. Nor has it shown much interest in how people use the media to communicate certain ideas and feelings with others. Popular and academic commentators have tended to focus instead on what media production techniques, coupled with the economic power of the television industry, have done to sports events and their audiences. There are good reasons for this, the most obvious being that, with television, audiences can see and hear sports events without attending the venue in which they are played. This has had far-reaching consequences; and television audiences have supplemented at-venue attendance and become a basic consideration for sports administrators. Television is thought to control every aspect of sports production, from scheduling and pre-game entertainment to rule modifications and player discipline. Many fans, however, remain nostalgic for rugby league as it was played and watched before television started to change how the game looked.

Against a condemnation of the media's effect on sport, TV has helped to eradicate excessive violence from contact sports including rugby league, Australian Rules football and rugby union. The visual qualities of the medium – replay, slow motion, close-up – may have made on-field violence unpalatable to audience members. It has certainly made the disciplinary apparatuses to which players are answerable much more effective. However, often it is assumed that modifications to rugby league were brought about by television, rather than by audiences. This assumption elides the space in which fans can be seen as active in demanding changes to the game. It also obscures the possibility of an ethics in the consumption of televised sport, making it difficult to ascribe agency to the practice of being a fan.

Watching sport is an active process, and by watching or refusing to watch TV, audiences can convey their tastes and demands to those responsible for the production of sports TV. Television doesn't make audiences disappear or eradicate the need for paying spectators, indeed it makes the audience more important, offering viewers a new means of engaging with sport. The media's involvement in sport opens up a new arena in which audiences can demonstrate their ethical commitment and in turn demand the same of media producers and the organisations that rule the game.

EMPOWERING MEDIA

I want to focus on two strategies used by Souths fans in building a coherent ethics of sports media consumption. The first of these, the formation of a community based around a specific set of consumption practices, used economic power as a resource with which to bind supporters together in pursuit of a common cause. Strategically, a well-articulated boycott demarcated both an objective and an enemy, and helped maintain the enthusiasm and morale of supporters. Souths fans consistently used their economic power in ways that would harm, hinder or shame the NRL and its sponsors. For example, a fan-produced web site urged *all* rugby league supporters to boycott any company connected to the NRL competition. Fans admitted that maintaining their boycott was difficult – the NRL's club sponsors numbered in the hundreds and included banks, energy companies and food producers – but nearly all the supporters I have spoken to felt that the boycott had a positive effect. When the *Daily Telegraph* revealed a drop in circulation in 2000, supporters claimed that their boycott was starting to bite. Matthew, a left-leaning Souths supporter I talked to in 2000, was keenly aware of the effect the boycott was having:

> *The* Tele *[Daily Telegraph] is atrocious. Obviously biased towards their own organisation, it's to be expected. But then I've noticed, it might just be me, but here we have anti-Souths editorial for much of '99, then, following that, we had a drop in circulation at the* Telegraph *by I think roughly 5 per cent – from, what I've seen, audited figures –*

> *then once those figures came out, coinciding with that drop in*
> *circulation, I've noticed a change in editorial stance within the Tele.*
> *I don't buy the Tele, I scan it and hear from other people and monitor*
> *it that way, and on the Internet. I've noticed the editorial tone towards*
> *Souths in the Tele has become neutral, has begun giving them some*
> *token coverage, and taking a not anti-Souths, a not pro-Souths point*
> *of view. I read that as the Tele's attempt to try and soothe the anger*
> *of Souths supporters, and try and win them back. I definitely see*
> *that happening.*

The selective purchasing of goods and services is a comparatively new strategy for expressing the concerns or desires of a community. Prior to the 1980s, left politics had concentrated mainly on the production side of economics and society, viewing consumption practices as individual, private and ineffectual for reshaping power relations between community and business.

Community solidarity is still central when attempting to extract better deals from the economically powerful, but the way in which this ethos is expressed is changing. There were some tenets of a traditional left politics in Souths' cause – for example, the logistical and symbolic support of the Construction, Forestry, Mining and Energy Union (representing Souths' claims of a blue-collar history) – but these were mainly used to amplify the ways Souths fans sought to wield consumer power. In a way that may seem shocking to a traditional left view, part of Souths' strategy was to focus on the club as a commodity, enabling supporters to participate as consumers. As part of the club's collateral, Souths' former CEO, Paul Dunn, lists excellent home crowds, strong merchandise sales, membership over 23 000, a solid sponsorship base, extensive media coverage, and a very marketable 'South Sydney brand'.[3] As Dunn suggests, the activism and enthusiasm of Souths fans have a commercial appeal to financial partners. Being a fan of a sports club involves more than going to matches and wearing the club colours around the house; it has become a way of engaging with corporations and media producers.

Souths fans' consumer boycott was subtle and sophisticated. It was relatively easy to blacklist all NRL and News Limited products (including Foxtel, the *Daily Telegraph* and the *Australian*), but supporters also pressured other media outlets, notably the *Sydney Morning Herald* and competing radio networks, to provide favourable coverage of their struggle by positioning themselves as a victim of a competing media company. For example, most supporters were aware that the *Sydney Morning Herald* had a commercial interest in pursuing Souths' story and stoking the passion displayed by Souths fans. In turn, fans used the knowledge that media ownership helps guide story selection as a kind of leverage to further their claim that the club ought to be re-admitted to the competition.

Frequently, fans had a keen awareness of how forcefully they (and potentially supportive media) could state Souths' case, finely balancing their support for the club, criticism of the NRL and News Limited, and not wanting to be perceived as unduly biased against other clubs. For instance, when I interviewed Matthew, a fan who had a letter published by the *Sydney Morning Herald* in 2000, he stated:

> *The* Herald's *been great. The* Herald's *been a champion of the Souths cause, I think, without being propagandist about it. The* Herald's *been smart in that they realise that if they support Souths' cause [they will win readers,] though I think they don't want to go too much overboard because it will actually do Souths more damage – if they become too supportive or too pro-Souths then they lose credibility. So the coverage they give Souths is credible. There's an interest in it for Fairfax [owners of the* Sydney Morning Herald*], sure: News Limited's a rival and if they can put the boot into News Limited, well and good. I suspect that's probably part of the reason why I got my letter published today, because indirectly I was putting the boot into News Limited as controller, as owner of the NRL.*

As this letter demonstrates, Souths fans were adept and committed users of the media. They were not simply acting *against* the actions of the NRL and News Limited, but were working to create a new and empowering sense of community in times of dramatic change. In framing Souths' fightback as a tight-knit community battling a vast media conglomerate it is easy to overlook the fact that Souths fans were themselves sophisticated users of certain media products. Two examples exemplify this: first, how televised sport, that is, a shared history of watching televised sport, was used to build a sense of community stretching well beyond the geographical boundaries of South Sydney. And second, how some Souths fans have promoted their club via the Internet.

ON WATCHING TV

It is a common argument that television prevents individuals from participating in social and cultural events; that when we stay at home to watch something on the television we are missing out on events happening somewhere in the 'real world'. The main problem with the idea that TV functions as an escape from social reality, or at best as a scripted account of that reality, is that it conceals the fact that the *use* of electronic media is itself a social activity. When we watch television we do so in the hope that we are going to be entertained or educated – both of which are deeply social activities. Critics, however, continue to assume that viewers passively consume the programs presented to them, form no opinions on what they see, and do not attempt to share these views with others.

One of the most interesting and important consequences of sports television has been the way it allows dedicated fans to share their passion with people who have little interest in a particular sport and who would never go to a venue to watch a game. This was the experience of George, a professionally employed man in his forties, who I met with his wife at the South Sydney club in 2000 at an information evening for supporters. Later, in an interview, George described watching televised matches with his father, who disapproved of the players' roughness and refused to watch a game live. George's parents had emigrated from Italy after World War II, settling in the South Sydney suburb of Botany. He was raised there at the height of Souths' success in the late 1960s and early 1970s. I asked George about the rest of his family's interest in rugby league.

MM: So, you were the only one who followed rugby league?

GD: Yeah, I was the only one. My father used to hate it. As I got older he used to sit down and watch it with me sometimes, but he thought it was too violent. He didn't like it. Sometimes, though, he'd be yelling at the TV and I'd say, 'Dad, what are you yelling at the TV for? I'm the supporter here, I thought you didn't like the game.' 'Oh they're too rough', he'd say. He didn't like Manly in those days.

Televised football gave George and his father a way of communicating across very different ideas about entertainment and cultural value. It facilitated a form of inter-generational dialogue. George's father would never go to a match but television allowed him to see what so stirred his son's interest. Willing to indulge his son's taste for the Rabbitohs, George's father invested something of himself in the televised images, trying to understand his son's enthusiasm for a bloodthirsty Australian sport. His acceptance of rugby league and George's interest in the game, however, had their limits: George recounts that he was not allowed to *play* rugby league, his parents preferring the less brutal, more European game of soccer. 'So be it. I think it's probably part of the reason why I'm letting my kids play [rugby league]: because I missed out.'

Far from being an isolating or antisocial technology, television allows for new and, at times, profoundly radical forms of social activity.[4] All too often, however, sports print writers and commentators forget that many people use television to follow their particular team. Viewing games on TV is social: not only does it occur largely in the company of friends and family, and hence requires negotiation and consensus, television producers are constantly refining the way sports events are presented to emphasise the sense that *all* viewers are sharing their appreciation of the sporting spectacle.

Televised sport is a basic building-block of community in a world where communities are formed through *symbolic* meanings much more than they are dictated by physical, geographical or ideological boundaries. South Sydney's supporter community is no longer strictly 'local' in the sense of being contained in a geographical area, if indeed it ever was. Processes of migration, media expansion and industrial change over several decades have meant that supporters of the South Sydney football club, along with other kinds of communities, have had to find new ways of talking to each other and making themselves heard. As a subscriber to a Rabbitohs supporter e-group, I got e-mails from supporters in western Sydney, Canberra, Perth and Brisbane, looking for other supporters with whom to watch Souths' matches on TV. Sometimes supporters would gather at a person's home in their city or town; but fans were often keen to find somewhere public to watch the game.

Supporters made much of the depth and geographical spread of support for Souths, insisting that the club ought not be excluded from the competition because it was a proven television ratings performer. At the rally in October 1999, Andrew Denton argued that the NRL was both callous and stupid in its disregard for the club. He tied the game's health to fans' support for particular clubs and claimed that Souths supporters were amongst the most loyal rugby league fans, pointing to the consistently high ratings figures for televised matches featuring the Rabbitohs. Statistics, of course, are notoriously malleable abstractions; and Souths were careful to use them in a way that emphasised the club's cultural heritage as a selling point. Former Souths player Bruce Longbottom, for example, describes how Aboriginal communities in country towns would gather to watch the club's matches on TV during the club's last great heyday of the 1960s and '70s.

> *Even when I go out to places like Kempsey and Wauchope, there's a lot of support. People in the country used to see a lot of that great Souths team on the match of the day on Channel Two. They were brought up wanting to support or play for Souths.*[5]

Laying claim to a long history of spectatorship was a critical part of Souths' case: such recollections made nostalgic support for the club an abiding, community-based activity, demonstrated the club's diversity and widespread appeal, and seemed also to suggest that support for Souths predated, and would outlive, the passing commercial interests of big business.

Key to Souths' success in their fight against the NRL and News Limited was the active support of thousands of fans. There always seemed to be supporters around when the club's struggle was being reported on television news bulletins, providing camera crews with a colourful and noisy backdrop. Support for Souths came from local suburbs, but was also spread throughout greater Sydney, regional New South Wales and other parts of Australia. Media reporting and the Internet enabled distant Souths supporters to participate in the club's struggle, even if this were confined to simply arguing the case with friends. News of Souths' victory in the Federal Appeals Court in July 2001 was e-mailed to hundreds of e-group subscribers within seconds of the announcement, thanks to a supporter who sent a text message via his mobile phone. The rapid dissemination of the verdict allowed fans to arrive at the leagues club well before club president George Piggins, providing evening news bulletins with dramatic images of a crowd of colourful fans devotedly waiting for their leader. I do not mean to romanticise community, or ordinary folks' ability to create it, but, rather, to show in practical terms how communities can transcend geographical distance by distributing information and advice.

GRASSROOTS INTERNET

Souths fans' use of the Internet also helped their supporter community express a precise set of demands about the behaviour of rugby league fans, administrators and commercial partners. Supplementing the club's official web site, www.souths.com.au, which at one point was the most popular football club site in Australia, supporters created a number of web sites devoted to publicising supporters' efforts to save their club. Over the course of the two-year campaign, more than a dozen pro-Souths web sites were in operation, providing mainstream media outlets with an easily accessible source of information and opinion. Most of these sites had a limited operational life, restricting themselves to documenting Souths' battle with the NRL through articles, opinion and pictures, and have since disappeared. As community-owned and operated outlets, however, these sites were a crucial part of supporters' activity. Most obviously, they demonstrated that the NRL was fighting a group of people who were passionate about Souths, committed to saving the club and willing to spend significant amounts of time, money and especially energy to publicise their struggle. The NRL's claim that fans hadn't been there when it mattered, that is, at games in the 1998 and 1999 seasons, simply didn't stack up when so much material on Souths was available, much of it on the Internet. Consisting of amateur graphics, photos and reporting, supporters' web sites helped give a home-grown feel to the club's campaign, something which exacerbated the popular belief that a 'people's game' was being taken from the people for whom it most mattered.

Against the large media companies, such as Telstra, Foxtel and News Limited, the fan-produced sites came from committed supporters speaking from the heart. Sites such as www.southsydneybravepages.com may have looked a bit rough and cheap compared with the slick professionalism of the NRL's web site, but the home-grown feel of the sites further signalled fans' protest against the managerial policies of the NRL. The NRL's site looks like it is devoted to a game administered by businesspeople. By contrast, the fan-produced sites express a popular, if slightly nostalgic, demand that ordinary supporters have significant input into rugby league's future.

The voluntary, community-based style of support displayed by Souths supporters was the key to the club's success. Certainly, Souths has experts in training, development, football management and marketing, but both club and supporters are quick to insist that such professionalism must leave room for participation by fans. After Souths were re-admitted to the competition in 2001, for example, a number of supporters emphasised the importance of tracking talented young players on behalf of the club. A few suggested using parents as 'a South Sydney recruiting resource'. One of the more developed proposals involved 'establishing a location on Souths and Souths juniors web pages' where parents could 'notify Souths of kids that display talent, that might one day wear the Red and Green'.[6]

CONCLUSION

Fans are the lifeblood of sport. They are also the lifeblood of sports media as the latter would not exist without consumers. But what it means to be a fan has changed, with supporters' sense of belonging or community expressed in more symbolic terms through their use of the media. As 'local' communities stretch well beyond their physical boundaries, sport is more often celebrated as a commodity. South Sydney fans are not alone in recognising that sport has to be produced and paid for *by* someone, and that it has an economy in which they are central players. Nor are Rabbitohs supporters unique in their understanding that the media, especially since the legalisation of pay TV in 1995, are central to this political economy. What is instructive about Souths fans' struggle with the NRL and News Limited is that this understanding guided every action they took, from the way supporters positioned them-selves as a television audience to the home-grown feel of supporter web pages. Even at its most fervent, Souths' campaign was never about doing away with the media, or even Foxtel. They were never going to be able to turn the clock back to a time when the media exerted little or no pressure on the structure of sports competitions. Instead, supporters insisted that room be found for them and their club, pushing themselves into the media spotlight and arguing for greater influence in shaping the decisions of global media companies.

While the battle to save South Sydney was ostensibly a battle to save a popular, if struggling, football team, the manner in which fans fought for their club brings into question prevailing ideas about populist ethics of media use. In the current climate of globalisation, sports communities are acutely aware of the need to reorganise the practices of fans around the brand of a particular club: the history it has produced, the ethical values contained in those images and narratives, and the sense of responsibility or commitment expressed in relation to those values. Supporters' faith in the administrators and financial backers of rugby league has been sorely tested since the early 1980s. As a result, fans have learnt to trust in themselves, their own sense of responsibility, and their own capacity for action.

Souths fans' struggle for the re-admission of their club to the NRL illustrates how an everyday ethics is created through their actions, particularly their use of the media. Important themes of responsibility, opportunity and respect for the emotional commitments of others are communicated through the consumption of media products, helping to build a community, willing to fight to save something that means a great deal to them.

NOTES

1   Paul Kent, *Sydney Morning Herald*, 11 October 1999, 25.
2   While the magistrate found there to be sufficient evidence to suggest that a jury might find Humphreys guilty, he decided that the evidence did not 'warrant the defendant being placed on an indictable offence'. The 'Big League' documentary screened six years later, however, traced the circumstances behind the dismissal of the charges against Humphreys and suggested that justice had been perverted by high-level judicial interference.
3   Paul Dunn, *The Red and Green Magazine*, South Sydney District Rugby League Football Club Limited (June 2002), 3.
4   It should be noted that the masculine hegemony within sports programming and sponsorship has been difficult to break for precisely this reason. Brian Cooney, a director of sports management company, International Management Group, explicitly condones the masculinism of sport, business and sponsorship: 'Sponsorship is about building relationships and with sport, blokes can do blokey things. You are with your mates having a few beers and a talk.' Cited in Douglas Booth and Colin Tatz, *One-Eyed: A View of Australian Sport* (Sydney: Allen & Unwin, 2000), 20.
5   Cited in Shayne Bugden, 'The Koori Konnection', in *Souths: The people's team*, commemorative edition of *League Week*, Australian Consolidated Press, 2002, 49.
6   From Rabbitohs e-group, September 2001.

13 Great Pretenders: Ethics and the Rise of Pranksterism

MILISSA DEITZ

ON THE FIRST DAY OF THE ANNUAL BRISBANE WRITERS' FESTIVAL IN 2000, festival-goers were treated to an aerial banner display, with the words 'Poetry Wrecks Lives' emblazoned across it. Down on the ground, approximately twenty people were gathered, protesting the 'irresponsible' promotion of poetry at the festival. Spokesperson for the group, who called themselves 'Young People Against Poetry', Ben Eltham, said that they were angry at the way Queensland's cultural elite continued to encourage young people to take up the dangerous activity of poetry. 'Most people think that poetry is nothing more than a frivolous pastime that young people can experiment with and will grow out of, but this is not the case', said Eltham. 'Many young people become trapped in a life of bohemian excess, wasting their talents and making no worthwhile contribution to society.'[1]

Their organised demeanour and serious tone had some members of the media confused until another spokesperson explained the real object of the stunt. It wasn't poetry the group had a problem with; it was their belief that the Brisbane Writers' Festival was dominated by an outdated and hierarchical understanding of literary culture.

Talking to Ian Townsend on ABC radio's *The World Today*, protester Mark Fula explained:

> Look, it's not poetry per se but it's what the Writers' Festival think of as poetry … Their insistence on promoting old creative forms is stifling the ability of the festival to promote what young people are really engaged in, which is exciting activities like hypertext writing, zine-making, legal

#230

graffiti, hip hop … It's only by challenging people's artistic preconcep-
tions that they can develop and grow and expand their horizons.[2]

The prank protest achieved something that reasoned, straightforward criticism of the festival couldn't – it got the views of an unknown group of young people publicity. And it did it by exploiting the mainstream media's weakness for polemic and novelty. The language in which the group denounced poetry is, of course, exactly the kind of language which current affairs programs routinely use to denounce the effects of drugs or pop music on 'today's youth'. And it's this media savvy which is one of the hallmarks of the postmodern media prankster.

The prank has a long history in Australian popular culture. The best known is the Ern Malley hoax, perpetrated in 1944 by Australian poets James McAuley and Harold Stewart with the aim of disparaging contemporary poetry. McAuley and Stewart concocted 'modern' poetry under the name of Ern Malley and sent it to the literary magazine *Angry Penguins*, where it was treated as genuine and published. As art critic Robert Hughes notes in the introduction to *The Ern Malley Affair*, the hoax marked the first time in Australian history that poetry became front-page news.[3]

The late 1990s saw a resurgence of pranksterism, targeting not obscure literary journals, but the most commercial of media. It was a trend which has been ignored in most recent debates about media ethics and yet it's one with real significance for the way we understand the relationship between media practitioners and their audiences.

Young people have traditionally been fodder for tabloid current affairs shows – they are portrayed as either being in need of protection or correction. Yet, it is precisely these younger, media-savvy generations who are familiar with the vocabulary, technology and formulas of the media, and who have been using this knowledge to both develop and deploy an auto-critique of the industry. The pranks and satirical commentaries they have aimed at mainstream media not only challenge assumptions about the passivity and gullibility of youth audiences, but, more importantly, suggest that any discussion of journalistic practices needs to be interactive. Journalists can no longer proceed on the assumption that the 'masses' are ignorant of the techniques and tropes of the mainstream media.

GENERATION AXED

In April 1994 a new handsome, gravel-voiced current affairs show host burst onto Australian TV screens with the words: 'Welcome to *Frontline*'. It wasn't until the show actually debuted that many viewers realised the promotion wasn't for another current affairs show, but a satire of the genre. Writer for the series, and actor in it, Rob Sitch, described the object of *Frontline*'s satire this way: 'Current affairs programs have always been highly manipulative. All the writing has been polemic in its nature, un-researched, generalised, full of unsubstantiated assertion.' *Frontline*, he said, was like a wind which 'blew up for a second and you saw their underwear'.[4]

If *Frontline* is the respectable elder statesman of satire when it comes to current affairs television (in New South Wales it's required viewing for the HSC syllabus), then John Safran is its bastard son. Safran is now a well-known media personality in Australia. But back in 1997, he was just another contestant on the ABC program *Race Around the World*, a program in which young contestants made short videos. Safran's work was instantly notable for the way in which he played with both genre and audience expectation. Satire is his *lingua franca*. For *Race Around the World*, Safran stripped in Jerusalem, insulted Walt's reputation at Disneyland and cast a voodoo curse on an ex-girlfriend.

But it is for a pilot made for the ABC in 1998, work that never made it to air, that Safran is perhaps most well known. In one segment of the pilot, Safran waylays a bemused executive on his way to work at the Phillip Morris conglomerate. He presents a marketing idea – a lone cigarette included in a 'Cheesesticks' packet. This way, Safran explains, when the six to 12-year-olds, who the cheesesticks are marketed at, are ready to move on, their first cigarette is there for them. (Phillip Morris markets cigarettes as well as cheese.) In another segment, Safran targets working bludgers rather than dole bludgers. Using the hidden camera technique used by tabloid current affairs shows, Safran follows staff from *A Current Affair* to the company canteen. He then filmed the workers 'doing bugger all'.

But it is the segment in which John Safran targets Ray Martin, a host for many years of *A Current Affair* and an Australian television icon, which is most infamous. Martin was the host of *A Current Affair* when the show ran a story about the Paxton family – a mother and her three teenage children – who were portrayed as a family of dole bludgers. The family was slammed by politicians and media commentators on a national scale – they were held up as figures of ridicule during a time of prolonged economic recession.[5]

When he set up camp outside Ray Martin's house to see what time Martin left home for work, Safran took Shane Paxton along as his timekeeper. Safran used the tabloid-style tactics that commercial current affairs reporters have relied on – 'doorstopping' (waiting on his doorstep), speaking directly to the camera, and feigning outrage at Martin's stance. Safran ended up in a scuffle with Martin and his wife. Although it can be seen on various Internet sites and has been screened at universities, to date the pilot has not been seen in its entirety on television.

The pilot's place in Australian prankster history was assured when the Ray Martin segment was shown on ABC's *Media Watch* in March of 1999. A week after screening the tape, *Media Watch* made an on-air apology for airing the controversial segment. At the time, *Media Watch* host, Richard Ackland, said the material was aired to demonstrate a point about thin-skinned journalists.

Roger Grant, then head of ABC Corporate Affairs, protested to the Independent Complaints Review Panel that the program was unfair and biased against Martin and failed to show the extent of intrusion into his privacy. The panel rejected that complaint but upheld Grant's other complaint that Martin had been unfairly portrayed by *Media Watch*.[6]

One of the most interesting aspects of the stunt, regardless of where you stand on Safran's intrusion into Martin's privacy, is the way it shows the power wielded by one individual armed with a handicam and a sense of humour. Ray Martin's standing in the industry undoubtedly contributed to the quick and public apology issued by *Media Watch*, and doubtless it left others in the industry wary of employing Safran. But clearly, anyone who has acted as the high-profile host of a current affairs program, which is known for using hidden camera techniques and walk-ups (where a journalist confronts a subject without prior warning), is open to being accused of hypocrisy if they complain about an invasion of their own privacy.

Interestingly, Shane Paxton, who accompanied Safran on his wake-up call to Martin, managed to parlay his media status as a pariah into a gig as a youth affairs reporter on the current affairs program *Today Tonight*, and a job on the ABC music show *Recovery*. The mauling Paxton received at the hands of the established media – mainly aimed at older viewers – worked in his favour when it came to securing a younger audience, many of whom were presumably sick of the youth-bashing that is one of the dominant tropes in commercial current affairs and newspaper culture.

DONE DIRT CHEAP

While Safran copped a lot of high-profile flak for his pranks, there are other media hoaxes in the archives that mainstream producers seem less than happy to publicise.

Matthew Thompson, now a *Sydney Morning Herald* journalist, was 21 when he wrote a letter to a Sydney newspaper claiming to object to youth culture. At the time, Thompson was an office junior whose boss liked to listen to Alan Jones' 2UE radio program. One morning Jones was complaining about the name of Sydney thrash band 'The Hard Ons' and, in Thompson's recollection, Jones commented that such a name was 'symptomatic of the moral decline evident in an element of youth culture'. Thompson decided to write a letter to the editor of Sydney's *Daily Telegraph-Mirror* (as it was then known). He introduced himself as the head of a growing movement called 'Young People Against Heavy Metal T-Shirts' (YPAHMTS). As the following excerpt from his letter shows, Thompson walked a fine line between parody and what one might read simply as conservative comment:

> *I think that young people have shown remarkable responsibility*
> *towards the environment, and now it is time for them to clean*
> *themselves up and act with equal respect for themselves and their*
> *elders. This means stopping socially and personally damaging activities*
> *such as smoking, drinking, swearing, taking drugs, easy sex and,*
> *in particular, wearing heavy metal T-shirts.*

Thompson went on to claim that YPAHMTS was established in New South Wales, Victoria and Queensland.[7]

The morning that the letter appeared, Thompson received calls from *Good Morning Australia*, *The Derryn Hinch Show*, *Daily Telegraph-Mirror* journalists and ABC radio. They were all journalists keen to garner the first coverage in their respective mediums, and they all wanted to know who they were against in their race for a scoop. As Thompson comments, 'Because I was the self-proclaimed head of some self-proclaimed group, I was presented as an authority figure. No one ever checked out the veracity of my claims about the size or activities of YPAHMTS.' It was, he says, 'kind of funny, especially when I was claiming to organise youth camps in the desert where youngsters learn to renounce labelism, and vow to read only the books I supplied'.[8]

On 15 April 1992, two days after Thompson's original letter appeared, the *Daily Telegraph-Mirror* published a short article relating to the original letter. The story, 'Teens shirty over row' by Scott Ellis, claimed that 'a storm is brewing among rival youth factions over one of the closest things to a teenager's heart – the T-shirt'.

When ABC radio rang to arrange an interview, Thompson says he made a point of telling them that YPAHMTS existed to change people's consciousness, not to have anything banned. Thompson was interviewed by Peter Luck on ABC radio station 2BL. He introduced Thompson as 'a bloke who wants to censor T-shirts', then read out segments from a newsletter supplied by Thompson.

Over the following half-hour of talkback, Thompson says, 'almost everyone missed my point of not wanting to ban anything. They were saying it was high time for sexist and violent imagery to be eliminated from popular culture. A few called me a "fundamentalist loon".' Thompson comments that his experience with the media:

> *showed how shallow the desire for freedom of speech is, and how*
> *shallow the understanding of it is. Most people mistakenly seem to*
> *think that there is legally guaranteed freedom of speech in Australia,*
> *and then many of those same people think freedom of speech means*
> *that people should be free to agree.*

Thompson's impromptu stunt also revealed how little research some journalists and producers bother to do: over and over again, media practitioners took his claim to be the head of a highly organised outfit at face value. When *The Derryn Hinch Show* asked if they could film a typical YPAHMTS meeting, Thompson went out and bought some heavy metal T-shirts to complain about, and briefed a few friends.

> *[When the segment was screened] everything too challenging*
> *was edited out – nothing remained about liberation from*
> *label consciousness – and all that went to air were tired*
> *old buzzwords like death, rape and destruction.*

Representatives from YPAHMTS were also asked to appear, and did so, on Couchman's talk show. At no stage, says Thompson, did he advocate the banning of T-shirts. Thompson says the experience taught him that:

if a person presents as an expert about an issue, the media and the audience will be more likely to believe whatever that person is saying. I gained credibility because I had an organisation behind me. YPAHMTS gave me credibility in the eyes of those listening, reading and watching. The fact that the organisation didn't exist escaped everyone. At no stage was I asked to produce evidence of the existence of the group, nor was I asked to back up or justify anything I was saying. The media and the audience simply reacted to my words.[9]

Thompson wrote an article detailing the entire hoax from beginning to end. The story was published in *Australian Style* magazine in 1996 and then again in 1998 in a Newcastle University student paper, *Pop Culture Experiment*. He sent the story to *Media Watch* in the hope that they would find it amusing and could give him a few ideas about where to get it published. He also sent in some video footage. *Media Watch* then put together their own short exposé on pranks perpetrated on the media. The prank was exposed but, according to Thompson, no one in the mainstream media, including those who had been hoaxed, reacted.

MAN BITES MEDIA

Thompson's prank was born out of a spur of the moment satirical impulse which snowballed. However, another notable prank, the Dole Army hoax, is an example of a far more deliberate, self-conscious targeting of what the group perceives as an ideological bias in the mainstream media's attitude to reporting youth unemployment.

The opening page of the Dole Army's web site carries the following disclaimer:

The information and content of this web site has been supplied to dolearmy.org from various individuals and sources. The information is reproduced for informational, research and educational purposes only. Dolearmy.org does not in any way promote or condone any action or conduct contained in this web site (heaven forbid).[10]

Much of the content of the web site covers information about what to do and who to contact if you have trouble receiving unemployment benefits from Centrelink, when it is appropriate to appeal against a Centrelink decision, how to appeal, along with information about Freedom of Information.

On 23 January 2002, the Dole Army contacted Channel Nine's *A Current Affair* and Channel Seven's *Today Tonight* via e-mail, claiming their 'Army' was made up of people who lived in tunnels below Melbourne and who only came out at night to forage for food in dumpsters. They said they ran a web site which detailed how to stay on the dole, avoid the work for the dole program, and generally beat the Centrelink system.

On the night of Monday, 4 February 2002, the story aired on both *A Current Affair* and *Today Tonight*. In promotional advertisements for *A Current Affair's* Monday night show, viewers were given glimpses of a 'rebel' army living in drains under the city of Melbourne, their sole purpose apparently being to teach the unemployed how to 'rip off the welfare system'. This apparently tipped *Today Tonight* off, who then contacted the group to also cover the story.[11]

'It's one of the country's best-kept secrets', says Norm Beaman to camera at the beginning of the Monday night program on 4 February.

> *A rebel army working deep beneath the city. They live in drainage tunnels under Melbourne and their goal is to teach people how to rip off the welfare system. Using a web site for communication with the outside world, the Dole Army details everything from defrauding the Work for the Dole scheme to tips on lying to Centrelink officers.*

With masks covering their faces, members of the Dole Army were then interviewed and explained that they were a group of people who met to 'discuss things. We talk about what's going on up there, we exchange food and ideas ... Some nights we sleep down there.' The reporter explains to the audience that the majority of the people in this group don't work – 'they could, but they simply do not want to'. Neither TV show made any mention of the web site's structural analysis of Australia's welfare system or how it could be changed.

The next day, the group calling themselves the Dole Army owned up to the hoax, saying that the stunt was perpetrated as a form of revenge on the news media for their prejudiced portrayal of the jobless and other disadvantaged groups in society. The *Australian* and the *Daily Telegraph* newspapers both ran stories about the hoax.[12]

In a piece on the ABC's *Lateline* on 5 February, journalist Mark Tamhane reported that as well as having fun fooling the two TV programs, the group had a serious message to deliver. A member calling himself Wombat said:

> *Those tabloid news programs basically will show anything that fits their point of view and we fitted their point of view because, for them, we were a bunch of dole bludgers living in a drain and that's their interpretation of what unemployed people are.*

Speaking to the *Sydney Morning Herald*, the group's leader, who called himself General Kool Keith, said that as soon as promotional advertisements for *A Current Affair* went to air, the Dole Army was contacted by *Today Tonight*, which he alleged offered the group $1000 for a spoiler story. He said his group took *Today Tonight* to a deserted brick factory to shoot the segment. There was no tour of the Army's headquarters, as reported by Norm Beaman of *Today Tonight*. *A Current Affair* claims that it did not pay any of the members of the Dole Army. The group, however, claims *A Current Affair* offered it $2000 not to talk to *Today Tonight* and handed over $360 worth of digital videotape.

After admitting the hoax, a Dole Army spokesman, calling himself General Kangaroo, said they did not live in drains and that most members had jobs. In interviews with the *Australian* and the *Daily Telegraph* a spokesperson for the group opined that: 'We've proved that there are a lot of people that get paid a lot of money to make really bad media with very little integrity'. The group also said that the con had publicised their web site, aimed at advising the jobless on the 'inhuman Centrelink bureaucracy'. General Kool Keith added:

> *We set out to expose the lazy, sensational standards of tabloid TV and to promote our web site. We achieved both goals. We had over 6000 hits over the weekend and the two programs have been held to accountability.*

In response to these allegations, *A Current Affair*'s producer, David Hurley, says the existence of the web site – and the fact that the office of Employment Minister Tony Abbott was aware of it – was reason enough to go ahead.[13]

While the publicity drew attention to the sloppy and polemic practices which characterise some current affairs journalism, it didn't necessarily serve to highlight the political issues the Dole Army sought to raise. Key aspects of the media release the Dole Army sent out after the hoax was exposed were largely ignored by the mainstream media. The release included information about current unemployment figures, that student benefits were up to 33 per cent below the poverty line, and that nearly 350 000 welfare recipients were punished with 'financially crippling breaches' for reasons such as arriving late to a Centrelink interview, not receiving Centrelink mail due to being homeless, or due to Centrelink's own mistakes.[14]

PAPER CHASE

While media pranks work, or conversely fall flat, because of how funny they are, they provide proof of an increasing trend. Underlying the pranks is clear evidence of both a sophisticated knowledge of the media, and a desire to make it do something other than reproduce clichés, especially when they are clichés about youth themselves. So on the one hand, it's increasingly obvious that young people are much more media savvy than previous generations. This is a point which has been argued again and again by media critics seeking to give young people some credit, and to raise their standing as full and active agents. While conservative research continues to portray youth as a group at risk from media fallout, especially in contentious areas, such as their use of porn or of violent material, other researchers are up-front about the power of youth to understand the dominant media, and more than that – to manipulate it.

In the words of Neer Korn, 'Speak to young Australians and the depth of their media and advertising nous is quickly apparent'. Korn is a director of the social and market research company Heartbeat, which conducts qualitative research with Australians on a broad range of issues. He has been closely involved in a major study of the media consumption habits of young Australians and he believes that the duping of two current affairs programs was a watershed moment.

Their constant exposure has enabled them to easily deconstruct the media, understand the devices the media use and the ratings forces that drive them. This is part of the wider trend as the young seek recourse

> *from what they see as self-serving key institutions:*
> *government, big business and big media.*[15]

This is a telling point. Less than the overt satire, we need to pay attention to the political project that fuels media pranks. Ever since the boomer generation grew up, it has become fashionable to remark in condescending terms about the supposed lack of political energy that characterises youth. Any number of named generations ('X', 'Y', 'Me') have all been branded as apolitical and pathetic in their purported desires only to consume and have fun. These critiques not only emanate from conservative circles, they are also mouthed by media critics and scholars. And there may be a lack of recognition on the part of older media scholars as to what constitutes radical critique of 'the system'. In his book *Celebrities, Culture and Cyberspace*, McKenzie Wark points out that while intellectuals who criticise the media and what's wrong with it abound, intellectuals who can 'conceptualise what can be done within the actual media' are less common.[16] Wark charts how:

> *In the '60s, critical media studies attacked the legitimacy of journalism,*
> *either in the name of its stated ideals of objectivity and independence,*
> *or in the name of a radical alternative … By the '90s, criticism still*
> *attacked the legitimacy of journalism, but mostly this served to*
> *legitimise the authority of the academic critic rather than advance*
> *a reforming or radical agenda.*[17]

From the point of view of the academic who casts his or her eye on the material I have described in this chapter, the pranks may look somewhat self-serving. But therein lies the point: amateur pranksters are helping themselves to cheaper media technologies, and are turning their cameras on the situation of youth, for once viewed from their perspective. The resulting picture sends up the ludicrous way in which any aspect of youth culture not readily understood by older generations is routinely dismissed. Be it in regards to heavy metal T-shirts, or the intricate and at times inane workings of bureaucracies such as Centrelink, pranksters perform a double-whammy. They send up these institutions and the received ideas of established figures, and then just as everyone starts laughing, the penny drops that these are in fact deeply serious issues.

In terms of both content and form, these prankster practices reveal an alternative view of what media ethics could mean. They obviously suggest a highly dynamic and interactive relationship between the media and some of its consumers. These examples speak to how, as if by osmosis, media techniques are now a part of a sub-cultural collective knowledge. However, they also demonstrate that it takes some skill to reproduce the look and feel of the nightly news or current affairs program – to copy and reproduce its overall effect. In this sense, the parody has to be understood as close critique based in familiarity. This differentiates pranksters from earlier critiques of the media that were evidently fuelled by disdain, and sometimes revealed a lack of knowledge of how a particular medium works. These pranksters don't hate TV. How could they when it has been such an accepted part of their lives? And it's not surprising that some, like Safran or Paxton, have gone on to make media careers for themselves, albeit in slightly off-centre formats.

While it is clear that much of the public is no longer satisfied to merely sit and let the news wash over them, established media practitioners need to acknowledge the capacity audiences have for critical readings of the media. While in many cases it is now an accepted part of commercial media practice to pick up on amateur videos – especially in cases of human or natural catastrophe – the increased ability of any one person to be a producer could have much more far-reaching implications for the current media environment. Imitation is not always flattery, and what the content of these pranks demonstrate is a refusal to buy into the dominant framing of issues that are close to the heart of younger generations. Like Safran stalking Martin, the media's heels are being nipped by the knowledgeable and audacious media practitioners of the future. As they increasingly turn the cameras on established truths and complacent media practices, the picture isn't pretty.

NOTES

1   Ben Eltham quoted in a press release from *Semper Floreat* magazine (University of Queensland newspaper) on 19 October 2000.
2   Mark Fula spoke to Ian Townsend on ABC radio's *The World Today*, 20 October 2000.
3   Michael Heywood, *The Ern Malley Affair* (St Lucia: University of Queensland Press, 1993), *xvii*.
4   John Casimir, 'Who would you believe?', *Sydney Morning Herald, The Guide*, 9 May 1994, 1–2.

5 Marcus Casey, 'Shock, horror, it's a tabloid TV scandal, *Daily Telegraph*, 7 February 2002, 27.

6 Jo Casamento and Margot Denney, '*Media Watch* says sorry', *Daily Telegraph*, 8 October 1999, 13.

7 The *Daily Telegraph-Mirror* published the letter on 13 April 1992, p. 20, under the headline 'Stamp out T-shirt terror'.

8 Thompson published his YPAHMTS experiences with the media in the December/January 1997 issue of *Australian Style* magazine as 'Tabloid whore', and then again in 1998 as 'Robot rape' in a Newcastle University Student Association's publication, *Pop Culture Experiment*.

9 Craig Garrett, 'Mischievous intent' http://www.loud.net.au accessed 15 August 2002. See loud7@enternet.com.au, created on 21 September 1997 and last modified on 10 Nov 1997; LOUDonline – http://www.loud.net.au – 10 April 1998, accessed 27 May 2002.

10 Accessed 7 May 2002.

11 Nick O'Malley, (ed.), 'Great story, this, if you don't dig too deeply', *Sydney Morning Herald*, 6 February 2002, 20.

12 See Andrew Dodd, 'Dole Army claims victory', *Australian*, 6 February 2002, 3; and Lisa Walker, 'Current affairs TV duped', *Daily Telegraph*, 6 February 2002, 17.

13 ibid.

14 http://www.dolearmy.org/Media/index.htm 5 February 2002, accessed 7 May 2002.

15 Neer Korn, 'Shooting the messenger and loving every minute of it', *Sydney Morning Herald*, 8 February 2002, 12.

16 McKenzie Wark, *Celebrities, Culture and Cyberspace* (Sydney: Pluto Press, 1998), 37.

17 ibid.

INTERVIEW WITH JOHN SAFRAN
THE LIMITS **OF SATIRE**
(TELEVISION PRESENTER AND WRITER)

How did you feel when the ABC decided not to air your pilot? Did you believe they had legitimate reasons for rejecting it at the time?

Well, at the time they just said it was a creative decision. They kind of put me in a position where I couldn't really argue without looking like I just couldn't wear the umpire's decision. In retrospect, it was a bit, I don't know what the word is, not nice. At first it was just me coming up with crazy conspiracy theories in my head, but then *Media Watch* did a segment on the pilot. They followed the paper trail and produced a memo from Roger Grant, Head of Corporate Affairs at the ABC, who was also on the board. So then there was actually a bit of circumstantial evidence that there had been some pressure to try to stop the pilot being shown. And I'd argue that I wasn't being totally crazy to have come up with conspiracy theories in the first place because it's not like you switch on the ABC, or any channel, and see topnotch, brilliant entertainment twenty-four hours a day, seven days a week. I mean, they'd gone to the trouble of filming it, so why not use it?

Roger Grant argued to the Independent Complaints Review panel that the piece was biased against Ray Martin and failed to show the extent of intrusion into his privacy. What do you think he meant by these comments?

I don't know if there's a legal definition of what invading privacy is so I couldn't talk from that perspective, but from a layperson's point of view, I guess we did

#243

invade his privacy. We went to his house and camped outside on the wall –
not overnight or anything, but for hours and hours.

**What did you take into consideration when you were editing
the Ray Martin segment? Did much happen other than what
was actually portrayed?**

I wasn't trying to make Shane [Paxton, John's co-host for the segment] or
myself look good. I didn't cut anything out that would have made us look bad.
I was just editing from a creative point of view, so there was obviously stuff that
we cut out, but nothing significant. But, things were totally played up in a
Chinese Whispers kind of way. People often say to me, 'Oh, you went through
his rubbish'. But all that happened was we noticed his recycling bin with
magazines on top while we were hanging around. In a joking way I said
things along the lines of, 'Mmm, I see *TV Week*. Has Ray Martin been filling
out his own Logie forms?' You know, just stuff like that. Then that became
this big thing like we'd gone through his rubbish bin seriously to try to find
private stuff.

How do you mean things were played up. By who?

I meant in a popular conscience kind of way. When they talk about the pilot,
most people say to me, 'Oh, you're the guy who went through Ray Martin's
rubbish'. Ray Martin was interviewed about the whole incident for a newspaper article and I noticed that everything he says in the article is pretty
accurate. He was straight down the line and reasonable. He didn't accuse us
of doing anything we hadn't done.[1]

**How do you think people reacted when they heard rumours
that Martin may have tried to stop your pilot from airing?
How did you react?**

I definitely got the impression that there were lots of people saying things like,
'Oh God, how ironic is that!', which is exactly what the point of the piece was.
But I also don't think that people really [understand] that somebody like Ray
Martin is just a person who is capable of getting upset, that he's not a cartoon
character.

What were you hoping to achieve when you first came up with your ideas for the pilot? Did you have specific objectives?

I guess most of my stuff is, you're kind of floating along, half gut reactions, half kind of knowing that what you're doing is adding up to something with subtext. So, for example, I look back on *John Safran: Media Tycoon* now and there are some bits where I say to myself, 'Oh what I just did then was instinct, I didn't plan that'. Because before *Race Around the World* I was just some guy with a job who didn't have anything to do with TV. I remember as soon as I started getting involved in TV, thinking, 'Man, there's so much editing and there's all this stuff you can do and TV is just not real.'

Of course, that's so bleeding obvious once you get involved and after a while things like that don't occur to you any more. When I was doing *Race Around the World* I filmed this piece about the way that Muslims slaughter their meat, halal, and how the Muslim dietary laws work. There was a scene in an abattoir where we showed how they killed the cows compared to how non-Muslims kill cows. When we were editing it, I remember the editor guy saying, 'Hey, we can get the sound of those cows in the field mooing and we can just chuck it in here and then it'll sound really dramatic, it'll sound like "moo moo moo!"' I remember being shocked. It was just so early in my career, and I said, 'You can't do that! That's just not the truth!' I was really quite anxious about it. Then you just kind of get used to the way things are done and two years later you're going into the sound booth and making the moo sounds yourself.

So I reckon *Media Tycoon* was kind of deconstructing the process of television, but I didn't really think about it that way at the time. I don't even know what I was thinking. I was just doing silly stuff, but I'm glad I got it out of my system because now when I do new stuff, like *Music Jamboree*, I don't feel obligated to have a grand mission. I just kind of trust myself. I think, well, I managed to add something to those segments for the pilot that made them a little more than superficial comedy, so I trust myself to be able to do that sort of thing again.

Why do you think the ABC hired you to do a pilot?

I think it was just because there'd been a lot of publicity about me and my *Race Around the World* stories, so people knew who I was. Looking back,

I think I went about [the pilot] the wrong way. With *Music Jamboree*, we're an independent production company, so we work out a deal and then drop the tape off on the desk of the TV station, rather than use all their facilities and their people, which I think just brings in all the problems I guess the pilots brought in. There's an aspect to doing things in-house where it has to be a wholly pragmatic thing, but it's not even about legal issues and not even really about creative issues. It's as simple as, for instance, doing *Music Jamboree*, if you find some young director who's just come out of Victorian College of the Arts and you think, 'He'd be cool to direct one of the little segments', you can just go ahead and get him to do it. If you're working within a TV station you just can't do that. Isn't that what the ABC should be all about – helping young people? Instead it's like, 'Oh, well, it's a bit more complicated than that, John. You have to use our people.' And I guess my style doesn't really click in with that.

Now that you have so much more industry experience, have your views of current affairs shows changed at all?

No, not at all. I remember someone telling me that the night after I'd been at Ray Martin's place filming he'd looked 'kind of shaky'. Then I watched it about two weeks later and there was a story where some guy was going into a real estate agent and doing the foot-in-the-door thing. So obviously I'd made no difference whatsoever.

Have your views on mainstream TV changed at all?

It's a bit hopeless in Australia. I mean, I don't want to discourage people but even though I just came out of this really great experience with *Music Jamboree*, I think it was a bit of an exception. But then again, it depends what people's aims are. I can't assume my creative aims are the same as everyone else's. I guess if you are coming in with a bit of a young, guerilla kind of attitude, television's probably not the first medium you should be looking at. Maybe you should think about film. I could talk about all these other mediums that I haven't had excessive involvement with and over-romanticise them, but there is a point when you're writing a film where some creative people are sitting in a room typing and working it all out, and things don't get compromised until later on. But there actually was that point where a bunch of people were sitting around being creative together. And if you're writing a book, there is a stage where you're working on it alone, doing exactly what you want to do before the publisher's editor tells you to change it. With TV, that stage never happens. It happens the other way round. You have a production company and then they approach creative people and say, 'Hey I've heard that Channel Ten's doing a life-style program. Let's try and get a life-style program up', or 'Hey, I think the new thing's going to be sketch comedy shows, so how about writing some sketch comedy?' When there is actually good stuff on TV it does seem to inspire people, but it seems like the laws of probability are that there's not going to be too much good stuff on Australian TV.

So you don't intentionally exploit what you see as the limits of television? Do you see TV as a limited medium?

No, not really. I'm kind of lucky in some way – I've never really watched too much TV. I mean, I watch *The Simpsons* and *Seinfeld*, but I can't really remember sitting around when I was young and thinking, 'Oh, what a great medium. I hope one day I work in this.' When I did *Race Around the World* I wasn't really sure what you were meant to be doing, and I think that probably helped out a bit in the long run. Although I always used to watch those trashy reality TV shows like *Cops* or even *Funniest Home Videos* and think to myself that they were really alternative except for the subject matter. They're kind of subversive because, for instance, *Cops* just set up a camera in a police car and followed these criminals around. It's the opposite of a show with slick production values and a conventional beginning, middle and end. I used to think that was really interesting except, obviously, the actual end result wasn't that interesting. So when I was doing *Race Around the World* stuff I was doing my version of that kind of reality TV.

Would you say current affairs shows or other parts of the industry are out of touch with audiences?

I don't think half the people in Australia are suckers who just believe everything and the other half are people who are really savvy and don't necessarily believe what they see. It's more likely that there are lots of different pockets of people, little different demographics that overlap. I guess you've just got to look at the ratings, and if things are rating then I guess whoever is responsible is relating to an audience. Sometimes I'll watch a current affairs show and think about the fact that from some people's perspective, it would be a show to take very seriously. It's easy to forget that.

Where do you think satire fits in terms of today's entertainment?

It's important because people really like it, or enough people really like it. There are plenty of mainstream examples now of satirical shows, the best ones being *The Simpsons* and *South Park*. That's probably one of the hardest things about alternative culture now. If you're working on your own little alternative cartoon, how do you make it more subversive than this thing that's put out by Rupert Murdoch's Fox?

Do you think satire has its limits as far as being able to critique the media?

I think satire contributes to a kind of liberal culture. In a very general sense it's good having all this satire on TV and in films and songs because it distinguishes what makes the good things about a liberal, Western culture. I don't know if it changes anything, though. I mean, has the existence of a show like *The Simpsons* harmed Rupert Murdoch at all? It's done the opposite. That subversive, satirical cartoon apparently saved his Fox network, to some extent. And I don't think that's really a contradiction. It's just that when it comes to single issues, I think it's pretty hard for satire to change things, but overall it helps add to a liberal kind of culture.

NOTES

1   Ray Martin responded to this interview with the following claims:
   - John Safran posed as a courier with an urgent package to gain entry to Ray Martin's house. This was omitted from the film.
   - Ray Martin never asked for, nor was ever given, the opportunity to cancel Safran's series. His only contact with anyone on the ABC Board was a phone-call of apology from the Chairman, Mr Donald McDonald. He is not a friend, nor an acquaintance, of Mr McDonald.

Index

#249